Crossing Frontiers

The Political Economy of Global Interdependence
Thomas D. Willett, Series Editor

Crossing Frontiers

Explorations in International Political Economy

Benjamin J. Cohen

Westview Press

BOULDER • SAN FRANCISCO • OXFORD

The Political Economy of Global Interdependence

Copyright © 1991 by Westview Press, Inc.

Published in 1991 in the United States of America by Westview Press, Inc., 5500 Central Avenue, Boulder, Colorado 80301, and in the United Kingdom by Westview Press, 36 Lonsdale Road, Summertown, Oxford OX2 7EW

Library of Congress Cataloging-in-Publication Data
Cohen, Benjamin J.
  Crossing frontiers : explorations in international political
economy / Benjamin J. Cohen.
    p. cm.—(The Political economy of global interdependence)
  ISBN 0-8133-7990-3
  1. International economic relations. 2. United States—Foreign
economic relations. 3. United States—Economic policy. 4. United
States—Monetary policy. 5. European Economic Community countries—
Foreign economic relations. I. Title. II. Series.
HF1359.C64 1991
337.73—dc20   90-43899
                                                                   CIP

Printed and bound in the United States of America

The paper used in this publication meets the requirements
of the American National Standard for Permanence of Paper
for Printed Library Materials Z39.48-1984.

10   9   8   7   6   5   4   3   2   1

For Jane
One frontier I've never regretted crossing.

Contents

Introduction

Frontiers, every beginning student of economics is taught, are the distinguishing characteristic of international economic relations. In most respects markets are the same whether they are local or global: trade and investment, wherever they occur, may be assumed to be responsive to the same underlying constraints and incentives and to reflect the same basic motivations and goals. There is only one significant difference when economic activity goes international—the existence of political frontiers separating sovereign nation-states from one another. But what a difference that is! Separate states imply separate policies, and separate national policies imply a range of influences on outcomes that are not only additional to but also quite distinct from those prevailing in purely domestic markets. A quarter of a century ago, when I first embarked on a career of academic scholarship following completion of my graduate training in economics, I had no doubt that my special interest lay in the realm of transactions that cross frontiers.

One frontier, however, at the time seemed insuperable—not a frontier between states, but rather a frontier between disciplines. Back in the 1960s, in the English-speaking world at least, little systematic communication existed between the disciplines of economics and political science, particularly in the area of my chosen specialty of international economic relations. Formal analysis of the political dimension of the world economy tended to be avoided by economists; the economic dimension of world politics, conversely, was largely discounted by political scientists. The result was a cognitive barrier between the two professions that appeared virtually unbridgeable. Exceptions could always be found, of course, but mostly among marxist commentators or others outside the mainstream of conventional Western scholarship. Within the intellectual mainstream, few challenged or even questioned the "disciplinary tunnel vision" that had tended to characterize the social sciences since the divorce of political science from economics in the latter half of the nineteenth century. "Academic astigmatism," Susan Strange called it in 1971.[1] The

1

essence of the problem was captured by Strange in the title of a key article that she had published a year earlier: "International Economics and International Relations: A Case of Mutual Neglect."[2]

In the years since, all that has changed. Today the study of International Political Economy (IPE) has become a recognized and respected research specialty in Western academic circles, complete with a formal scholarly literature that has grown by leaps and bounds since the first scattered seeds were sown in the late 1960s and early 1970s. Some of the earliest contributions were made by economists, including most notably Richard Cooper,[3] Charles Kindleberger,[4] and Albert Hirschman (in his rediscovered classic, *National Power and the Structure of Foreign Trade*, originally published in 1945).[5] Most of the spadework in more recent years, however, has been done by political scientists, beginning with such innovative and imaginative pioneers as Robert Keohane and Joseph Nye,[6] Robert Gilpin,[7] Stephen Krasner,[8] and Peter Katzenstein,[9] and continuing thereafter with an ever widening cadre of adventurous scholars and students. Only a relatively few economists have continued to labor in this particular vineyard, overcoming the disinclination of their increasingly mathematically oriented profession to take on messy questions of politics and power. With some pride I include myself among the small number of economists who, despite the difficulties inherent in cross-disciplinary work, have persisted in attempting to add their insights to the development of the IPE field.

Almost from the start of my academic career, I found myself drawn to exploring theoretical and policy issues at the frontier between the specialties of international economics and world politics. Topics that I have addressed, at one time or another, encompass some of the most central themes of the contemporary literature on International Political Economy—in particular, the relationship between commercial and political interests in the conduct of foreign policy, the origins of economic imperialism, the organization of international monetary and financial relations, and the evolving nature of foreign economic policymaking in the United States and Europe. The purpose of this volume is to bring together in one location a representative sample of my diverse efforts to advance analysis of each of these themes written over a span of more than two decades. Since, happily, most of the dozen essays in this collection seem to have withstood the test of time reasonably well, all are reprinted essentially as they originally appeared with only minor extraneous material excised in a few cases. Together they provide an easily accessible, and, I hope, illuminating introduction to what much of IPE today is all about.

Methodological Themes

International Political Economy has been usefully defined by Gilpin as "the reciprocal and dynamic interaction in international relations in the pursuit of wealth and the pursuit of power."[10] The hallmark of IPE as a distinctive area of scholarly inquiry is its emphasis on the formal *integration* of market and political analyses in the realm of international affairs. It is not merely a matter of studying the autonomous role of politics in setting the framework for economic activity across national frontiers, which tends to be the approach of conventional economics. Nor is it solely a question of the independent role that international markets may play in affecting the attainment of political goals, which has always been the typical approach of political science. In IPE, both economics and politics are treated as endogenous variables (determined by systematic process) rather than as exogenous parameters (given by arbitrary assumption). And central attention is paid to the key role played by governments, since the fundamental unit of authority in the international system still remains the sovereign state. The core issues of the field are considered to be questions of public policy.

Two broad sets of questions have tended to dominate the IPE research agenda. One set of questions has to do directly with the behavior of individual governments: What motivates states in foreign economic relations, and how are their policies best explained and analyzed? The other set has to do, more broadly, with system management—how relations between governments are organized collectively to cope with the consequences of economic interdependence. How do state actors manage (or fail to manage) their conflicts, and what determines whether they cooperate or fail to cooperate to achieve common objectives? Methodologies applied to these questions vary, of course, depending on both the professional training of the individual scholar and the circumstances of the specific issue under consideration. Serious efforts to cross the frontier between established disciplines must often be pragmatic, not to say eclectic, if they are to add substantially to our understanding.

Certainly pragmatism has been characteristic of my own explorations in IPE, which at different times have employed a variety of conceptual and analytical approaches depending on the particular issue at hand. For precisely that reason, I believe that my work has had something of value to offer to more traditional specialists in both economics and political science. Conventional economists could learn more about the complex interplay of interests and power in global economic relations and how these systematically affect, and are affected by, purely market outcomes. Political scientists, conversely, could learn more about the usefulness of selected elements of formal economic theory when applied to questions of either national decisionmaking or international governance. Both sides could benefit from a greater sensitization to issues and variables largely ignored by their respective conceptual frameworks.

The pragmatism of my work has to a large extent been dictated by personal taste and, most particularly, by an early recognition on my part that my professional interests lay more in the direction of applied analysis than in any sort of purely abstract theorizing or model-building. Only rarely, since my graduate-school days, have I been moved to undertake an exercise based primarily on deductive reasoning from a priori premises and principles. For the most part, my preference has been to focus on the challenges of practical and serious problem-solving: explication and evaluation of issues of genuine importance in the real world. Not that this choice has necessarily required any sacrifice of intellectual rigor. In fact, I have always tried, as the essays in this volume testify, to set the issue at hand—be it a question of national policy behavior or a question of international systemic reform—firmly within an appropriate theoretical and conceptual framework, although admittedly the approach has implied a willingness at times to trade off a certain degree of analytical parsimony for the sake of greater realism or relevance.

Through my nearly quarter-century of applied work, a number of common methodological themes can be discerned. None of these themes, to be sure, are by themselves unique in the IPE literature; indeed, by now some have come to be widely stressed by a more recent generation of scholars. Taken together, however, they may be regarded as summarizing and defining the distinctive character of my own personal contributions to the field.

First is a central emphasis on the *strategic interdependence* inherent in international economic relations—the fact that when transactions cross national frontiers, governments necessarily become involved in interdependent decisionmaking. In two of the essays in this volume I make the point explicit by drawing an analogy between the behavior of states in the global economy and that of competing firms in an oligopolistic market. Both situations are apt examples of what in game theory would be described as a mixed-motive nonzero-sum game, in which elements of common interest as well as of rivalry are inevitably present. Potential implications of this strategic interdependence inform most of my research and writing over the years. Indeed, it is precisely the fact that states are caught up in such games, simultaneously both competitive and mutually dependent, that makes IPE so interesting as an area of scholarly inquiry.

Connected to this point is a second theme that is common to most of my work—a recurrent emphasis on the *two-level* nature of the games that states play in the international economy. Strategic interdependence is characteristic not only of their external relations but, inherently, of their internal decisionmaking processes as well. That is the reason for the domestic dimension of analysis that is stressed in many of the essays in this volume. Governments are necessarily involved in political interactions not only with one another but also with influential actors in their own domestic societies. Moreover, the nature of the relationship between the two levels of behavior is necessarily reciprocal rather than unidirectional. Formal modeling of all these interactions is of course extraordinarily difficult. Here again a basic trade-off is required between analytical parsimony and greater realism. In my own efforts I have consistently aimed to highlight *all* the variables that would seem to matter in foreign economic policymaking.

Also connected to the theme of strategic interdependence is a third theme in my work—a recurrent emphasis on the *endogenous role of power* in international economic relations. The capabilities of actors, including decisionmakers outside as well as inside government, obviously are a major determinant of the outcomes of games at both the domestic and international level. The point is hardly controversial and is underscored in virtually all writing in the IPE field. But actor capabilities are not exogenous: they may also *be determined by* the outcomes of games. It is important to stress, as a number of the essays in this volume do, that this relationship too—the link between power and outcomes—is reciprocal, not unidirectional. An assertion that "Power changes" is true whether the verb is understood to be transitive or reflexive.

A final methodological theme common to my work is an emphasis on the *multiplicity of policy objectives* that states bring to the games they play in economic relations. Sovereign interests are not defined exclusively in terms of some measure of materialistic welfare, as most conventional models of international economic theory tend to assume; nor solely in terms of some equally narrow concept of physical security, as implied by the Realist paradigm of international-relations theory. In fact, it is fair to assume that governments effectively define state utility in terms of both economic welfare and national security, and may well formally or informally include other goals as well involving the self-interest of public officials, income distribution at home, status and prestige abroad, or even preservation of the stability of the international system as a whole. Direct implications of this complexity in the ordering of state preferences figure prominently in most of the essays in this volume.

Substantive Contributions

Reflecting the fact that over the years my work has moved back and forth between aspects of both main sets of questions on the IPE agenda—government behavior and system management—the selections in this volume are arranged by their substantive content rather than in chronological order. The first eight essays explore issues in the formulation and implementation of foreign economic policy by individual states, looking at examples drawn from the experiences of both the United States and key governments of Western Europe. The final four essays focus more on systemic issues in the organization and management of international economic relations, with particular emphasis on the underlying sources of conflict that hinder effective cooperation between states. Individually, these essays may claim to have usefully furthered scholarly debate on the diverse subjects they address and to having generated a fair number of novel ideas and insights. Together, I would modestly argue, they constitute an instructive survey of some of the central themes in the field of IPE today.

"Foreign Economic Policy: Some General Principles of Analysis," the earliest of the selections in this volume, aims to develop in broad terms a systematic conceptual framework for the analysis of foreign economic policy in a single country. Reflecting my formal training as an economist, the proposed approach relies most heavily on concepts and tools derived from standard microeconomic theory, treating states as rational, self-interested ("egoistic"), and essentially unitary actors. The strength of the framework is its ability to accommodate in a relatively parsimonious fashion the political as well as economic objectives of policy. Its greatest weakness is its failure to open the "black box" of the state to evaluate the relevant *domestic* decision processes. Using the familiar terminology of Kenneth Waltz,[11] the analysis is strictly "third image"—system-level (or structural-level) analysis, locating the sources of state behavior solely in constraints and incentives that derive from the broader structure of inter-state relations. "Second-image," or unit-level, factors influencing policymaking (specifically, domestic politics and institutions) are largely ignored.

The same is also true of my essay on "United States Monetary Policy and Economic Nationalism," which explores connections between narrow self-interest and broader systemic interest in U.S. international monetary policy in the first three decades after World War II. My argument in this essay is that U.S. policy was always egoistic to a degree, even at the height of the Bretton Woods era in the 1950s and 1960s. The appearance of intensified American nationalism in the 1970s was due more to a change in the structural *context* of U.S. policy—namely, the decline of America's global monetary hegemony—than to any change of its substantive *content*. In practical terms, this essay is noteworthy for its emphasis on the theme of the endogeneity of power. (This theme, stressing ways in which the gradual erosion of America's post-World War II hegemony in economic affairs has influenced U.S. policy behavior, reappears in a number of other essays in this volume as well.) In analytical terms, however, this essay, like the previous one, remains strictly third image in its deemphasis of the domestic dimension of decisionmaking.

The next six essays, by contrast, put much more emphasis on that domestic dimension, concentrating as much on the internal characteristics of nations as on their external environment. "International Debt and Linkage Strategies," for instance, is very much in the tradition of second-image analysis, with its specific focus on societal factors at home that might influence the ability of a government (in this case, the U.S. government) to formulate and implement coherent policy strategies abroad. My particular interest in this essay, which originally appeared in 1985, is the impact of the global debt problem—involving, as it did, many U.S. private-sector creditors—on the ability of public officials in Washington at the time to realize expressed foreign-policy preferences. Debt, the essay argues, creates link-ages in foreign policy that may either constrain or enhance the government's broader capabilities in external affairs, depending on the circumstances. Some of the more relevant of these circum-stances, which effectively highlight the two-level nature of the games that states play in the international economy, are identified by exploration of a selection of recent experiences, including the Polish debt crisis of 1981-82 and the beginning of the Latin American debt crisis (or crises) in 1982-83.[12]

In the next two essays, system and unit levels of analysis are explicitly blended by examining selected aspects of U.S. foreign economic policy in the specific context of relations with other advanced industrial nations. "The Revolution in Atlantic Economic Relations: A Bargain Comes Unstuck" is primarily concerned with the sharp changes that occurred in America's economic relationship with Europe following the breakup of the Bretton Woods system at the start of the 1970s. Earlier in the postwar period, I argue, an "implicit bargain" had been struck between Washington and our allies in Western Europe. The Europeans "acquiesced in a system which accorded the United States special privileges to act abroad unilaterally to promote U.S. interests. The United States, in turn, condoned Europe's use of the system to promote its own regional economic prosperity, even if this happened to come largely at the expense of the United States." At the time this essay was written, in 1974, the nature of transatlantic economic relations had never before been articulated in quite this way. Since then, following wider popularization by Marina Whitman among others,[13] the idea of an implicit bargain has become part of the conventional wis-dom on this subject. Reasons for the dissolution of the bargain are found in key domestic factors, including both bureaucratic politics within the U.S. government and a revival of protectionist sentiment in American society at large, as well as in the evolving balance of power at the international level.

Similarly, "An Explosion in the Kitchen?" probes internal as well as external influences on the economic policies of the first five years of the Reagan administration, in relation to our political allies in Europe, Canada, and Japan. Of particular interest is the extent to which this analysis confirms an idea of mine concerning underlying rhythms in the historical record of U.S. foreign economic policy in recent decades. Despite the surface appearance of substantial discontinuities in government behavior, I argue here, there have in fact been discernible regularities in the cycle of policy from administration to administration. Each of our most recent administrations, it seems, has entered office initially inclined toward an activist reaffirmation of America's traditional influence over economic events, only to become increasingly frustrated by growing limits on American power both at home and abroad, and ultimately to be driven into a posture of either bellicose confrontation (e.g., President Nixon's suspension of the dollar's convertibility into gold in August 1971) or mutual accommodation (e.g., the Reagan administration's return to cooperative exchange-rate management in the Plaza Accord of September 1985). My basic point is that these swings of the pendulum should not be at all surprising, since they in fact are a systematic endogenous response to a familiar combination of internal and external influences. This idea, which was first presented in an earlier version of this same essay published in 1983, has also now become part of the conventional wisdom on the subject as a result of wider popularization by such authors as Fred Bergsten and Randall Henning.[14]

A blend of system and unit levels of analysis also permeates the next three essays, though here the spotlight is shifted from the United States to the European side of the Atlantic. "Britain's Decision to Join the Common Market" traces the roots of the British government's dramatic policy transformation in 1971 to significant changes in the international economic environment as well as to alterations in the attitudes and perceptions of key domestic elites in British society and government. Likewise, "Europe's Money, America's Problem" lays stress on systemic as well as more parochial motivations for the 1978 decision by a majority of the members of the European Community (EC) to create the European Monetary System. The Europeans, clearly, were driven as much by their desire to reduce their external dependence on the U.S. dollar as they were by internal pressures for a closer monetary union. And in similar fashion, "European Financial Integration and National Banking Interests," written in 1989, searches at both the Community level and the national level for explanations why EC members, despite previous rhetorical commitments, had not at that time yet succeeded in creating a single market for commercial banking in Europe. Careful specification of the problem in game-theoretic terms, with creation of a unified banking market treated analytically as a kind of public good in scarce supply, suggests that inhibitions were derived from domestic structures as well as from systemic considerations and were complicated by reciprocal interactions between influences at the two different levels. In all three of these selections, once again, the importance of second-image as well as third-image factors is evident.

The final four selections in this volume concentrate more on systemic issues in international economic relations. The first three focus on various aspects of the evolving international monetary system. The last essay addresses the underlying nature of relations between rich and poor countries in the global economy.

Of the three monetary essays, "The Political Economy of Monetary Reform Today," originally published in 1976, is the most broadly conceived, asking why comprehensive reform of the global monetary system then seemed (and, for that matter, still does seem) so difficult to achieve. The answer, I suggest here, is to be found in the fundamental political dilemma lurking behind all the purely economic and technical aspects of exchange rates, international liquidity, and the like—the problem of how to ensure, in the absence of world government, at least a minimum degree of *compatibility* among the policy objectives of separate sovereign states in order to reduce significantly the risk of costly policy conflict. (This formalization of what I label the consistency problem, which serves to underscore the mixed-motive nonzero-sum nature of international economic relations, is developed most fully in my book, *Organizing the World's Money*, published in 1977.)[15]   Well before widespread acceptance of the notion of international "regimes" in the IPE literature, I was already wrestling with the question of how legal or conventional frameworks can be developed to provide some measure of "governance" in the world economy. The answer, I decided, essentially lay in a choice among four alternative organizing principles: (1) automaticity, a self-disciplining system of rules and norms binding for all nations; (2) supranationality, a system founded on collective adherence to the decisions of some autonomous international organization; (3) hegemony, a system organized around a single country with acknowledged responsibilities and privileges as leader; and (4) negotiation, a system of shared responsibility and decisionmaking. Any international regime, I argued back in the mid-1970s, had to be based on one or some combination of these four basic principles. At the time, only a couple of other scholars were thinking along similar lines.[16] Today, the logic of the consistency problem is widely applied in discussions of regime issues.

The next two essays, by contrast, are conceived rather more narrowly and focus in greater detail on a more limited range of issues in monetary relations. "Balance-of-Payments Financing: Evolution of a Regime" asks how we are to understand the major innovations that occurred in the 1970s and early 1980s in institutional arrangements for the provision of international liquidity to governments. At issue during this period was the emergence of commercial banking institutions as a major source of financial assistance for many deficit nations. This development may be best comprehended, I argue, as a change of degree rather than a transformation of kind—an example of "norm-governed" evolution in the international monetary regime, driven in particular by structural changes on both the demand and supply side of private credit markets. "A Global Chapter 11," published initially in 1989, in turn addresses the question of Third World debt and asks: How could we overcome the obstacles to effective resolution of the difficulties of hard-pressed debtor countries? The persistence of their difficulties throughout the 1980s, the essay contends, could most accurately be attributed to underlying configurations of power in the political arena, both within individual debtor countries and in their broader strategic interaction with creditors. Major changes in the political equation conditioning creditor-debtor relations, therefore, are required to achieve a truly effective solution; I argue that this could best be achieved through imaginative institutional innovation modelled on Chapter 11 of the U.S. Bankruptcy Code or analogous regulations elsewhere. Much of the essay is taken up with a detailed elaboration of what such a "Global Chapter 11" might look like—something that had not previously been attempted by any other commentator. Although in this instance it would be far from accurate to claim that this idea too has become part of the conventional wisdom, the Chapter 11 proposal has at least managed to receive enough favorable attention in relevant circles to be included in recent policy debates on the debt issue.

An emphasis on power relationships leads directly to the final essay included in this volume, "Toward a General Theory of Imperialism," which originally appeared as the last chapter of my book, *The Question of Imperialism*, published in 1973. The aim of that book was to critically evaluate various "nonorthodox" theories purporting to explain the essential nature of relations between rich and poor countries—the "imperialism" of dominance-dependence relationships. Most of those theories, I tried to demonstrate, could be challenged both at the level of logic and the level of empirical observation. This last selection accordingly offers an alternative explanation for the "taproot" of imperialism, developed in terms of third-image analysis rather than the second-image analysis favored by most marxists or other radical theorists. The "urge to dominion," I contend, derives from the anarchic nature of the system of political relations *between* states rather than from the capitalist nature of social and economic structures *within* states. In short, imperialism derives first and foremost from the insecurities of "the good old game of power politics"—nations contending with nations to preserve their territorial integrity and political independence—rather than from any presumed imperatives of class struggle or the material needs of capitalism.

When I wrote *The Question of Imperialism* back in the early 1970s, there was hardly a conventional social scientist to be found who showed the slightest interest in marxist or radical analyses of relations between rich and poor countries. Indeed, even today that books remains one of the few efforts by someone trained in standard Western academic techniques to systematically comprehend and evaluate the so-called economic theories of imperialism. The originality of my own alternative theory lies less in its emphasis on power politics (other writers have also stressed the theme of power politics in this connection) than it does in my attempt to go behind the "urge to dominion" to identify more fundamental sources of motivations.

In effect, my approach helps to reintegrate the notion of imperialism as such into the broader mainstream of IPE scholarship, treating the phenomenon of dominance-dependence relationships as a not illogical response to the underlying nature of the broad international system. In this, as in the other selections in this volume, my main ambition has been to push out a bit at the frontiers of our understanding of crucial issues in International Political Economy. But it is perhaps best left to others to offer final judgment regarding just how useful or enduring any of this work may eventually turn out to be.

* * *

For their instrumental roles in helping to put this volume together, I wish to thank Tom Willett, editor of the Political Economy of Global Interdependence Series; Spencer Carr and Jane Raese of Westview Press; and my secretary Charlotte McIver, who prepared the final manuscript for publication. I am also grateful to the several publications and publishers who kindly gave their permission to reprint the essays collected here. And most of all I am grateful to my wife Jane De Hart, whose decision to join me in crossing the frontier of matrimony not so long ago started me on the most pleasurable exploration of all.

Notes

1. Susan Strange, *Sterling and British Policy: A Political Study of an International Currency in Decline* (London: Oxford Univer-sity Press, 1971), p. 3.
2. *International Affairs*, vol. 46, no. 2 (April 1970), pp. 304-315.
3. Richard N. Cooper, *The Economics of Interdependence: Economic Policy in the Atlantic Community* (New York: McGraw-Hill, 1968).
4. Charles P. Kindleberger, *Power and Money: The Politics of International Politics* (New York: Basic Books, 1970).
5. Albert O. Hirschman, *National Power and the Structure of Foreign Trade* (Berkeley: University of California Press, 1945, reprinted in 1969 and 1980).

6.   Robert O. Keohane and Joseph S. Nye (eds.), *Transnational Relations and World Politics* (Cambridge, MA: Harvard University.

PART ONE

Actor Behavior in International Economic Relations

1

Foreign Economic Policy:
Some General Principles of Analysis*

Foreign economic policy is not an end in itself. It is part of a country's total foreign policy and to some extent serves the same goals. Yet foreign economic policy is not often discussed from this point of view. Economics deals primarily with the allocation of scarce resources and political science deals primarily with power relations. Most economists and political scientists act as if "never the twain shall meet." In their surveys and studies of international affairs, neither economists nor political scientists have devoted much serious thought to developing a systematic conceptual framework of analysis that would permit discussions of the allocation of scarce resources in support of power relations. The purpose of this essay is to start to lay the foundation of such an analytical framework. I begin in the first section with a brief, general review of some basic principles of foreign policy. The second section examines in greater detail the specific role, potentialities, and limitations of foreign economic policy and describes the proposed analytical framework.

---

*From *American Foreign Economic Policy: Essays and Comments* (New York: Harper and Row, 1968), Part I.

17

Principles of Foreign Policy

If there were one world government, there would be no need to study foreign policy—unless of course we were in communication with life on other planets. As it is, we study foreign policy because the globe is segmented into numerous nation-states, social communities organized within a particular constitutional order prevailing over some specific geographical terrain. These communities are, in a world of innumerable and overlapping organizations, the focal point of political power. All of them claim the right to exercise complete sovereignty over their own internal affairs. Consequently, no one of them can exercise anything even approximating complete sovereignty except within its own borders. The nation-state individually can attempt only to *influence* the external environment, using whatever instruments are at its command. All such actions intended to affect situations beyond the national jurisdiction represent together the foreign policy of the nation-state.

Ideally, foreign policy might be regarded as the reasoned product of creative leadership—concerted, purposive action arising out of a rational perception of the fundamental interests of the nation-state. Policy can mean this and often does, but often it does not, because the political processes out of which policies normally spring are not nearly so simple. To repeat, the nation-state is a social community organized into groups of all kinds, many with extensive foreign as well as domestic interests, and every one with its provisional conception of the overall national interest related ideologically to its own special interest. To the extent that interest is institutionalized, particular interest expresses itself with political power; and out of governmental processes of tension, conflict, and domination, the national interest and the foreign policy of the state emerge—a consensus of purposes and actions that are essentially the end products of a system of domestic power relationships.[1]

No wonder, then, that foreign policy so often seems the product of random, haphazard, or even irrational forces or events. Frequently it is an uneasy compromise formula, the result of deadlocked judgments. And frequently a country has no foreign policy at all, but, owing to indecision or the unwillingness or inability to act, simply drifts with events. Always, though, foreign policy is a function of specific lesser interests within the nation, the offspring of the interplay of powerful institutions, each trying to achieve its own particular ambitions and goals. One interesting implication of this is that the foreign policy of any single state is unlikely to serve the interests of the world community as well as it does those of the national community, for it is an inherent tendency of any collectivity of diverse interests to reconcile conflicts among their separate ambitions, as much as possible, at the expense of outsiders. After all, foreigners don't vote, but citizens do.

But foreign policy is not only a function of specific lesser interests within the nation. To insist on that view alone is to lose sight of the forest for the trees.[2] The foreign policy of a state must ultimately be legitimized by the state's national interest, and its national interest, however specifically defined, encompasses a set of general purposes that transcend the particular ambitions of domestic institutions. In managing the affairs of the nation in relation to its external environment, the government of the state acts as trustee of the separate, often disparate interests within the community, but it also acts as trustee of the interests of the community itself, the most basic of which is self-preservation—*survival*. Nothing is more important to the nation-state than the ability to defend itself against outside attack and to protect itself from outside control. National security must be the ultimate goal of all foreign policies, the irreducible core of every nation's idea of the national interest. As Nicholas Spykman has written, "the basic objective of the foreign policy of all states is the preservation of territorial integrity and political independence."[3]

Thus, even while the foreign-policymakers of the state are expected in their regular operations to promote and protect the specific interests of domestic institutions, they are first of all responsible for the survival of the sovereign nation itself. To the extent that foreign policy is in fact the "reasoned product of creative leadership," it is designed to maximize that single objective: national security. The basic problem of foreign policy is twofold. First, it is necessary to choose a strategy of foreign policy—that is, to identify a series of proximate goals and an action pattern appropriate to them that will ensure the ultimate objective of national security. And second, it is necessary to make the correct choices among the instruments of foreign policy—to allocate means to ends. These are not easy tasks, nor, as we shall see, are they entirely discrete tasks.

The latter problem, that of allocating means to ends, is fundamentally a technical affair. The instruments available to policymakers must be evaluated for their potentiality, both in overall quantitative terms and qualitatively in terms of their suitability for specific tasks. How effective are they, and how interchangeable in practice? It is also necessary to evaluate the costs associated with each instrument of policy. What are likely to be the alternative opportunities foregone when one particular end is sought? And, finally, it is necessary to make the actual allocation itself, hopefully to maximize policy objectives at least cost. This kind of calculus is quite familiar to economists; it is presumably what economics is all about, and it is certainly much of what the making of foreign economic policy is all about. We shall return to this problem below.

For now, let us turn our attention to the other problem of foreign policy—the problem of translating the ultimate objective of national security into an operational strategy of foreign policy. This is a difficult matter, for the concept of national security is not a precise, meaningful guide for action; it is subjective rather than objective in content and consequently rather ambiguous.[4] The presence or absence of external threats to the state's independence and territory can never be measured objectively. It must always remain a matter of subjective evaluation and speculation. National security is measured by the absence of *fear* or external threats, and fear is an idiosyncratic element in international affairs. It is well known that, for reasons only partly explained by special interest, groups within nations and even nations themselves differ widely in their reaction to one and the same external situation. We should not be surprised, therefore, that they differ in their choice of preferred foreign-policy strategy as well.

Likewise, we should not be surprised that their preferences differ when we note that the concept of national security is usually interpreted to imply not only protection of national independence and territorial integrity, but also the preservation of minimum national "core values." For the nation-state as for the individual, physical survival is not usually valued highly unless accompanied by cultural survival as well. In fact, nations have been known as collectivities to risk biological extinction through war rather than risk cultural extinction in peace. And even short of war, they tend to design and implement their foreign policies to protect not only their sovereignty and their borders, but also a certain range of previously acquired values, such as rank, prestige, material possessions, and special privileges. The problem for foreign policy is that such values are by definition subjective. Not only are nations and groups within nations likely to differ in their estimation of the range of values to be considered "basic"; even for any one nation or group that range is apt to prove elastic over time. For instance, it is a familiar phenomenon that military bases, security zones, foreign investments, or commercial concessions may be sought and acquired by a nation for the purpose of protecting basic national values, and that they then become new national values requiring protection themselves. Pushed to its logical conclusion, such extension of the range of values to include more and more marginal values does not stop short of the goal of complete world domination.

Fortunately, from the point of view of world peace, complete world domination is, at any single moment of history, an operative goal in the foreign policies of very few, if any, nation-states, although it is certainly true as well that there are always a number of governments behaving in a manner that can be described as predatory or coercive. However, most governments do not push the logic of national security quite so far and rely instead on less ambitious strategies of foreign policy. To see why, we might draw an analogy between the behavior of states in the international arena and that of competing firms in an oligopolistic market. Like the community of nations, the oligopolistic market is characterized by interdependence and uncertainty: the competitors are sufficiently few in number so that the behavior of any one has an appreciable effect on at least some of its rivals; in turn, the actions and reactions of its rivals cannot be predicted with certainty. This results in an interdependence of decisionmaking, compelling each firm to be noticeably preoccupied with problems of strategy. True, the oligopolist wants to make profits and consequently cannot afford to ignore such important matters as consumer tastes and factor costs. But, above all, he wants to maintain his share of the market and perhaps, if possible, to increase it—in other words, he wants to survive. This means that he must pay particular attention to long-run strategic considerations. He must scrutinize his every move for its effects on the long-term market position of his firm, for its implications concerning the firm's future freedom of action, and for the probable countermoves of the firm's rivals. Rarely is any move undertaken that is likely to threaten seriously the firm's existence.

For the individual oligopolist, a position of monopoly would obviously be preferable to the uncertainty and risk of his current status. But the goal of complete market domination is not an operative goal in the competitive strategies of many firms, for each knows that its rivals, singly or collectively, are also strongly armed with the weapons of price reductions, aggressive advertising, and product improvement. True, one does occasionally observe oligopolistic firms attempting to improve their position or to dominate a large part of the market by means of such predatory policies as price-cutting, monopolizing raw materials or distributive outlets, tying arrangements, and so on. However, most oligopolists prefer to rely on less aggressive strategies that are correspondingly less likely to provoke challenge and retaliation.[5] Some of the larger firms, for example, seem content to settle for a position of previously acquired preeminence, which may be considerably short of complete dominance, but which is in any event acknowledged by at least a part of the market as one of price leadership. Their strategy is to maintain their position, not augment it. Smaller firms find security in associating themselves publicly with the acknowledged price leader and conforming readily to the latter's observed market behavior. Still others, both large and small, enter tacitly or explicitly into collusive arrangements for setting prices and dividing markets; their strategy is to ensure individual survival through mutual compromise and accommodation. And still others adopt a policy of maximum independence, eschewing any consultation or prior agreements with groups of rivals in the process of deciding on their output and prices; their strategy is to ensure survival through neutrality.

To be sure, there are many variations on these few themes, but the important point is that they represent the basic poles of conduct in an oligopolistic market. They also represent the basic strategies of conduct in international affairs: predation, preservation of existing hegemonies, association with a Great Power, compromise agreements and alliances, and neutrality. The question is: What determines the choice of basic strategy? Clearly, a multitude of variables is operative. In an oligopolistic market, the ideological inclinations and moral convictions of the corporate management are not unimportant. Nor are expectations concerning psychological and commercial developments elsewhere in the market. But perhaps most important of all is the market power that the firm can bring to bear to achieve its ends. For the individual firm, the main problem is to choose a set of proximate goals consistent with the resources at its disposal. A small firm, for instance, with little public enthusiasm for its product, no monopoly of any raw material or distributive outlets, and no special access to financial backing, is hardly in a position to elect a policy of immediate market domination. Such behavior would not be rational; much more rational would be a policy of slow accumulation of market power through price "followership" or perhaps tacit collusion. Conversely, a very large firm in a dominant market position cannot adopt a policy of maximum independence, since its actions have such an immediate effect upon and hence are so closely watched by all of its rivals. For such a firm, predation or accepting the role of price leader would be more rational choices.

Firms in the market place tend, of course, to be much more rational in their behavior than states in the international arena. It has already been emphasized that foreign policy, being very largely the product of an internal political process, often seems anything but rational. All kinds of variables enter into the determination of foreign policy, too. Even so, in its role as trustee of the interests of the national community, the government must steer the state away from destruction. National survival is its first responsibility. Therefore, even though there is a wide latitude for the introduction of irrational elements into foreign policy, that latitude is not without limits. Weak, small states cannot rationally aspire to dominate the world, and strong, large states cannot effectively isolate themselves. The proximate goals of foreign policy must fit the resources available, however tenuously. Ultimately, national power sets the limits to the nation-state's choice of a strategy of foreign policy, just as market power sets the limits to the oligopolist's choice of a strategy of competition.

The key word here is choice. In a situation of competition, interdependence, and uncertainty, the survival of any one unit is very much a function of the range of alternative strategies available to it. The oligopolistic firm with only one strategic option leads a precarious existence: if that strategy fails to result in profit, the firm will disappear. Likewise, the nation-state with only one strategic option can never truly be secure: if that strategy fails, the state will disappear or be absorbed by others or, what is more likely, be compelled to abandon certain of its national core values.[6] For both the firm and the state, the rational solution is to broaden its range of options—that is, *to maximize its power position*, since power sets the limits to the choice of strategy. This does not mean that more power must be accumulated than is available to any of one's rivals, nor does it imply that the power must be used coercively. It means only that power must be accumulated *to the extent possible* in order to maximize the range of available strategies. This is the conduct we observe of firms in an oligopolistic market. To the extent that government processes are rational, it is also the conduct we observe of states in the international arena.

What constitutes national power, and what determines the extent to which it can be accumulated? Essentially, power represents the ability to control or at least influence the behavior of others. This ability need not be exercised; it need only be acknowledged by others to be effective. Basically, national power derives from the entire range of the nation's resources, available or potential, and in particular from those resources that have been or could be placed at the disposal of the state's foreign-policymakers. Foremost among these resources, of course, is the military establishment—the organizational and physical entity that wages war. But national power is more than just "forces in being"; it is a function of all of the nation's other resources as well—its industries, population, geographic location and terrain, natural resources, scientific, managerial, and diplomatic skills, and so on. In addition, it is a function of the resources available to the nation's principal rivals, for power is potent only insofar as it balances or outweighs power elsewhere. What truly matters is not so much influence in absolute terms as influence in relation to that of others. True, taking all of these resources into account necessarily implies that national power must remain an ambiguous concept; no one has yet developed satisfactory criteria for measuring its components and ranking them. Nevertheless, each state must, and in practice does, form an approximate idea of its own power and that of its main competitors. Even though the risk of miscalculation is considerable, these estimates are indispensable. They are the necessary raw material from which the choice of foreign-policy strategy is fashioned.

The extent to which national power can be accumulated is implied by the definition of that concept, ambiguous as it may be. National power can be accumulated to the extent permitted by the resources of the state. These set an upper limit. The problem of the state's foreign-policymakers is to maximize national power subject to this constraint—that is, to make most effective use of the available resources in pursuit of the state's proximate foreign-policy goals. It is clear that these goals cannot exceed the sum of resources available. Conversely, it is clear that the available resources must be qualitatively appropriate to the chosen ends. In a real sense, therefore, national power not only sets the limits to the selection of proximate foreign-policy goals; it also provides the instruments for their achievement. This is the sense in which the two basic problems of foreign policy are interrelated: through the sum total of national resources that can be employed to influence the external environment and ensure the ultimate objective of national security. Nowhere is this interrelation more apparent than in the determination of that subset of general foreign policy labeled foreign economic policy, to which we now turn.

Analyzing Foreign Economic Policy

Foreign economic policy represents the sum total of actions by the nation-state intended to affect the economic environment beyond the national jurisdiction. As such it is a hybrid, combining elements of foreign policy in general as well as of economic policy in general.

On the one hand, like *economic* policy in general, foreign economic policy is concerned with the allocation of scarce resources. Ultimately, one of its objectives is to help employ national resources in the most efficient manner possible in order to maximize the production of goods and services available for domestic absorption. The problem for the makers of the state's foreign economic policy is not necessarily to optimize the pattern of foreign trade and investment according to cosmopolitan criteria, for this might leave the nation with fewer goods and services that it could potentially attain. Rather, their problem is, in an immediate sense, to organize foreign trade and investment in whatever pattern is necessary to maximize national income. In a more fundamental sense, their rational long-term objective is to maximize national wealth—the sum total of the nation's productive possessions—since it is from these material resources that the stream of current income derives.

On the other hand, like *foreign* policy in general, foreign economic policy is also concerned with national security. Ultimately, another of its objectives is to help ensure the self-preservation of the political community. In this regard, the problem for the makers of foreign economic policy is, in an immediate sense, to provide maximum support for the chosen strategy of the state's general foreign policy. In a more fundamental sense, their rational long-term objective is to maximize the national power position, since national power plays the same role in relation to foreign economic policy in particular as it does in relation to foreign policy in general. That is, national power both sets the limits to the selection of the proximate goals of foreign economic policy and provides the instruments for their achievement.

Even though foreign economic policy is concerned with the maximization of national power, it can actually operate on only one single element of national power—national *economic* power. What constitutes this particular element of national power? Essentially, national economic power represents the ability to control or influence the behavior of others *in economic matters*. The possibility for influence in economic matters derives from the fact that the world economy, being based on a rather elaborate international division of labor, is in fact a system of inter-relationships in which to a greater or lesser extent every nation is dependent on others—dependent for commodities and services of various kinds, for markets and investments, for technology and skills. These dependencies are tolerated because policymakers, presumably having learned some international economic theory, are generally aware of the tremendous benefits to be had from foreign trade and investment: the availability of goods and services that either cannot be produced at home or can be produced only at relatively high cost, the access to external sources of capital and to foreign investment opportunities, the spread of scientific knowledge. Together, these benefits enrich each nation-state and increase its material wealth. The price to be paid for these gains is dependence on others.

The dependence of one state on another gives the latter influence through its control over that for which the former depends on it. That is, if A depends on B for, say, oil, B can influence A through its ability to control—and *in extremis* to halt—the flow of oil to A. True, B may do itself harm in the process. But if in greater measure A requires oil and cannot locate alternative sources of supply, B's influence over A is effective. Likewise, even in the absence of effective control of the flow of any important commodities or services to A, B can nevertheless exercise effective influence over A if, alternatively, it either provides essential markets for A's production or supplies A with vitally needed investments or foreign aid. With respect to each of these kinds of international economic relationship, A is continuously exposed to the potential threat of a stoppage by B. Herein lies the essence of national economic power. As Albert Hirschman has pointed out, "Thus, the power to interrupt commercial or financial relations with any country, considered as an attribute of national sovereignty, is the root cause of the influence or power position which a country acquires in other countries. . . ."[7]

Ceteris paribus, the greater a state's power to interrupt commercial or financial relations, the stronger its position in international economic affairs. Conversely, the more exposed a state is to potential interruptions of commercial or financial relations—i.e., the greater its dependence on others—the weaker its position in international economic affairs.

No state, not even the United States, has unlimited economic power. On the other hand, we might note that there are some small states so weak in international economic affairs, so overwhelmingly dependent on a single large neighbor, that they essentially have no choice but to rely for their national survival on the latter's tolerance and patronage. In return for assurances of their right to exist as nominally independent political entities, they yield to the patron all effective control of their own economy. The transfer of dominion may be tacit rather than explicit, thus preserving at least the appearance of economic sovereignty, as in the cases, say, of Botswana and Malawi in southern Africa. Or it may be unambiguously confirmed in a formal economic union or other written agreement, as in the cases, say, of Bhutan in Asia, of Andorra, Liechtenstein, Monaco, and San Marino in Europe, and of several island-states scattered about the world's oceans. How the transfer is effected is unimportant in this context. What matters is that in all such cases, national security can be assured only by acquiescing totally in the economic hegemony of another state—in effect, by entering knowingly into the most intimate of associations with a Great (or greater) Power.

However, most states are not nearly so weak in international economic affairs. Hence, for them such intimate associations are either impossible or repugnant. In the first place, there may be no convenient patron on which to rely. The situation just outlined requires that the discrepancy between the economic power of the two neighbors be obvious and overwhelming. Such instances are limited in number; more normally, disparities between neighbors are discernible but not decisive. Furthermore, the situation requires that there be only one logical choice of patron. In fact, many relatively small states find themselves positioned between two or more Great (or greater) Powers, between whom it would be difficult to choose without upsetting the international power balance—and perhaps the domestic power balance as well. In any event, political communities in practice prefer to determine their own destinies. Except under extreme compulsion, most are quite evidently reluctant to surrender control of the national economy to a foreign government. They want economic sovereignty as well as political recognition.

These facts are significant. Since most states neither can nor want to abdicate direction of their economic affairs, they have no alternative but to confront squarely the fact of their dependence on the international economy. If they are to enhance their national security, they must, to the extent permitted by the resources available to them, try to use their foreign economic policies to reduce that dependence—that is, to reduce the potential threat of stoppages in their commercial and financial relations. Furthermore, to counterbalance forms of dependence that cannot be avoided, they must try to increase their own influence on others. By so doing, each state individually will hope to enhance its net influence in the international economy by creating conditions that make interruptions of trade and financial flows of less concern to itself than to others. In short, each state will hope to enhance its national economic power.

This does not mean, though, that each state will necessarily hope to *maximize* its national economic power. In this regard, as already indicated, the rational objective of foreign economic policy is to maximize *national power in general*, of which economic power is only one single element. National power embodies political, military, geographic, and other elements as well, and while it is certainly true that all of these elements are often mutually reinforcing, it is also true that they are not always perfect substitutes. Consequently, the problem for policymakers is to estimate costs and allocate means to ends, hopefully to achieve overall policy goals at the least total cost. At times it may seem necessary to sacrifice one element of national power in order to exploit the more attractive possibilities of another. This is no less true of the element of economic power than of any other. Thus some less developed countries, eager to import the latest in military hardware, have in recent years been willing to sacrifice much of their economic independence by indebting themselves heavily to one or another Great Power, in the expectation that on balance this would increase their overall national power. Likewise, in past years the United States willingly sacrificed a good part of its economic influence in Western Europe by promoting local programs of regional integration, in the expectation that this would enhance our joint political power in confrontation with the Soviet Union. Whether either of these specific strategies was especially wise is a matter best left for evaluation elsewhere. What we must stress here is that the objective of foreign economic policy provides maximum support for the chosen strategy of the state's general foreign policy.

However, foreign economic policy is also, we have said, supposed to provide maximum support for the state's general economic policy; its rational objective is to maximize national wealth, too. To what extent are these two objectives—national power and national wealth—the same? Superficially, they seem to be identical; it seems intuitively obvious that it is the rich who are powerful, the poor who are weak. And indeed often they are. But such is not always the case. Great Britain, for example, is one of the wealthiest nations on the face of the earth, yet in her dealings with the economically underdeveloped Arab states and sheikdoms of the Middle East, absymmally poor except in oil, she does not appear to operate from a position of marked strength. The Arab's ability to control or even halt the international flow of oil gives them a considerable influence over the British. Likewise, the United States is a far richer country than France, yet the French have been able to neutralize and at times even prevail over American strength in the prolonged negotiations on world monetary reform. Apparently France's influence stems from her recent large balance-of-payments surpluses and resulting accumulations of reserves, which have given her the ability to threaten interruptions of international financial relations.

In other words, wealth per se is not sufficient to exercise effective power in international relations: national wealth and national power are not in fact identical. Of course, it is clear that a minimum level of wealth of some sort is a prerequisite, a necessary condition, for the disposition of power. Those without any wealth of any sort have no power at all. The Arabs must be able to produce oil, the French must be able to produce balance-of-payments surpluses. But it is equally clear that the mere possession of wealth is not a guarantee of power. What matters is how that wealth fits into the overall distribution of dependence and influence in international affairs.

These facts have important implications for the analysis of foreign economic policy. Over a broad range of policies, there can be no doubt that the two objectives of national wealth and national power are functionally equal, complementary rather than competing. Many policies that add to the nation's material possessions are also likely to add directly to its net influence in international affairs.   But there is also no doubt that over a certain range of foreign economic policies, the two objectives are in direct conflict. Within this range a choice must be made, as even Adam Smith recognized, admitting that to some extent "defence . . . is of much more importance than opulence. . . ."[8]

Following Smith's advice, states often may choose to forego a certain amount of national wealth if they can thereby augment their national power. Certainly we observe much behavior of this kind in the world economy. We observe states maintaining extremely protectionist commercial policies, despite the familiar arguments stressing the gains from modified free trade. We observe states savoring balance-of-payments surpluses, despite the implied reduction of real domestic absorption relative to national income. We observe states reluctant to admit private investments or public assistance from abroad, despite the attractive charms of foreign capital and imported technology. In all these instances, current income, hence future wealth, is sacrificed for the sake of national power and security.

At the same time, we observe in many instances that states may choose to sacrifice a certain amount of national power for the sake of current income and future wealth. Policies of this kind are not at all uncommon, either. The problem for the makers of foreign economic policy is to sacrifice as little power as possible, since power cannot be foregone without limit if national survival is to be ensured, and to sacrifice as little wealth as possible, since wealth cannot be foregone without limit if the disposition of power is to be effective. In other words, the problem is to maximize jointly two objectives. This in reality is what foreign economic policy is all about.[9]

Several years ago, Harry Johnson planted the seeds of a general analytical approach to the problem of foreign economic policy.[10] It remains for us to harvest the fruits of his efforts, for even though Johnson himself wrote specifically of only one branch of foreign economic policy—commercial policy—his analytical apparatus can be readily generalized. His article begins by noting that the traditional approach to the theory of commercial policy, like all of conventional economic analysis, is based on a clear distinction between "economic" and "noneconomic" objectives. There is, supposedly, only one valid objective of policy—the economic objective of maximizing real income, identifiable with the utility derived by individuals from their personal consumption of goods and services. Noneconomic objectives are irrelevant, since they are *ex hypothesi* irrational. This distinction keeps the analysis neat, but unfortunately it also means, as Johnson writes, that "the economist is left without a theory capable of explaining a variety of important and observable phenomena, such as the nature of tariff bargaining, the commercial policies adopted by various countries, the conditions under which countries are willing to embark on customs unions, and the arguments and considerations that have weight in persuading countries to change their commercial policies."[11]

In order to make the conventional analysis more operationally useful, Johnson abandons the traditional distinction between economic and noneconomic objectives, which as he points out is ethically biased in favor of private consumption as the exclusive measure of welfare. We might also point out that it is politically unrealistic, since it totally ignores power relations. Instead of the traditional distinction, Johnson emphasizes two other distinctions. The first is between private consumption goods and public consumption goods, the latter being commodities and services that are consumed collectively and can be provided only through the government at the cost of sacrifices of private consumption. The second is between "real income" in the sense of utility enjoyed from both private and public consumption, and "real product" defined conventionally as total production of privately appropriable commodities and services. He then assumes that there exists a collective preference for industrial production, in the sense that industrial production appears as a collective consumption good yielding a flow of satisfaction to the public independent of the satisfaction individuals derive directly from the consumption of industrial products. It follows, on the assumption of rationality of government processes, that the makers of the state's foreign economic policy will protect domestic industrial production by imposing tariffs and in general carrying protection to the point where the value of the marginal collective utility derived from collective consumption of domestic industrial activity is just equal to the marginal excess private cost (product foregone) of protected industrial production. Real income will be maximized, though real product will not, since maximization of real income requires sacrificing real product in order to gratify the preference for collective consumption of industrial production. In equilibrium, the proportional marginal excess private cost of protected production measures the marginal "degree of preference" for industrial production.

To generalize Johnson's analysis, let us first substitute for his assumed collective preference for industrial production a preference for the collective consumption of national power (including economic power). By definition, national power can, within a certain range of foreign economic policies, be provided only through the government at the cost of sacrifices of private consumption. We have already explained, from the perspective of political science, why rational policymakers would in fact adopt this public consumption good as an immediate objective; in addition, we need only assume that the public itself shares the government's concern for national survival. Meanwhile, let us preserve Johnson's assumption that a second objective of national policy is to maximize what Johnson labels "real product," since in fact this corresponds to what conventional economic analysis stresses as the immediate objective of rational policymakers. And finally, let us assume that the overall objective of foreign economic policy is to maximize "real income" in the sense of the utility enjoyed from both private consumption of real product and collective consumption of national power. From these assumptions together with the assumption of rationality of government processes, it follows that, within that range where the objectives of national power and real product are in conflict, foreign economic policies will necessarily depart from the standard production-maximization precepts of economic analysis: within that range current income will be sacrificed for the sake of national security *up to the point where the value of the marginal collective utility derived from collective consumption of national power is just equal to its marginal excess private cost.* Real income will be maximized, though real product will not. In equilibrium, the proportional marginal excess private cost of national power measures the marginal "degree of preference" for national power.

Of course, government processes are not at all as rational as this implies. It cannot be emphasized too often that policy, being very largely the product of an internal political process, in fact frequently seems anything but rational. Nevertheless, since it is in their interest to maximize policy objectives at least cost, policymakers do manifestly attempt at least a rough approximation of the sort of calculus just outlined. In formal language, they try to ensure that the marginal excess private cost of national power does not exceed the marginal degree of preference for national power. More simply, they try not to pay for net influence in the world more than they think it is worth.

This analytical approach to the problem of foreign economic policy can be very useful operationally. Its insights help to explain a variety of important and observable phenomena in this area of study. For instance, they help us to understand why, in confronting the fact of their dependence on the world economy, nations do not simply seek to avoid every form of dependence by refusing to participate at all in international economic affairs. This is the policy of autarky—total economic isolation and self-sufficiency—and it certainly does exclude the threat of interruptions of commercial and financial relations, but it does so negatively by eliminating the relations rather than the threat. This is akin to throwing the baby out with the bath water. In the view of most states, autarky represents economic security purchased at too high a price; it is just not worth foregoing all of the gains from foreign trade and investment, particularly since some of them at least should be expected to increase rather than decrease the state's net international influence.

As a matter of fact, no state in modern times has ever achieved total segregation from the world economy. Not even the Soviet Union, in the most autarkic phases of its development, ever felt that it could afford to forego all of the benefits of international economic specialization. True, for decades the Soviets officially regarded foreign trade as no more than an unavoidable residual— a means for uncorking bottlenecks in the domestic planning mechanism. The price they were willing to pay for minimizing foreign influence was quite high. But it is noteworthy that in more recent years, that price has fallen dramatically. Indeed, these very same Soviets have now actually renounced autarky as an official policy. Instead, they are beginning to preach the advantages of an international division of labor, albeit a "socialist" international division of labor.[12] Presumably this seemingly ideological qualification is in fact a practical one reflecting the discrepancy between the Soviet Union's preponderant economic influence within the Communist bloc and its rather limited influence elsewhere. To that extent, the Soviet Union's behavior represents a rational effort to maximize national power at least cost and is wholly consistent with the analytical approach outlined.

In summary, the overall objective of foreign economic policy is the joint maximization of the state's current income and its net influence in international affairs. The practical problem of foreign economic policy is to allocate means to ends—that is, to make most effective use of all available national resources in pursuit of the overall objective, the idea being ultimately to provide maximum support for the general foreign policy of the state. National resources here are defined as broadly as possible to include all means and instruments that can be employed in the interest of the state to influence the external economic environment. Generally, these resources can be grouped under four principal policy headings: (1) commercial policy, (2) foreign-investment policy, (3) foreign-aid policy, and (4) balance-of-payments policy.[13] Each of these can be discussed separately.

Commercial Policy. Commercial policy represents the sum total of actions by the state intended to affect the extent, composition, and direction of its imports and exports of goods and services. These actions include not only the familiar direct interventions in international trade, such as tariffs, subsidies, quotas, exchange controls, official procurement policies, state trading, and the like, but also the many indirect interventions, ranging from domestic revenue taxes and pricing policies to sanitary regulations, advertising restrictions, and packaging requirements. They might also be said to include a variety of private business practices, such as market allocation among the domestic and foreign affiliates of large national corporations.

International economic theory teaches that given all the Pareto optimality conditions of the perfectly competitive market, free trade maximizes world income. However, if the individual state exercises any degree of monopoly-monopsony power in world markets, its own income is not maximized, and even if the state lacks such power, its own income is likely to fall short of the potential maximum if there are significant departures from Pareto optimality. Consequently, some interventions in foreign trade can be justified on conventional economic grounds as means for improving the state's terms of trade or as "second-best" corrections of domestic "distortions."[14] Most interventions, though, cannot be justified so easily. Most are plainly the product of special-interest legislation, the outcome of the efforts of powerful domestic institutions to achieve their own particular ambitions and goals at the expense of the general welfare of the national community as well as of the outside world. As a result, most forms of trade intervention are notoriously "sticky": once enacted, they take on a life of their own and are difficult—if not impossible—to remove.

Even so, the makers of a state's commercial policy are not completely without room for maneuver. Most forms of trade intervention can be at least manipulated in the interest of the national community, and many can in fact be negotiated away in return for significant concessions from others. The problem is to manipulate and negotiate to affect the extent, composition, and direction of the state's foreign trade in such a way that, subject to the constraint of special-interest legislation that remains, the state's net international influence is jointly maximized along with its current income. If there were no special-interest legislation at all, any interventions lowering rather than raising income would be justified solely as the price to be paid for maximizing this aspect of national power.

An almost infinite variety of manipulations and negotiations of commercial policy is possible, depending on the resources available to the state and the proximate goals of its general foreign policy. Assume, for instance, a small state—small in population, in geographic area, and in natural resources—trying to follow a path of political neutrality in international affairs. Being small, it is likely to be rather highly specialized in the relatively few lines of production in which it enjoys a comparative advantage. Consequently, it is likely as well to be rather highly dependent on foreign trade, as measured by the proportion of exports and imports to total national production. Being neutral, however, it presumably wishes to minimize the influence on itself of the outside world in general and of any single Great Power in particular. It will therefore use its commercial policy defensively to minimize the danger to itself of stoppages in any part of its foreign trade. Its first aim will be to diversify the national production structure. This will not only reduce the state's overall dependence on foreign trade, thereby reducing its dependence on the outside world; it will also alter the commodity composition of its foreign trade, increasing the range of exports while probably decreasing that of imports, thereby reducing the state's specific dependence on any single trade item. In addition, the state will use its commercial policy to diversify the geographic composition of its trade, in order to ensure that no single large trading partner will control too great a share of its foreign markets or sources of supply.[15]

Now, in contrast, assume a large state trying to follow a path of political predation or preservation of existing hegemonies. This state will use its commercial policy aggressively rather than defensively.[16] It will attempt to exploit the fact that, being large, it is likely already to be an important influence in world trade, even though, in relation to its own total production, its exports and imports may be rather small. Logically, its aim will be to maximize its power to threaten interruptions of the commercial relations of others, particularly of those others it wishes to dominate (or continue to dominate), at least cost to itself. Thus this state will, first of all, oppose all efforts by others to restrict or divert international trade in general, on the principle that this could diminish the power it derives from its domination of individual markets either as buyer or seller. Second, it will itself seek to divert its own trade away from states larger and richer than itself to states smaller and poorer, on the principle that this creates conditions that make the interruption of mutual trade of much graver concern to each of its trading partners than to itself. Third, it may also promote exports of highly differentiated industrial products in place of primary commodities, on the principle that importing countries can in the event of stoppage less easily switch suppliers of the former type of good than of the latter type. And last, it may offer special price or other advantages to some of its own suppliers, on the principle that this renders more painful the diversion of a trading partner's exports to third countries.

For a final, intermediate case, assume a state that, being neither small enough to be neutral and innocuous nor large enough to be predatory or hegemonic, seeks to preserve its national security through a general foreign policy of compromise agreements and alliances. In support of this policy it is likely to direct its trade toward its friends and allies, since this would minimize the threat of potential stoppages of its trade with more hostile trading partners. It may even agree to a free-trade area or customs-union arrangement, since this would in addition maximize the group's joint power to bargain and to threaten interruptions of the trade of others. In unity there is strength. In unity there is also relatively little—if any—economic cost. In this case, the price of national security is the sacrifice of a certain degree of economic sovereignty.

These are the three principal lines of commercial policy. It seems readily apparent that in the real world virtually all states do in fact follow one or another or some combination of them. Many of the less developed countries, for example, follow the first line of policy, for the most part because of their general interest in nonalignment with any of the large power blocs, but also simply because of their political failure in almost all cases to agree on an effective approach along the third line of policy. Likewise, the first line of policy is preferred by a few of the more advanced countries, mainly those like Japan and Australia that happen to be relatively isolated at the fringes of the developed world. Most of the advanced countries, though, are more partial to the third line of policy. This is particularly true of Canada and of the small and medium-sized states of Europe on either side of the disintegrating Iron Curtain, for whom the key to survival has become compromise and alliance. The very largest countries, of course, whose principal desire is to preserve or extend existing hegemonies, favor the second line of policy, albeit modified in some proportion by the third in the interest of maintaining local alliances or strengthening bargaining power. And finally, we should not forget the very smallest countries, whose extreme application of the third line of policy has already been alluded to.

Foreign-Investment Policy. Foreign-investment policy represents the sum total of actions by the state intended to affect the extent, composition, and direction of private direct and portfolio investments both by residents abroad and by foreigners domestically. These actions include principally taxes and administrative regulations of various kinds, but also monetary policy to a certain extent. Their purpose is to manipulate the stock as well as the flow of private international investments in such a way as to jointly maximize the state's national power and current income.

There can be little doubt that with respect to the problem of maximizing current income, international investments benefit both capital-exporting and capital-importing countries. Otherwise, we would hardly expect to find such large flows of private capital as we do observe in the world today. For the host countries, foreign investments can bring not only short-run support of the balance-of-payments position, but also supplements to domestic savings, permitting them higher levels of gross capital formation than would otherwise be possible. For the investing countries, meanwhile, foreign investments can provide alternative outlets for domestic savings yielding higher marginal returns than investments at home, as well as eventually produce a reflow of income that can provide support to the balance of payments in the longer run. In these respects, capital-exporting and capital-importing countries share certain interests in common.

However, with respect to the problem of maximizing national power, the same is only partially true at best—and utterly false at worst. A basic motive of foreign investment is to minimize the danger of stoppages in the capital-exporting country's foreign trade by increasing the reliability of markets for exports and sources of supply for imports.[17] This ambition coincides with the security interests of the capital-importing country only if the latter is not disinclined toward close economic and political association with the capital exporter. If, contrarily, the capital importer prefers a policy of neutrality, the investments may not be welcomed at all, except possibly as a counterweight to investments from other sources. And the investments may be actively opposed if the capital importer prefers association not with the capital exporter at all but rather with some third party. Moreover, even if the capital importer is not disinclined toward a close relationship with the capital exporter, such investments may be restricted if they threaten foreign domination of important sectors of the domestic economy.

Thus a capital-importing country will often, on security

grounds, seek to constrain the flow of private investments from abroad below the level that might otherwise be dictated by purely market criteria. As a result, clear economic benefits are lost both to it and to the capital exporter. We should note, however, that there is a discrepancy in the gains foregone. Whereas the capital exporter loses only the extra profits that would have accrued from investments abroad rather than at home or in some third country, the capital importer loses the entire investment together with the increased production and improved technology that might have resulted from it. This implies that in the field of policy relating to the flow of private foreign investments, the capital-exporting country maintains one basic advantage: it has the resources; the capital importer does not. This advantage gives the capital-exporting country a considerable influence over the capital importer, since it can be used to withhold new investments, to bargain over their composition and the conditions affecting them, or even to divert them when necessary to less hostile recipients.

On the other hand, in the field of policy relating to the already existing stock of private foreign investments, the capital-importing country maintains one basic advantage: it has direct political control over the investment; the capital exporter does not. This advantage gives the capital-importing country a considerable advantage over the capital exporter, since it can be used to restrict or supervise the activities of the investment, or even to halt its operation or confiscate it when necessary. Obviously, this directly negates the basic motive of foreign investment in the first place, which was to minimize the danger of stoppages in trade. The capital exporter's rational response to such threats is to attempt, to the extent possible, to diversify the composition of foreign investments and to disperse them geographically. Where this is difficult because of specificity of investment needs or of supply or market possibilities, the stage is set for a conflict of policies between capital exporter and capital importer, the outcome of which will depend ultimately on the price each is willing to pay for this aspect of national power.

Foreign-Aid Policy. Foreign-aid policy represents the sum total of actions by the state intended to affect the extent, composition, and direction of foreign public assistance given or received. Like other foreign economic policies, its purpose is to maximize jointly the state's national power and current income. Its analysis is fairly straightforward since the main economic gains all accrue to the recipient while the main political benefits all accrue to the donor. Thus the recipient will seek to maximize the benefits of foreign aid obtained at least cost in terms of dependence on other states, while the donor will seek to maximize its influence abroad at least cost in terms of foregone alternative uses of public capital. This helps to explain why, for example, recipients favor multilateral aid programs while donors favor bilateral ones, and also why donors try to concentrate their aid efforts geographically while recipients try to diversify the sources of the help they receive. And of course it certainly helps to explain why, from the point of view of the recipients, who are preoccupied with the problem of development, the donors' efforts never seem adequate.

Balance-of-Payments Policy. Balance-of-payments policy represents the sum total of actions by the state intended to affect the net demand or supply of foreign exchange. These actions include all of those listed under the three other categories of policy insofar as they bear upon the international payments adjustment process, as well as any other monetary, fiscal, or administrative device that influences, either directly or through its effect on private market behavior, the surplus or deficit in the balance of payments. In addition, they include all actions affecting the composition of the state's international monetary reserves.

International economic theory teaches that balance-of-payments surpluses are not inherently desirable, since they imply a reduction of real domestic absorption relative to national income. Conversely, deficits are not inherently undesirable, since they permit a nation to "live beyond its means." Nevertheless, the makers of foreign economic policy abhor deficits and prefer surpluses whenever possible. The reason is simple and relates to the inadequacies of the international payments adjustment mechanism under a regime of relatively fixed exchange rates. To begin with, it is evident that under this type of regime, persistent payments imbalances can emerge only because of conflicts within individual countries between the policies that are considered appropriate for the current state of the domestic economy and the policies that are considered appropriate for the current state of the balance of payments. If there were no such conflicts within separate countries, the payments imbalances between them would disappear. For instance, if a

mutual imbalance reflected a combination of deficit and inflation in A and a combination of surplus and recession in B, there
would be no internal policy conflict for either country. A would
deflate, B would reflate, and balance would be restored. However, a problem arises if, as is so often the case, deficits are
associated with recession (or absence of inflation) and surpluses
with inflation (or absence of recession). Then there is a conflict
within each country between its domestic and balance-of-
payments policies—a conflict most governments prefer to resolve
in favor of the former. As a result, the internal policy conflict
gets translated into an international policy conflict. The conflict
will persist for as long as the mutual imbalance of payments can
be financed by the flow of gold and foreign-exchange reserves.

Now, there is virtually no limit to how long a surplus country
can accumulate reserves. On the other hand, there is a distinct
limit to how long a deficit country can deplete its reserves, a
limit determined by the size of its reserve stock plus its access to
external credit facilities. The pressures on the deficit and
surplus countries are not symmetrical. Consequently, the deficit
country is, more often than not, the one forced to take the initial
steps to resolve the international policy conflict, usually at its
own expense.[18]   In this sense, the surplus country exercises an
important influence over the economy and policies of the deficit
country. The influence may be implicit in the former country's
accumulation of the latter country's reserves, or it may be made
explicit in the form of conditions and "strings" attached to the
extension of credit facilities or balance-of-payments support.
Either way, the situation represents for the deficit country a
form of dependence that it would prefer to circumvent. The
easiest way for it to do so is to become a surplus country itself,
capable of exercising an influence of its own. That is why the
makers of foreign economic policy generally prefer surpluses to
deficits, despite the evident cost in terms of real domestic
absorption foregone. This cost measures the price they are
willing to pay for maximizing this aspect of national power.
Sometimes the price they are willing to pay is strikingly high,
as in the case of France in most years after General de Gaulle
first came to power in the 1960s.

For reserve-currency countries, the situation has another dimension. A reserve-currency country functions as a sort of banker for
the world: its money is held by other states as part of their
international reserves. There are several reasons why some

states want to hold the money of another. In the past they were all based on the essential assumption of a fixed-price relationship between the reserve currency and gold, which all states considered the ultimate in international currency. Significantly, the right to alter the gold value of the reserve currency—in other words, its exchange rate—rested solely with the reserve-currency country. This right gave the reserve-currency country a considerable influence over its "depositors"—in fact, a sort of hegemony in monetary affairs—and under appropriate circumstances could largely free it from balance-of-payments constraints. For rather than risk forcing a devaluation of the reserve currency in terms of gold, the depositors were often willing to "lend" to the reserve-currency country—that is, accept balances of its currency—to the amount of any deficit the latter happened to incur; further, they were often willing to resolve the international policy conflict themselves at their own expense. In such cases, the influence afforded states by surpluses in their payments balances was neutralized by the unique advantages afforded the reserve-currency country by its control over the gold value of its own money.

However, if the reserve-currency country's deficits persisted for too long, its depositors were not apt to remain quite so passive. Significantly, any single depositor had the right to convert its own reserve balance, despite the risk that by so exercising the influence afforded it by current payments surpluses or past reserve accumulations, it might be seriously jeopardizing the gold value of the balances of remaining depositors. From the point of view of the rebellious depositor, the risk might have been worthwhile if it could thereby increase its net influence vis-à-vis the reserve-currency country. From the point of view of the reserve-currency country, the problem was to decide what price it was willing to pay in order to maintain its hegemonic position in world monetary affairs. That price could be counted in terms of the deviations from present domestic policies that would have been required to reduce or eliminate its deficits, or in terms of the concessions—monetary or otherwise—that would have been required to prevent remaining depositors from following the example of the rebel. In its current confrontation with France in the 1960s, a most rebellious depositor, the United States, the world's principal reserve-currency country, appeared willing to pay a strikingly high price, indeed as high as General de Gaulle seemed prepared to pay for his surpluses. This was not surprising, since the stakes for both were so great: in effect, predominance in Europe. Here was dramatic confirmation of the basic fact that the ultimate role of foreign economic policy is to provide maximum support for the general foreign policy of the nation-state.

Notes

1. A foremost exponent of this point of view is Anthony Downs, who argues that all government actions (not only foreign policy) are motivated exclusively by a desire to maximize votes; policies are merely means toward this end. It therefore follows, assuming rationality on the part of decisionmakers, that general policy never represents anything more than the largest possible coalition of particular interests. See his *An Economic Theory of Democracy* (New York: Harper & Row, 1957). However, it should be noted that Downs's perspective is much too narrowly defined, for he fails to recognize that the nation-state itself may have certain general interests transcending the specific interests of domestic institutions.

2. See Paul Seabury, *Power, Freedom and Diplomacy: The Foreign Policy of the United States of America* (New York: Random House, 1963), Ch. 4.

3. Nicholas Spykman, *America's Strategy in World Politics* (New York: Harcourt, Brace & World, 1942), p. 17.

4. See Arnold Wolfers, "'National Security' as an Ambiguous Symbol," *Political Science Quarterly*, LXVII (December, 1952), pp. 481-502.

5. See Joe S. Bain, *Industrial Organization* (New York: John Wiley, 1959), Ch. 8.

6. In economics, clearly, the standard of success or failure is much more visible and "objective" than it is in politics. Profits can be measured, and when they are negative the firm will be liquidated; for even while the owners of an enterprise value its survival highly, they will be willing to see it go out of business if it produces only losses. The citizens of a nation-state, however, are rarely willing to see their country "go out of business," come what may. Rather, they prefer to contract their range of core values, often quite drastically, for the sake of national survival. But since values are by definition subjective, it is a

most difficult problem to know precisely when the state is producing "losses."

7. Albert O. Hirschman, *National Power and the Structure of Foreign Trade* (Berkeley: University of California Press, 1945), p. 16.

8. Adam Smith, *The Wealth of Nations* (Modern Library ed.; New York: Random House, 1937), p. 431.

9. Even the mercantilists of the seventeenth and eighteenth centuries regarded wealth and power as joint objectives. According to a popular misconception, power was for the mercantilists the sole end of foreign economic policy, with wealth valued mainly as a necessary means toward that end. But in fact there is remarkably little evidence to support this interpretation of mercantilist thought and practice; most of the evidence indicates that wealth, like power, was regarded as valuable simply for its own sake. See Jacob Viner, "Power versus Plenty as Objecitves of Foreign Policy in the Seventeenth and Eighteenth Centuries," *World Politics*, I (October, 1948), pp. 1-29.

10. Harry G. Johnson, "An Economic Theory of Protectionism, Tariff Bargaining, and the Formation of Customs Unions," *Journal of Political Economy*, LXXIII (June, 1965), pp. 256-283.

11. Ibid., p. 257.

12. See, e.g., V. P. Sergeyev, "Economic Principles of the Foreign Trade of Socialist States," in R. F. Harrod and D. C. Hague (eds.), *International Trade Theory in a Developing World* (New York: St. Martin's, 1963), pp. 277-296.

13. As a fifth category, we might also list immigration policy, defined to include actions by the state affecting the outward as well as inward movement of labor (human capital). However, we have decided to exclude discussion of this category here on the grounds that in practice policymakers treat it primarily as a social problem rather than as a matter of economic analysis.

14. Harry G. Johnson, "Optimal Trade Intervention in the Presence of Domestic Distortions," in Robert E. Baldwin, et al., *Trade, Growth and the Balance of Payments* (Chicago: Rand McNally, 1965), pp. 3-34.

15. Hirschman describes this last aim as "an elementary defensive principle of the smaller trading countries." Hirschman, *National Power*, p. 31.

16. Ibid., Ch. 2.

17. Alternatively, this motive can be expressed as a desire on the part of investing enterprises to avoid uncertainty by

reducing their competition; effectively, this emerges as a desire to maintain or augment oligopolistic market shares. See Stephen Hymer, "Direct Foreign Investment and International Oligopoly," June, 1965 (Yale University, Economic Growth Center: mimeo).

18. Actually, this statement is accurate only as a first approximation. In fact, the problem of who initiates the adjustment process and who pays the costs of adjustment is a much more complicated matter. See Benjamin J. Cohen, *Adjustment Costs and the Distribution of New Reserves*, Princeton Studies in International Finance, no. 18 (Princeton: International Finance Section, 1966).

2

United States Monetary Policy and Economic Nationalism*

Is United States monetary policy becoming more nationalistic? In this essay I shall argue that American policy is *not* becoming more nationalistic—for the simple reason that *it always has been nationalistic*. In international monetary affairs, America has always acted out of an instinct for self-interest. That has not changed. What has changed is the willingness of other countries to acquiesce in America's pursuit of its self-interest: others no longer see this as being in their own interest as well. And so what they once regarded as world leadership by the United States, they now brand as economic nationalism. In fact, this says more about the changes in their own attitudes and perceptions—and about changes in the international monetary system in general—than it does about the specifics of United States monetary policy. It is not so much the *content* as the *context* of American policy that has really changed.

Two Key Phrases

The above remarks will be substantiated in the remainder of this chapter. But to begin with, it would be useful if I make clear what I mean by the two key phrases of my initial question.

Monetary Policy. In the domestic context, where the underlying structure of the monetary system normally tends to be relatively stable, monetary policy can be understood simply to describe the use of variations in the quantity of money and/or level of interest rates to tighten or ease monetary conditions and hence to lower or raise aggregate demand. In the international context,

---

*From Otto Hieronymi (ed.), *The New Economic Nationalism* (London: Macmillan, 1980), ch. 3.

however, things tend to be a bit more complicated. Unlike the domestic monetary system, the underlying structure of the international monetary system cannot be assumed to be stable, even for comparatively short periods of time. In this context, therefore, monetary policy must be understood to operate on two levels, not just one—on the level of "structure" as well as on the level of "process." (Process level refers to the conduct of policy *within* a given set of institutions and "rules of the game"; structure level refers to policies designed to *change* given institutions and rules of the game.) At the process level, monetary policy operates (in conjunction with fiscal policy) to achieve the purposes of *macroeconomic management*; its principle concerns are the rate of real economic growth and/or unemployment, the rate of inflation, the balance of payments and the exchange rate. At the structure level, by contrast, monetary policy operates to achieve the purposes of *monetary reform*, its principal concerns being the mechanism of balance-of-payments adjustment and the mechanism for creation and control of the supply of international reserves and payments financing. When speaking of monetary policy, it is important to keep both these levels of operation in mind.

Economic Nationalism. There tends to be an ambiguity about this phrase. Popularly it is understood to apply to any policy motivated by pursuit of self-interest. But by that definition virtually all policies must be described as nationalistic, since virtually all states have well defined policy objectives— economic welfare, political security, domestic autonomy, international prestige—and purposefully design and implement their policy instruments to achieve them. What, then, is the problem? The problem—and the source of the ambiguity—is the lack of a qualifying adjective. Economic nationalism may be, broadly speaking, either "malign" or "benign." Malign nationalism seeks national goals relentlessly, even at the expense of others; benign nationalism, by contrast, is prepared to compromise national policy priorities where necessary to accommodate the interests of others. The difference between these two types of nationalism lies in the willingness of a country to identify its own national interest with an interest in the stability of the overall international system. Benign nationalism acknowledges a connection between self-interest and systemic interest; malign nationalism ignores or denies it. When speaking of economic nationalism, it is important to keep this distinction in mind as well.

Benign Nationalism

Having defined these two key phrases, now consider again our initial question: Is United States monetary policy becoming more nationalistic? The answer, I have suggested, is that American policy has always been nationalistic. But in that case, to paraphrase Gertrude Stein, what is the question?[1] The question is, is the nationalism of United States policy becoming more malign?

The reason that American policy has always been nationalistic is that while the United States is clearly the paramount state actor in global economic relations, and has been throughout much of the twentieth century, it is also one of the world's most closed national economies, whose main orientation is still basically inward rather than outward. These two facts combine to establish a fundamental American bias toward maintenance of policy autonomy in monetary matters. As a leading economy, the United States naturally prizes its ability to act unilaterally to promote objectives believed to be in the national interest. As a closed economy, the United States accords a lesser priority to external considerations relative to domestic policy needs. The key objective of American policy, therefore, has always been to minimize any balance-of-payments constraint on the government's decisionmaking capacity, in order to maximize the country's self-interested freedom of action in domestic and foreign affairs. That was, of course, the great advantage of the old Bretton Woods system from the United States' point of view. Because of the central role of the dollar in monetary affairs, there was relatively little effective external discipline on American policy autonomy. Ever since the breakdown of the Bretton Woods system in 1971, America's manifest goal has been to preserve as much as possible of the special privileges it had learned to enjoy in the years after World War II. At both process level and structure level, American policy since 1971 has continued to be framed with that basic vested interest in mind.

But that does not mean that American policy has been, or is necessarily becoming, malign. To understand why this is so, it is necessary to go back to first principles—in this instance, to the so-called "n-1 principle" of international monetary theory, also known as the "redundancy problem."[2] In a world of n sovereign states and currencies, there are only n-1 exchange rates. Therefore, only n-1 balance-of-payments policies (be they expressed in

terms of exchange-rate targets in a floating world or in terms of
reserve targets in a pegged-rate world) can be independently
determined. One country (the nth country) is redundant. If all n
countries try to set their policies independently, these policies
will almost certainly be inconsistent (technically, the system
will be overdetermined), and, as a result, the stability of the
system itself will be threatened. To preserve monetary stability,
some means must be found—some organizing principle—that will
ensure consistency among national policies and reduce the risk of
policy conflict. The history of international monetary relations
is written in the succession of attempts by the international
community to find such an organizing principle.[3]

   In theory, four alternative organizing principles are possible.
These are:

   1. *Automaticity.* A self disciplining regime of rules and conventions binding for all nations (for example, a gold standard or pure floating exchange rates).
   2. *Supranationality.* A regime founded on collective adherence to the decisions of some autonomous international organization (for example, a world central bank).
   3. *Hegemony.* A regime organized around a single country
   with acknowledged responsibilities (and privileges) as
   leader.
   4. *Negotiation.* A regime of shared responsibility and
   decisionmaking.

   In practice, only one of these four has ever actually succeeded
for any length of time in preserving international monetary
stability. That one is the principle of hegemony, which underlay operation of both the classical gold standard in the last
decades before World War I and the Bretton Woods system in the
first decades after World War II. In each case the monetary
system was effectively organized around a single hegemonic
leader—Great Britain in the earlier period, the United States in
the later. In both cases the comparative lack of policy conflict
was directly attributable to the stabilizing influence of the
dominant national power.

   Recent historical analysis has amply demonstrated that the
classical gold standard, far from being the politically symmetrical system of conventional textbook models, was in fact
distinctly hierarchical, dominated at the top by Great Britain,

the supreme economic power of the day.[4]   Stability in the gold standard was ensured through a trio of roles that only Britain at the time had the resources to play: (1) maintaining a relatively open market for the exports of countries in balance-of-payments difficulties; (2) providing contracyclical foreign long-term lending; and (3) acting as lender of last resort in times of exchange crisis. These were not roles that the British deliberately sought or even particularly welcomed. As far as the Bank of England was concerned, its monetary policies were dictated solely by the need to protect its narrow reserves and the gold convertibility of the pound. It did not regard itself as responsible for global monetary stabilization. Yet this is precisely the responsibility that was thrust upon it in practice—acquired, like the British Empire itself, more or less in a fit of absence of mind. This was truly a hegemonic regime, in the sense that Britain not only dominated the system but also gave monetary relations whatever degree of inherent stability they possessed.

A parallel role was played by the United States after World War II. As dominant then as Britain had been in the nineteenth century, America rapidly assumed the same three managerial roles—in effect, taking over as money manager of the world. Since international monetary reserves were everywhere in short supply, the United States itself became the residual source of global liquidity through its balance-of-payments deficits. At war's end, America owned almost three-quarters of the world's existing monetary gold, and prospects for new gold production were obviously limited by the physical constraints of nature. The rest of the world, therefore, was more than willing to economize on this scarce gold supply by accumulating dollars instead. The United States was accorded the unique privilege of liability-financing its deficits; the dollar became enshrined not only as the principal "vehicle currency" for international trade and investment but also as the principal reserve asset for central banks. In the early postwar years, America's deficits became the universal solvent to keep the machinery of Bretton Woods running. The Bretton Woods system became synonymous with a hegemonic regime centered on the dollar.

In effect, the United States became the worlds nth country, abjuring any balance-of-payments target of its own. Other countries set independent payments targets; consistency in global monetary relations was ensured by the fact that America could be counted upon to play a passive role in the international adjustment process. American policy was freed to concentrate largely on domestic stabilization objectives. Its only express international monetary objective was to maintain the fixed dollar price of gold—although, implicitly, the United States also had an obligation to manage its domestic policies with the needs of the rest of the world in mind. Given America's weight in the global economy, conditions inside the United States inevitably had a considerable influence on the pace of economic developments elsewhere as well. America was the balance wheel of the world economy. (The only recourses other countries had to adjust to movements of the balance wheel were either to modify their balance-of-payments targets or else to alter the par values of their currencies against the dollar and gold.) Keeping the balance wheel moving stably was what the responsibility of being world money manager was all about.

Like the British in the nineteenth century, the Americans did not deliberately seek this responsibility. On the other hand, unlike the British, once they found themselves with it, they soon came to welcome it, for reasons that clearly were not unrelated to self-interest. Being money manager of the world fit in well with America's newfound leadership role in the Western Alliance. The Cold War had begun, and the United States perceived the need to promote the economic recovery of potential allies in Europe and Japan, as well as to maintain a sizable and potent military establishment overseas. All of this cost money: The privilege of liability-financing deficits meant that America was effectively freed from all balance-of-payments constraints and could spend as freely as it thought necessary to promote objectives believed to be in the national interest. The United States could issue the world's principal vehicle and reserve currency in amounts presumed to be consistent with its own policy priorities—and not necessarily those of foreign dollar holders. Foreign dollar holders conceded this policy autonomy to the United States because it also contributed directly to their own economic rehabilitation. America's pursuit of self-interest was seen as being in their interest as well.

In effect, an implicit bargain was struck. Washington's allies acquiesced in a hegemonic system that accorded the United States special privileges to act unilaterally to promote American interests. The United States, in turn, condoned its allies' use of the system to promote their own economic prosperity, even if this happened to come occasionally at the short-term expense of the United States. American policy was demonstrably nationalistic—but it was a nationalism that could credibly be described as benign rather than malign. The situation was characterized best by a phrase that became fashionable near the end of the Bretton Woods era: "benign neglect." The United States acknowledged the connection between its own interest and the stability of the overall system—and acted accordingly.

Systemic Changes

Since the breakdown of the Bretton Woods system, the United States has continued to act in a demonstrably nationalistic fashion. At the process level, America's monetary policy has continued to be focused almost exclusively on domestic stabilization objectives. During the Bretton Woods period, the Federal Reserve routinely sterilized the internal monetary consequences of external deficits: that has not changed since 1971. Nor has there been any significant change in the priority accorded domestic considerations in the management of the nation's monetary aggregates and credit conditions. (The raising of interest rates in December 1977 in response to the accelerating depreciation of the dollar was a highly unusual exception.) Likewise at the structure level, American policy continues to be motivated by a desire to preserve as much freedom of action in monetary affairs as possible. This explains, for example, America's strong support of the present regime of floating exchange rates. (Floating rates are especially convenient to a large, closed economy like the United States.) It also explains America's determined resistance to all global reform proposals that might reduce the central reserve role of the dollar. Why submit to more external discipline than necessary? Such an attitude obviously underlay Washington's expressed preference in the Committee of Twenty both for a "tight" adjustment process (presumably intended to relieve some of the pressures to alter domestic American policies that might arise in the event of future payments deficits) and a "loose" settlement system (presumably intended to allow more cumulative deficits in the future). Suspension in 1971 of the dollar's gold convertibility eliminated the one major weapon that foreign governments had for restricting America's freedom of action. The United States has not been eager to submit to effective new constraints on its decisionmaking capacity.

At only one point, however, has America's persistent nationalism threatened to become malign rather than benign. That was in the pivotal year 1971, when the Bretton Woods system was brought down by America's own aggressive actions. Toward the end of the 1960s, the United States had begun to feel severely constrained by a growing threat of conversions of official dollar balances into gold. Although most observers agreed that the dollar had become overvalued, America felt powerless to alter the value of the dollar unilaterally. (All the United States could do was alter the dollar price of gold: it was up to other countries to make the devaluation effective by intervening in the exchange market at appropriate new rates in terms of their own currencies.) Yet America also felt powerless to persuade surplus countries to revalue. And meanwhile the US deficit was widening rapidly. Ultimately it was the Americans themselves who decided to force the issue, by the measures announced on 15 August. The purpose of these measures—in particular, the "temporary" suspension of the dollar's convertibility and the 10 per cent surcharge on imports—was to compel the major surplus countries to accept a mutual exchange rate adjustment that would correct the over-valuation of the dollar. That purpose was ostensibly accomplished by the currency realignment agreed upon at the Smithsonian Institution in December 1971.

Although the currency realignment itself collapsed in little more than a year, the Smithsonian Agreement was successful at least in defusing a potentially nasty political confrontation. By the time the Committee of Twenty was established in mid-1972, United States policy had already returned to its more traditional posture of benignity. American policymakers were frankly shocked by the disruptive consequences of their own actions. John Connally (the combative Treasury Secretary who was the chief architect of the 1971 measures) may have cared little about avoiding destabilizing behavior. But his successors have been only too cognizant of the close identity of America's interests with the stability of the system as a whole. In the years since, they have needed little encouragement to try to act more "responsibly" in monetary affairs.

If the nationalism of American policy has not changed, what then *has* changed? What has changed is the system itself—more specifically, the conditions required to organize and maintain a hegemonic system like Bretton Woods. Two conditions are essential. First, hegemonic leadership must in fact be "responsible"—that is, the economic policy of the world's money manager must truly be stabilizing, imparting neither inflationary nor deflationary impulses to the rest of the world. And second, hegemonic leadership must be regarded as "legitimate," generating neither resentment nor policy conflict over the benefits and costs of the system. Today, neither of these conditions may be said to be satisfied.

Consider the first condition. What assurance is there that the United States will in fact always act "responsibly"? The answer is—no assurance at all. America's policymakers may indeed be cognizant of the country's role as balance wheel of the world economy; they may be fully aware of the obligation of the world's money manager to provide a stable standard of economic performance (especially price performance) around which other countries can organize their own policy priorities. But there is still no certainty that such an obligation will actually be honored—precisely because, by definition, in a hegemonic regime there is no effective external discipline on the leader. Given the absence of any formal deterrent, the possibility always exists that, sooner or later, accidentally or deliberately, the leader will take advantage of its special position to initiate policies that destabilize the world economy. In the case of the United States, this is indeed precisely what did happen following escalation of military hostilities in Vietnam after 1965. Before 1965, America clearly had the best long-term record of price stability of any industrial country; even for some time after 1958 the United States could not be justly accused of "exporting" inflation, however much some governments were complaining about a dollar glut. But then President Johnson made a decision to fight a war in Vietnam and a War on Poverty simultaneously. As a result, America's economy quickly began to overheat. The virus of inflation began to spread, and ultimately the whole world was infected, setting the stage for the dramatic events of 1971. In the years since, America's policy seems to have regained some semblance of "responsibility." But now the genie is out of the bottle. American leadership has proved once to be destabilizing. Can anyone doubt that history might one day repeat itself?

In any event, American hegemony is no longer regarded as legitimate. Objective circumstances have changed too much since the years immediately after World War II when the foundations of the Bretton Woods system were laid. In those days the United States bestrode the world economy like a colossus. Other countries may have had reservations about America's leadership role; weakened as they were by war and destruction, however, they were hardly in a position to question it. Today, by contrast, the political and economic conditions that originally made American hegemony acceptable—or, at any rate, tolerable—no longer exist. America's relative position in the international hierarchy has declined enormously. Foreign economies are no longer so weak and uncompetitive as they were immediately after the war, and foreign governments (in Europe, Japan, and even OPEC) are no longer satisfied to accept a political role subordinate to that of the United States. America's leadership role has come under increasing challenge. The United States is still acknowledged as *primus inter pares* in the world economy. But it is by no means still universally accepted as *primus motor*.

Proof of these changed attitudes and perceptions can be found in the current debate between the United States and its major allies over the so-called "locomotive" approach to recovery from the "Great Recession" of 1974-5. As always, America's own monetary policy—which until recently was generally expansionary in tone—has been guided essentially by domestic considerations. But since expansion at home could credibly be argued to aid recovery abroad also, the United States has been urging other "locomotive" economies like Germany and Japan to follow America's lead, stimulating their own growth rates as well, in hopes that this would help to pull weaker economies out of the general stagnation that has persisted since 1975. Once, America's leadership in this regard might have been heeded. Today, however, it is resisted. The result is frustration and deadlock. Germany and Japan argue that further expansion of their economies may be neither desirable (because of the inflationary pressures that might be generated) nor even possible (because of domestic political and institutional constraints on policy); and that in any event the stimulative impact on weaker economies would probably be comparatively small. Instead, they criticize the United States for allowing its balance of payments to get out of control and its currency to depreciate sharply in the exchange markets. In some quarters, America is even accused of trying to use dollar depreciation to gain an unfair competitive advantage—malign nationalism at its worst.

But *is* this malign nationalism? I would argue, rather, the reverse—that America's relatively passive exchange rate policy is precisely the posture required to resolve the global redundancy problem in today's floating rate world. In fact America is still playing the *n*th-country role in the international monetary system. Other countries pursue their independent payments targets through direct or indirect intervention in the exchange market; the residual of all their targets emerges in net movements of the dollar's effective exchange rate. This is the main reason why serious inconsistency in monetary relations has been avoided since the breakdown of the Bretton Woods system.

Not that this should be surprising. A country still as large and powerful as the United States needs little incentive to avoid destabilizing behavior whenever possible. Its ability to disrupt is too evident; as American policymakers since John Connally have recognized, the nation's self-interest is too closely identified with stability of the overall system for them to try deliberately to act "irresponsibly." (This of course does not rule out accidental "irresponsibility.") Smaller and less powerful countries, by contrast, need a correspondingly greater incentive to act "responsibly," since the identification of self-interest and systemic interest is for them relatively less clear. One of the few luxuries afforded small countries in an international hierarchy is the privilege to pursue narrow national priorities without regard for the stability of the system as a whole. Such "free-rider" behavior does not threaten systemic stability so long as it is indulged in only sporadically or by just a few countries. But it can be threatening if indulged in by a greater number of countries, and it may be very threatening indeed if indulged in systematically by countries further up on the scale of size and power—countries like Germany and Japan, for example. If such countries fail to recognize the damage they can do by pursuing goals divergent from the interest of the system as a whole, stability in international relations will be very difficult to preserve.

Essentially, this is the problem that we face in monetary relations today. Conditions are no longer propitious for an American hegemony, yet Germany and Japan have so far resisted America's blandishments to share in the responsibility for global monetary stabilization. Some organizing principle, as I have argued, is necessary to ensure consistency among national policies and reduce the risk of policy conflict. If the community of nations is unwilling to submit to the rigors of automatic rules or a world central bank, then, in current circumstances, the solution must be found in a regime of shared responsibility and decisionmaking. Some means must be found to enable the locomotives all to pull in the same direction. If not, the train may never leave the station.

Notes

1. Stein, on her deathbed, is reported to have muttered: "What is the answer?" When no one replied, she continued: "In that case, what is the question?"—and died.

2. The "n-1 principle" or "redundancy problem" was first enunciated by Robert Mundell. See his *International Economics* (New York: Macmillan, 1968), pp. 195-8.

3. The problems of international monetary organization are treated at greater length in my book *Organizing the World's Money* (New York: Basic Books, 1977). I have drawn from this source for some of the arguments developed in the present essay.

4. See, for example, C.P. Kindleberger, *The World in Depression, 1929-1939* (Berkeley and Los Angeles: University of California Press, 1973).

3

International Debt and Linkage Strategies: Some Foreign-Policy Implications for the United States*

Recent debt crises in Eastern Europe and the Third World have vividly highlighted the close connections between high finance and high politics. "Money brings honor, friends, conquest, and realms," said John Milton; or, as the old French proverb puts it, "l'argent fait le jeu"—money talks. The connections, however, are anything but simple. Money may talk but it does so, as it were, out of both sides of its mouth. The game that money makes is a highly complex one in which it is not at all clear who conquers, who is conquered, or even what conquest means.

My purpose in this essay is to explore some of the foreign policy implications of international debt from the point of view of a major creditor country. Specifically, my focus is on the United States, whose banks have been among the heaviest lenders to sovereign borrowers in recent years. Foreign policy, in this analysis, is understood to encompass the full range of strategies and actions developed by the U.S. government's decisionmakers in America's relations with other nations. Foreign policy aims to achieve specific goals defined in terms of national interests as

*From *International Organization*, vol. 39, no. 4 (Autumn 1985), pp. 699-727.

decisionmakers themselves perceive them. National interests may include economic objectives no less than political or security concerns. The central issue for analysis is the extent to which, if at all, the global debt problem has influenced the power of the U.S. government in foreign affairs, power being understood to imply leverage or control not only over resources and actors but also over the outcome of events.

Has the global debt problem altered the ability of public officials in Washington to realize their foreign-policy preferences?

What makes this question analytically interesting is the fact that most international debt is owed to private creditors rather than to governments or multilateral agencies. Following the first oil shock in 1973 the private financial markets, and in particular the major commercial banks, became the principal source of external finance for much of Eastern Europe and the Third World, and banks have been intimately involved in all of the major debt crises of recent years. In short, banks have become full participants in the realm of foreign policy: they are now important independent actors on the world stage. Yet there is no assurance at all that the banks' interpretation of their private interests in the marketplace will necessarily converge with the public interest as interpreted by policymakers in Washington. As one astute observer has commented, "U.S. foreign policy actions and the overseas activities of the private banks have come increasingly to overlap. The interests of the two sides do not always coincide and indeed may at times be contradictory."[1] Or to quote Ronald Reagan's first under secretary of state for economic affairs,

> There are areas of shared interests . . . as well as areas of potential friction. . . . The bankers must be guided by the interests of their stockholders. . . . Governments, on the other hand, are guided by a mix of political, humanitarian, strategic and economic objectives. . . . Banks may differ with government in their assessment of political factors. . . .[2]

In formal terms the situation described here corresponds to Robert Keohane and Joseph Nye's "complex interdependence," in which direct interstate relations are affected by the presence of important transnational actors, including banks. As Keohane and Nye write, "These actors are important not only because of their activities in pursuit of their own interests, but also because they act as transmission belts, making government policies in various countries more sensitive to one another."[3] Certainly the lending practices of banks, insofar as they contributed to the origin or exacerbation of the debt problem, have increased the mutual sensitivities of the United States and major sovereign debtors and complicated considerably the U.S. government's pursuit of policy objectives in relation to those countries. Complex interdependence, Keohane and Nye remind us, means that power in foreign policy must be exercised through a political bargaining process. The participation of banks in the process, with their own interests to pursue, can significantly affect outcomes. Through their ongoing commercial decisions vis-à-vis sovereign debtors, the banks affect the general foreign-policy environment—and their effects may substantially alter the issues of salience for policy or the nature and scope of policy options available to government officials.

In short, high finance intersects with high politics. Strategic interactions between governments—the traditional focus of foreign-policy analysis—are increasingly linked with strategic interactions between public and private institutions in both debtor and creditor countries. The roster of players in the "money game" is rich and varied.

From the point of view of a major creditor country such as the United States, the principal impact of these interactions is on the number and substance of potential "linkages" in foreign policy (that is, the joining for bargaining purposes of otherwise unrelated policy instruments or issues). Policymakers may be forced to make connections between different policy instruments or issues that might not otherwise have been felt necessary; opportunities for connections may be created that might not otherwise have been thought possible. In a world of complex interdependence, power in foreign affairs is very much a function of a government's "linkage strategies"—that is, how well the government can make use of instruments or issues where its bargaining position is relatively strong in order to promote or defend interests where it is weaker.[4] These considerations shape the analysis to follow. My discussion will center on the implications that the global debt problem holds for the linkage strategies of the United States as a major creditor country.

I start by introducing some general considerations that bear on the relationship between international debt and the foreign-policy capabilities of the United States. The discussion is deliberately abstract, in effect creating a set of empty analytic "boxes." In the following three sections I attempt to put some empirical content into those boxes by looking at a limited selection of recent experiences—the Polish debt crisis of 1981-82, the Latin American debt crisis (or crises) of 1982-83, and the International Monetary Fund quota increase of 1983. In all three cases the cutoff point for discussion is mid-1984. The treatment in the three sections is necessarily cursory but nonetheless suggestive. I conclude the essay with a brief summary of conclusions and implications for the politics of stabilization of the international financial system.

Debt and Foreign Policy

The intersection of high finance and high politics in the context of the global debt problem highlights the potential for reciprocal influences between governments and banks.[5] Changes that banks induce in a government's decisionmaking environment may alter foreign-policy capabilities; in turn, a government may be able to supplement its power resources by relating bank decisions, directly or indirectly, to foreign-policy considerations. Either form of influence could affect the power of a government in foreign affairs, but neither can be predicted a priori with any confidence.

Some observers do not doubt that the banks' lending practices in Eastern Europe and the Third World have weakened the ability of the U.S. government to realize its foreign-policy preferences. By their decisions affecting sovereign borrowers—to lend or reschedule debt? to which countries? how much? when? at what cost? under what conditions (if any)?—banks establish priorities among capital-importing nations that amount, in effect, to decisions about foreign aid. And since these decisions may depart quite substantially from the goals and priorities of official policy, they can significantly hamper the effectiveness of existing policy instruments. The government may find it more difficult to support or reward its friends or to thwart or punish its enemies. Generous debt assistance to countries with poor records on human rights, for instance, or to regimes that support international terrorism may easily undermine efforts by Washington to exercise influence through the withholding of public moneys; states deemed vital to U.S. security interests may be seriously destabilized if they are suddenly "red-lined" by the financial community. Contends Congressman Jim Leach of Iowa, "The large money center banks are the true foreign aid policy-makers of the United States."[6]

Clearly, there is some truth in this charge. As the *Banker* has commented, "bankers assume a political role . . . through the mere act of lending on any large scale. The provision of finance to sovereign borrowers . . . immediately involves financial inter-mediaries in passively helping to determine priorities."[7] But equally clearly, it is an exaggeration to argue, as Jack Zwick and Richard Goeltz do, that therefore "private banks are effec-tively making United States foreign economic policy."[8] Public officials still make policy. What has changed is the nature of the constraints and opportunities that now confront those public officials in the international arena. It is not at all clear that these changes are, on balance, necessarily disadvantageous for foreign policy.

In the first place is an empirical question: How serious is the problem? The fact that banks may establish priorities at vari-ance with the goals of official policy does not mean that they inevitably will do so. Banks naturally pay attention to foreign relations in the ordinary course of business and, to some extent at least, tailor their commercial decisions accordingly. It is obvious that insofar as movements of money correlate positively with movements of the diplomatic barometer, bank decisions may actually enhance rather than diminish the effectiveness of existing foreign-policy instruments. The drying up of private credits in Chile, for example, undoubtedly strengthened the Nixon administration's campaign against Salvador Allende after his election in 1971. Current U.S. government support of such strategic allies as South Korea and the Philippines is undoubtedly reinforced by a continued high level of bank lending there. Sometimes private and public interests converge and sometimes, as we shall see in the discussions of Poland and Latin America, they do not.

Furthermore, even where bank operations appear to diverge from official priorities, the resulting impacts on policy effec-tiveness could turn out to be little more than trivial. To say that policy could be affected is not to say that any such influences are necessarily significant. That remains to be seen.

Finally, and most importantly, any impacts on foreign-policy capabilities will depend a great deal on the policy linkages that bank decisions generate. Debt-service difficulties are a natural breeding ground for policy linkages. When key sovereign borrowers get into trouble, Washington may feel forced to respond, however reluctantly, with some sort of support—in effect, to underwrite the debts in some way. Some borrowers are considered crucial for U.S. interests and cannot be ignored. As the Senate Foreign Relations Committee staff has written, America "has important security interests in other debtor countries. . . . It can hardly afford to stand by and watch the economies of these countries collapse, or to have their governments undermined politically by financial difficulties."[9] In other cases borrowers may stimulate concerns about possible repercussions on the health and stability of American banks or the wider financial or economic system. Either way, debtors gain a new kind of political leverage to extract from the U.S. government concessions that might not otherwise be obtainable. These concessions may be financial, trade, or even political.

Financial concessions are the most familiar variety. Back in 1979, for example, at a time of near-bankruptcy, Turkey was able to exploit its strategic position within NATO to persuade the United States and other Western allies to come to its rescue with pledges of special assistance totaling nearly one billion dollars. Subsequent aid packages for similar amounts were pledged for 1980 and 1981 as well.[10] Likewise, more recently, financial assistance has been arranged for several Latin American debtors when they had trouble meeting their obligations to foreign creditors.

There may also be trade concessions, which have been increasingly mooted lately despite strongly protectionist domestic pressures. U.S. policymakers have been forced to acknowledge the obvious linkage between trade and finance—that import liberalization by industrialized countries may be the only way to enable major borrowers to earn their way out of their debt morass. In the words of Meyer Rashish:

> We must face the interdependence of the financial trading systems. External debt only makes sense if the borrower has a reasonable prospect for servicing the debt by exporting goods and services to the lenders. . . . Ultimately, we, the lenders, will be confronted with a decision—either to open our markets in order to provide

outlets to the borrowers for their exports, thus generating revenues in the borrowing countries for debt repayment, or to yield to protectionist pressures and be forced to deal with resultant financial failures. . . ."[11]

Finally, even political concessions may be felt necessary. In 1977 the Senate Foreign Relations Committee staff worried that "there appears to be a direct correlation between economic hardship and political repression in many countries. The Carter Administration may therefore have to choose between pressing its international human rights effort, and supporting creditor demands for drastic austerity programs that can only be achieved at the expense of civil liberties in the countries that undertake them."[12] In the first half of the 1980s this dilemma confronted the Reagan administration as well, in Latin America and elsewhere. In the case of the Philippines, for example, Asia's second-largest debtor to the banks, the United States clearly chose to maintain support for the martial law "New Society" of Ferdinand Marcos on broad foreign-policy grounds. U.S. policymakers justified strict Filipino controls, including the continued stifling of political opposition, by the need to preserve the financial viability of an important strategic ally.

Can we generalize about the implications of these policy linkages for the foreign-policy capabilities of the United States? I shall stress three considerations that bear on this question. First is the nature of the concessions themselves. Concessions are not necessarily disadvantageous. In fact, the constraints and opportunities created for the U.S. government's linkage strategies in individual instances may actually enhance rather than diminish U.S. power in foreign affairs. The constraints imposed by the debt problem are evident—the risks of possible financial disruption, loss of export markets, souring of political relations, or instability or disorder in areas of vital strategic importance. But opportunities to promote U.S. policy preferences may be generated as well. The key is whether debt-related concessions may be regarded as advantageous outside the immediate area of financial relations. Do the concessions, while effectively underwriting debt, also serve to reinforce other U.S. policy interests? Or do they work at cross-purposes, demanding trade-offs among interests? Concessions will be disadvantageous only when inconsistent with other foreign-policy objectives.

Of crucial importance in this connection is whether U.S.

relations with troubled debtors are adversarial or not. Where relations are adversarial, as they were in the case of Poland, efforts to cope with debt-service difficulties may actually undermine the effectiveness or credibility of other policy measures, weakening U.S. power in foreign affairs. Concessions in such instances may be regarded as disadvantageous. But where relations are nonconflictual, as in Latin America, helping others can, under appropriate circumstances, also help ourselves. Concessions may be of mutual benefit and may even lead to matching political or economic concessions from debtor governments. In such instances a potential certainly exists for promoting foreign-policy preferences.

A second consideration bearing on policy linkages is whether, or to what extent, the government may be able to supplement its own power resources by relating bank decisions, directly or indirectly, to foreign-policy considerations. Insofar as bank behavior has a significant influence on the general foreign-policy environment, public officials could, hypothetically at least, try to alter that behavior to conform more closely to policy objectives—in effect, to deploy the banks as part of the government's broader linkage strategies. How effective are such attempts likely to be in reality?

In principle the international activities of American banks are supposed to be independent of politics. But in practice political considerations are rarely absent, even if in most instances they remain fairly subtle. At times they become overt. The U.S. government has long had an arsenal of policy instruments available in order, when deemed appropriate, to relate the commercial activities of U.S. banks to foreign-policy questions; among those instruments are loan guarantee programs, restrictions, and outright prohibitions as well as prudential supervision, general monetary policy, and "moral suasion." During the years of the Cold War, for instance, loans to communist governments were strictly prohibited on political grounds (as they still are to Cambodia, Cuba, North Korea, and Vietnam). The prohibitions were reversed with the coming of détente. At their summit conference in 1972 Leonid Brezhnev and Richard Nixon declared that "the USA and the USSR regard commercial and economic ties as an important and necessary element in the strengthening of their bilateral relations and thus will actively promote the growth of such ties." Quite clearly the activity was to include promotion of credits from American and other Western banks. By mid-1982 U.S. banks alone had built up an exposure in Soviet-bloc countries in excess of $7 billion. The exposure of all Western (including Japanese) creditors was in excess of $60 billion.

Other examples can also be cited. Prohibitions on lending were employed in support of UN sanctions against Rhodesia, for instance, in the years following that colony's unilateral declaration of independence as well as in support of Washington's economic sanctions against the revolutionary government of Iran during the months of the hostage crisis. Conversely, in early 1982 the State Department went out of its way to make plain its hope that banks would keep open their credit lines to Yugoslavia, lest that nation be driven closer to the Soviet Union.[13] But the fact that such efforts are not unprecedented does not mean that they are uncontroversial. On the contrary, any attempts by Washington to influence bank behavior on foreign-policy grounds—either to encourage or discourage lending, to individual debtor countries or in general—have tended to generate lively public debate. Some observers, indeed, feel that the only problem is that the U.S. government has not gone far enough to link foreign policy and the commercial decisions of American banks. As Zwick and Goeltz argue, "This step must be taken to preserve not only the financial integrity of the banking system but also the discretion of the Government in the formulation of foreign policy."[14] For others, Robert Russell among them, the problem is precisely the opposite: "It would seem better to keep public policy and private investment at arm's length to the extent possible. . . . Injecting foreign policy considerations into private bank decisionmaking . . . seems likely to exacerbate both the problems of foreign policy and bank soundness."[15]

The key issue here is effectiveness. Can public officials effectively influence the commercial decisions of banks? In an era when much of the international activity of American banks takes place beyond Washington's direct jurisdictional reach in an almost totally unregulated environment (the Eurocurrency market), the answer is no simple matter. Today most foreign lending takes the form of bank credits booked through financial centers where official supervision is by definition minimal. Moreover, with the evolution of the Eurocurrency market has come a blurring of the strictly national identity of banking institutions. The largest part of bank credits is now the product of syndicates of mixed nationality. The ease and intimacy with which financiers from different countries work together today would have seemed unthinkable, if not treasonous, three-quarters of a century ago. As a result it is difficult indeed for Washington effectively to control or manipulate bank behavior on foreign-policy grounds.

But it is not impossible: government officials are not entirely without leverage. In the first place, while national identity may have become blurred it has certainly not been forgotten. As Herbert Feis wrote half a century ago, "Bankers are subject to the force of national feeling as are their fellow men."[16] The men and women who run America's largest banks can still be moved by "moral suasion" when the national interest appears to be at stake. Furthermore, despite the extent of their overseas operations, the banks are still ultimately dependent on a domestic financial base and subject to the influence of domestic monetary policy and prudential supervision. What is implied, however, is that any government attempts at leverage are likely to be effective only within rather broad limits—that is, control is likely to be "loose" rather than "tight." As we shall see, control is especially likely to be loose when the government aims in individual instances to encourage rather than to discourage lending.

The third and final consideration bearing on the question of policy linkages is whether, or to what extent, Washington might be able to supplement its power resources by pursuing policy objectives through the intermediation of a multilateral agency such as the International Monetary Fund—in effect, to deploy the Fund as part of the government's broader linkage strategies. Because of the global debt problem, the IMF has gained considerable leverage over the behavior of both debtor governments and banks. But the Fund itself is subject to substantial leverage from the U.S. government, which still retains unparalleled influence over IMF decisionmaking. In effect, therefore, an opportunity seems to have been created for U.S. policymakers to accomplish indirectly, via the IMF, what they cannot accomplish (or can accomplish only at a higher economic or political cost) on a direct, bilateral basis.

Solidarity Suppressed

The Polish debt crisis of 1981-82 provides a particularly apt case for empirical investigation. Rarely in recent American experience have the complex connections between high finance and high politics been quite so manifest. After the rise of the Solidarity trade union movement in 1980, Poland became the touchstone for U.S. foreign policy in Eastern Europe. Yet Washington's ability to exercise leverage over the course of events in that troubled country was plainly compromised by the high level of Western bank exposure in Poland. Polish debt added to the difficulties experienced by the United States in trying to prevent suppression of Solidarity after martial law was declared in December 1981.

Even before December 1981 Polish debt was becoming a problem. As early as 1979 Poland's economy had stopped growing, in good part because of a deterioration of export revenues; and in 1980 and 1981 national income actually dropped at a rate of 5 percent a year. To maintain imports, Warsaw resorted to accelerated borrowing from the West. As a result, between 1978 and 1981 Polish foreign debt increased by nearly half, from under $18 billion to an estimated $26 billion; and its debt-service ratio (the ratio of interest and amortization to export revenues) more than doubled, from an already high 79 percent to an incredible 173 percent.[17] By the start of 1981 it was an open secret that Poland could not meet its scheduled obligations. Warsaw formally notified its creditors in March that it would no longer be able to guarantee debt service.

At the time the attitude of the U.S. government was clear: do everything possible to avoid destabilizing the situation inside Poland, and do nothing to jeopardize the achievements of Solidarity. Throughout 1981, therefore, Washington maintained an essentially benevolent posture toward the Polish debt problem. While it contemplated no massive new credits, it did undertake several actions to ease Warsaw's financial difficulties. As early as the previous summer, in an obvious attempt at a linkage strategy. Washington had openly pressured American banks to keep a substantial refinancing loan from failing. (Washington was not alone in this instance: in Bonn the West German chancellor, Helmut Schmidt, personally telephoned the presidents of the three largest German banks to back a similar Polish loan.) And in April 1981 the United States joined with fourteen other industrial nations (later fifteen) in agreeing to postpone for four years $2.3 billion of Polish debt payments due in 1981 to official creditors. In the first week of December, after some difficult negotiations, there followed an agreement among Western banks to reschedule $2.4 billion of commercial debt due in 1981 as well. The concurrence of Western banks was crucial inasmuch as almost two-thirds of Poland's debt—some $16 billion—was owed to private lenders, reflecting a decade's growth in Western bank lending to the East. West German banks held the largest amount—about $6 billion. American banks accounted for about $3 billion.[18] The December 1981 rescheduling was made contingent on Poland's payment of $500 million in interest obligations for the last three months of 1981.

In addition, in the spring of 1981 the Commodity Credit Corporation (CCC) of the U.S. Department of Agriculture raised the interest-rate guarantee for private agricultural export credits to Poland (used to finance grain sales) from 8 percent to 12 percent; this exceptional provision for the Poles was not generalized to any other country. And even as late as early December plans were going forward for $100 million of new CCC credits that would have fully guaranteed, for the first time and for any country, all interest payments as well as principal.[19]

But then came General Jaruzelski's declaration of martial law on 13 December 1981, followed by suppression of Solidarity. Washington's attitude quickly hardened. Western governments immediately suspended talks with the Jaruzelski regime about a possible rescheduling of Poland's 1982 debt to official creditors, at Washington's behest, and numerous other economic sanctions were levied against both Poland and the Soviet Union, including termination of all subsidized food shipments and most U.S. government-guaranteed bank credits to Poland (including the planned new CCC credits), restrictions on Polish fishing rights in American waters, suspension of talks (due to have begun in February 1982) with the Soviet Union on a new long-term grain agreement, and an embargo on materials for Russia's natural-gas pipeline from Siberia to Western Europe. The aims of the sanctions were clear—to persuade Poland and its patron the Soviet Union to end martial law, free all political prisoners, and restore Solidarity to its previous domestic status. Pressure would be maintained, the Reagan administration insisted, until these goals were achieved. In the words of assistant secretary of state at the time, Robert Hormats,

> In these circumstances, our continuing objective is to apply sustained pressure on both Poland and the Soviet

Union to have martial law lifted, the prisoners released, and the dialog between the government, the church and Solidarity begun in earnest in a free atmosphere. In short, our goal is the restoration of the process of reform and renewal in Poland.[20]

The impact of the sanctions, however, was diluted by the continuing problem of Poland's debt. For 1982 alone the country was estimated to owe Western creditors a total of $10.4 billion in principal and interest—yet Warsaw had still not even gotten current on the interest due for its rescheduled 1981 debt.[21] Clearly, some additional relief would be required if default were to be avoided, and Washington had no desire to precipitate a Western banking crisis. It was recognized, of course, that the direct exposure of Western banks was not large (certainly not as compared with their exposure in Latin America or the Far East). Of the $16 billion of outstanding bank claims on Poland, almost half (about $7 billion) was guaranteed by creditor governments. Of the $3 billion owed to American banks, the CCC guaranteed $1.6 billion, and the remainder was spread so thinly among some sixty institutions that for most American banks guarantee-adjusted exposure amounted to less than 5 percent of capital.[22] The fear of financial disruption was nevertheless genuine. Who knew what might happen if a major debtor like Poland were compelled to default?

The biggest question was whether a default could be contained. Many U.S. officials were concerned about the possibility of a "domino effect"—a scramble by banks to reduce their exposure elsewhere in Eastern Europe, which might lead to a chain reaction of defaults throughout the region, and perhaps in other areas of the world as well, endangering the entire Western banking structure. The flow of new bank credits to other Soviet bloc countries, as well as to Yugoslavia, had already started drying up as a result of Poland's debt-service difficulties.[23] American policymakers were convinced by their conversations with bankers that their fears of a regional "contagion" were not unfounded.[24] Banks, after all, had their own interests to protect.

Indeed, Washington's concern was such that despite its tough rhetoric, it even started servicing some of Poland's debt itself when Warsaw failed to meet payments due on part of its $1.6 billion of CCC-guaranteed credits beginning in January 1982.[25] In such an instance creditor banks would ordinarily have been required to declare the debtor formally in default in order to qualify for CCC payments. But in this case, for the first time ever, the Reagan administration circumvented the legal requirement by quietly adopting an emergency waiver to avoid triggering cross-default clauses in other bank loans to Poland. In effect, by meeting the CCC's guarantees and then transferring the overdue credits to its own books, the U.S. government unilaterally rescheduled a portion of Poland's debt. Most importantly, it did so *unconditionally*, without extracting any price from Warsaw—no formal default, no attempt to attach Polish assets, not even a public announcement. From a foreign-policy point of view this action was undoubtedly the turning point of the whole affair.

The CCC decision did not go unopposed within the administration. Defense Department officials in particular, led by Under Secretary for Policy Fred Iklé, argued vigorously for maintaining the hardest possible line vis-à-vis Poland, up to and including a formal declaration of default. But the prevailing view among policymakers, reflecting a de facto coalition of the Treasury and State departments, ruled out default under almost any circumstance, for three principal reasons. First was the fear of financial disruption, described above. Second was a fear of political disruption in the Western alliance, reflecting Western Europe's far greater loan exposure in Poland (amounting, in fact, to about three-quarters of all Polish debt). Given that West European banks and governments had so much more of an investment to protect, there was a considerable risk that they might respond favorably to any Polish overture to negotiate a separate deal. American bankers were especially concerned about the prospect. As a confidential working document prepared by one large U.S. bank warned, "There is every reason to believe that European banks and governments would cooperate with the Poles. . . . There is [therefore] not only a significant probability that such a default action would fail, but it would also impose massive costs on the alliance."[26]

Finally, there was a fear of losing a possible instrument of leverage over the Poles. Policy makers reasoned that by taking over the debt itself, Washington could actually hope to reinforce its pressure on the Jaruzelski regime—"keep Poland's feet to the fire," to quote a leaked State Department memorandum. With new lending at a standstill, Warsaw's interest payments represented a net transfer of financial resources *to the West*. A formal declaration of default, however satisfying to the emotions, would only have relieved the Poles of that burden. The Jaruzelski regime would no longer have had to find precious foreign exchange to meet debt-service obligations to Western banks. Instead, the martial-law regime would have been freed to consolidate its authority with even greater force and harshness. According to one administration official, "keeping the pressure on this way is the real hard line."[27]   The view was summarized by assistant treasury secretary Marc Leland:

> What should we do about the debt? Our feeling is that we should try to collect it. The more pressure we can thereby put on the East Europeans, particularly on the Soviet Union, to come up with the funds to help Poland, the better. . .
>
> To maintain maximum leverage . . . they should be held to the normal commercial concept that they owe us this money, so they should come up with it. . . .
>
> In this way we hope to maintain the maximum amount of pressure on them to try to roll back the actions of December 13th and to enter into an internal political dialog.[28]

The proof of the pudding, however, is not to be found in the chef's fine words. In practice this "real hard line" proved scarcely effective at all, and it may even have been counterproductive in Washington's attempt to exercise leverage over the Poles. For once having signaled the depth of its apprehensions about default in its decision to pay off CCC-guaranteed credits unconditionally, the U.S. administration actually made itself *more* vulnerable to the threat of financial disruption; and the Jaruzelski regime was not above making veiled hints about possible default as a form of policy leverage of its own.[29] Washington's constraint, in effect, became Warsaw's opportunity. Western bank assets could be held as a sort of hostage, and perhaps a wedge could be driven between the U.S. government and its West European allies. The CCC decision handed the Poles, despite their desperate economic straits, some additional room for maneuver.

At a minimum, the action strained the credibility of the Reagan administration's commitment to sanctions. The key question at the time was why the CCC guarantees were paid off unconditionally. Observers were entitled to ask why no quid pro quo of any kind was demanded of the Poles, for instance, by attaching some of their foreign assets as collateral for eventual repayment. Officials argued that few such assets were available; perhaps a few airplanes and ships plus some meager hard-currency reserves. But their response missed the symbolic value of the opportunity thus lost. Psychologically, the appearance of vacillation by policymakers quickly dissipated the impact of Washington's sanctions. What was left was an impression—right or wrong—that the administration, simply put, was more concerned about a Western banking crisis than it was about the future of Solidarity. Public perceptions at the time were accurately, if colorfully, summarized by columnist William Safire:

> The secret regulation giving the junta extraordinarily lenient treatment makes a mockery of pretensions of pressure.
> In an eyeball-to-eyeball confrontation, the Reagan administration has just blinked. Poland's rulers can afford to dismiss the Reagan rhetoric because they have seen that the U.S. is ready to do regulatory nip-ups to save them from default.[30]

In the end, of course, as we know, the administration achieved few of its goals. Poland neither "came up with the money" nor "rolled back" the actions of 13 December. Martial law was formally lifted after two years, to be sure, but many of its key features still remained, now incorporated into Polish civil law. And while most political prisoners were released in 1984, Solidarity still remained an outlawed organization, replaced by tame government-sponsored trade unions. In short, the process of "reform and renewal" was not restored. Yet, one by one, most the sanctions imposed so dramatically in 1981 were either eased or eliminated. In July 1983 a new long-term grain agreement with the Soviet Union was announced. In November 1983 the most stringent sanctions directed against the Soviet gas pipeline were lifted, and restrictions on Polish fishing rights were relaxed. And the following month Washington joined other Western governments in reopening the suspended talks with Poland on rescheduling some of its debt to official creditors.

Admittedly, apprehensions about default were by no means the only—or even the most important—reason for such seemingly conciliatory behavior. The Soviet grain agreement, for example, was best understood in terms of President Reagan's 1980 campaign promises to American farmers. Similarly, the easing of sanctions against the Soviet pipeline was most evidently motivated by a desire to improve roiled relations with Western European allies. Even the reopening of debt negotiations was a response, at least in part, to growing discontent on the part of other Western governments that viewed Washington's continued refusal to talk as essentially self-defeating. From the time discussions were first cut off, following the declaration of martial law, Warsaw had suspended all payments of interest as well as principal on its official debt (although interest payments to banks were maintained, albeit with delays). As a result, U.S. allies began to argue, Poland was actually able to save precious foreign exchange, in effect at the expense of Western taxpayers. Other Western governments had initially gone along with the suspension of negotiations.[31] But as the situation dragged on, they eventually started to lobby the Reagan administration vigorously for agreement to an early resumption of talks.[32]

It must also be admitted that the easing of sanctions might have occurred even *without* apprehensions about default. The use of economic sanctions in pursuit of foreign-policy goals is a tricky business in the best circumstances. The success rate of sanctions varies greatly, depending among other factors on the type of goals being pursued.[33] The more modest the policy changes targeted, the greater is the probability of success. Conversely, in instances where "major" policy changes have been sought, as in the Polish case, the evidence suggests that economic sanctions have rarely been effective. Washington was fighting an uphill battle. Even with *no* Western bank exposure in Poland, the Reagan administration would have experienced difficulties in trying to prevent the suppression of Solidarity.

Poland's debt, therefore, cannot be blamed per se for the evident failure of the administration's policies. Washington's leverage in the situation was at best limited. But debt can be blamed for adding to the administration's difficulties, by undermining the effectiveness and credibility of its other policy initiatives. The effort to avoid Polish default worked at cross-purposes with other policy interests. I would not go so far as to argue with John Van Meer that the default issue thus "allowed the tyranny of the debtor to replace the tyranny of police-state Communism as the key to Western calculations."[34]   But I would contend that debt helped to undercut whatever power the U.S. government might otherwise have had in its confrontation with Warsaw. The negative effect of the linkage may have been only marginal, but it was not trivial. Foreign-policy capabilities were indeed diminished.

Debt Storm in Latin America

In Latin America the situation was different. Although here too Washington feared financial disruption—indeed, such fears were rampant—the U.S. government's foreign-policy capabilities in the region were, for a time at least, enhanced rather than diminished by the sudden explosion of a debt crisis in 1982. The principal reason seems to have been that U.S. relations with the major Latin borrowers were at the time not adversarial, as they had been with Poland. Initially, this general sense of cooperation created an opportunity for Washington, through a series of financial concessions, to win considerable goodwill and influence for itself at comparatively little economic or political cost. Over time, however, these gains proved essentially transient. As the region's debt crisis wore on, and particularly as Washington's efforts to revive private lending to Latin America proved largely ineffective, relations grew gradually more strained. Two years after the crisis began, in mid-1984, the continued goodwill of our hemispheric neighbors appeared to depend on new concessions of some kind from Washington. Foreign-policy leverage, it seemed, needed nourishment to remain effective.

The roots of the Latin American crisis go back at least to the late 1960s, when a number of governments made a deliberate decision to finance accelerated domestic investment with borrowing from private and public institutions abroad—"indebted industrialization," in Jeff Frieden's phrase.[35] Then came the first oil shock, which spurred further borrowing to pay for higher-priced oil imports, and after 1976 a trend toward negative real interest rates in global financial markets, which whetted appetites even further. By the time of the second oil shock, at the end of the decade, many Latin governments had seemingly become addicted to foreign finance, and debt was piling up at a dizzying pace. By mid-1982 total debt in the region had swollen to an estimated $295 billion, including $90 billion in Mexico, $75 billion in Brazil, $30 billion each in

Argentina and Venezuela, and $15 billion in Chile.[36] Two-thirds of the total was owed to private banks.

The banks, not surprisingly, were getting worried. Two years earlier they had already begun to shorten the maturities of new credits, hoping to position themselves to get their money out quickly should something go wrong. The policy would have been rational for any one creditor acting alone. With all banks doing the same thing, however, the practice merely added to the risks of lending in the region by greatly increasing the aggregate amount of debt that repeatedly had to be rolled over. By mid-1982, according to Morgan Guaranty Bank, the debt-service ratio (including amortization) of the five largest debtors had grown to 179 percent for Argentina, 129 percent for Mexico, 122 percent for Brazil, 116 percent for Chile, and 95 percent for Venezuela.[37] Interest payments alone for these five were expected to eat up from 35 to 45 percent of export revenues. Clearly, a storm was brewing.

The first threatening clouds appeared in early 1982, during the Falklands/Malvinas conflict, when Argentina began to fall behind on its debt service because of the British government's freeze of Argentinian assets in London. But the really rough weather did not set in until the middle of the year, when political and economic uncertainties in Mexico sparked a major capital flight. In June 1982 the Mexicans had still been able to raise $2.5 billion in the Eurocurrency market, albeit with considerable difficulty. By August, new private lending had ceased, the peso had to be devalued, and the government was forced to announce that it could no longer meet its scheduled repayments of principal on external public debt. Suddenly, one of the Third World's two largest debtors seemed on the edge of default, and the tempest had broken.

Like the cavalry of old the U.S. government rushed to the rescue (but this time *on   behalf* of the Mexicans), quickly providing more than $2.5 billion of emergency assistance—$700 million via the Federal Reserve's swap arrangement with the Bank of Mexico, $1 billion from the Commodity Credit Corporation, and an advance payment of $1 billion on oil purchases by the Department of Energy for the U.S. Strategic Petroleum Reserve. In addition, the Treasury department's Exchange Stabilization Fund (ESF) and the Federal Reserve together contributed about half of a $1.85 billion bridging facility provided through the Bank for International Settlements. And Washington also backed a proposed

$3.9 billion credit from the International Monetary Fund.[38]   By September the Mexican situation seemed, for the moment at least, in hand.

But the storm kept spreading. Largely because of the Mexican crisis, bank confidence sagged, new private lending dried up throughout Latin America, and soon other debtors in the region were finding themselves deep in trouble too. More rescue packages had to be organized. In the latter part of 1982 the ESF made some $1.23 billion available to Brazil. And in December and January bridging loans were arranged through the Bank for International Settlements, with substantial U.S. participation, for both Brazil and Argentina.[39] In addition banks were constantly exhorted by Treasury and Federal Reserve officials, in the name of the public interest, to resume their lending in the region despite already high exposure levels. Typical was a well-publicized speech by Federal Reserve chairman Paul Volcker in November 1982, in which he laid great stress on easing the difficulties of major Latin borrowers. "In such cases," he said, "new credits should not be subject to supervisory criticism."[40] Translated, his message was that considerations of banking prudence would not be allowed to prevail over the objective of keeping key debtors afloat. On the contrary, banks were reportedly threatened with closer scrutiny of their books if they did *not* go along with fresh loans for countries like Mexico.[41] The pressures on the banks were not inconsiderable.

Nonetheless, they proved largely ineffective. Banks simply did not regard it as in their own interest to increase their exposure in the region significantly. In 1980 and 1981 total bank claims in Latin America had risen by some $30 billion a year. In the eighteen months from June 1982 to December 1983, by contrast, they increased by no more than $9 billion in all, less than the total of so-called "involuntary" lending arranged in connection with parallel IMF credits (discussed below), meaning that there was absolutely no "spontaneous" new lending at all.[42] Accordingly, no important borrower in the region was able to maintain debt service without some difficulty. All had to enter into protracted and difficult negotiations with private and public creditors, and most were forced to initiate painful—as well as politically risky—domestic austerity measures. In the words of Pedro-Pablo Kuczynski, "Undoubtedly, the interruption of significant new lending by commercial banks has been the major stimulus for such measures."[43]

Still, Washington continued to press the banks for a more accommodating attitude. One example was Argentina in late 1983 after that country's presidential election. According to *The New York Times*:

> The bankers . . . said that they were already coming under pressure from the United States . . . to aid the country's new democracy after nearly eight years of military rule. Many are resigned to making some concessions.
> "We don't want to look like the bad guys," one American banker said.[44]

Officials also urged the banks to consider limiting the interest rates they charged on loans to hard-pressed debtors. In another well-publicized speech in early 1984 Federal Reserve chairman Volcker suggested that "one of the things certainly worth looking at is what arrangements could be made so that one particular important threat to their financial stability, the continued rise in interest rates, could be dealt with."[45] What he had in mind was some kind of a cap on interest payments, with any excess of market rates over the cap being added to loan principal ("capitalization"). A specific proposal along these lines, for a cap tied to real interest rates, was floated by the Federal Reserve Bank of New York at a meeting of central bankers in May 1984, though nothing ever came of the idea.[46]

Moreover, to encourage the banks Washington continued to put its own money where its mouth was, for example in the U.S. contribution to the IMF quota increase, finally approved by Congress in late 1983. Another example was the decision of the Export-Import Bank in the summer of 1983 to extend new loan guarantees of up to $1.5 billion to Brazil and $500 million to Mexico—the largest such package ever proposed by the Bank. William Draper, the Bank's president, made no secret of official intentions to prompt further private lending in these and other Latin countries. "We expect the proposed financing will strengthen the Mexican and Brazilian recovery," he said, "by acting as a catalyst for continuing support by the international financial community."[47] What was highly unusual about this initiative was that, unlike most guarantee proposals, these guarantees were not tied to specific projects. Clearly, the U.S. government wanted to send a signal.

It is not difficult to discern why the government took such an active role in the crisis. Latin America has always been regarded on broad foreign-policy grounds as a region vital to U.S. national interest. From the moment Mexico's difficulties began, there was never any doubt among policymakers that America's own security, not just Mexico's, was at stake—that the United States too would be threatened by serious economic or political instabilities south of its border. Nor was there any doubt that the contagion might spread to other Latin American nations as well. Washington simply could not ignore the potential for disorder in its own backyard that financial default might have sparked. As *The Economist* commented at the time:

> How to resolve these difficulties is one of the biggest foreign policy questions facing Washington, for behind Mexico there stretches a line of other burrodollar [*sic*] debtors. Brazil, Argentina and Venezuela between them owe $140 billion. The United States dare not risk the political consequences of calling default on any of them. . . . Those in the Reagan administration who have calmly contemplated pulling the plug on Poland's debt, which is only a third of Mexico's, have to recognize that the problem facing them in Latin America is far bigger.[48]

More narrowly, of course, policymakers were also worried about the direct risks to American banks, particularly the large money-center banks, whose loan exposure in Latin America far exceeded that in Poland. For Mexico alone, at the end of 1982, exposure in relation to capital exceeded 40 percent in nine of the twelve largest U.S. banks. Taking Latin America's five biggest borrowers (Argentina, Brazil, Chile, Mexico, and Venezuela) together, the exposure of these same dozen banks ranged from a low of 82.5 percent of capital (Security Pacific) to a high of 262.8 percent (Manufacturers Hanover); most banks fell in a range of 140 to 180 percent.[49] The banking system was clearly vulnerable. If Poland had provoked fears of financial disruption, Latin America triggered nightmares.

Finally, there was also concern about U.S. trade interests in Latin America. By 1982 the region had surpassed all but Western Europe as a market for U.S. goods; Mexico alone was America's third-largest customer. Once the Mexican crisis broke, commerce and real-estate markets throughout the American Southwest were seriously damaged.[50] U.S. government officials never tired of stressing how many exports, and hence jobs, would be lost if something were not done for troubled debtors. Washington's motives were neatly summarized by Paul Volcker: "The effort to manage the international debt problem goes beyond vague and generalized concerns about political and economic stability of borrowing countries. . . . The effort encompasses also the protection of our own financial stability and the markets for what we produce best."[51]

It is hardly surprising, then, that the government would take so active a role. Nor is it surprising, given the reluctance of private banks to resume lending in the region, that Washington's concerns might give debtors the leverage to extract official concessions of some sort. What is striking is how much goodwill and influence were initially generated for the United States, and therefore how much easier it became to realize U.S. foreign-policy preferences. Officials in Washington reported a marked shift on the part of Latin governments toward a more accommodating spirit on various international issues.[52] The United States was now in a position to say, when looking for cooperation, that "we were there when you needed us, now we need you." In Brazil, Washington's efforts to help out financially were reported to have given the United States "more leverage . . . than it has enjoyed in more than a decade."[53] Suddenly the Brazilians were willing to talk about problems that had been roiling relations with the United States for years, most important among them nuclear policy and military cooperation. Likewise diplomats noted that Mexico toned down criticisms of U.S. policy in Central America; and also the Department of Energy was given permission to buy even more oil than originally agreed, at attractive prices, for the U.S. Strategic Petroleum Reserve.[54] In the short run Washington's investment in these countries' financial stability seemed to yield significant foreign-policy dividends.

But it did so only in the short run. As the debt crisis wore on, and domestic resistance to prolonged austerity measures grew, Latin governments were bound to grow more impatient. Riots and street demonstrations, as well as election results, suggested a decreasing tolerance for belt tightening in the region. Latin governments increasingly asked why the burden of adjustment should fall entirely on the shoulders of the debtors. What was first perceived as generosity on Washington's part came to be viewed more as miserliness and insensitivity. U.S. concessions, it was noted, had been strictly financial and, for the most part, strictly short-term. (All of the loans included in the emergency packages for Argentina, Brazil, and Mexico, for example, had to be repaid within one year.) No trade concessions had been forthcoming at all—indeed barriers to key imports from Latin America, such as copper and steel, were on the rise—while at the same time rising U.S. interest rates, universally blamed on the Reagan administration's huge budget deficits, were adding to current debt-service burdens. Washington's emphasis on domestic "stabilization" translated, to Latin observers, into nothing more than retarded development, increased unemployment, and declining living standards. The risk was that this changing mood might eventually push Latin American governments toward alienation and confrontation with the United States. It could even lead to their replacement by regimes far less friendly to U.S. economic or security interests.

By 1984 the straws were in the wind. In May the presidents of four of the region's largest debtors—Argentina, Brazil, Colombia, and Mexico—meeting in Buenos Aires issued a joint statement warning that they "cannot indefinitely" accept the "hazards" of current approaches to the debt crisis. Expressing concern over the effects of "successive interest rate increases, prospects of new hikes and the proliferation and intensity of protectionist measures," they cautioned that "their peoples' yearning for development, the progress of democracy in their region and the economic security of their continent are seriously jeopardized."[55] Such sentiments were emphasized when eleven Latin debtors met in Cartagena, Columbia, in June and concluded with a plea to the United States and other creditor countries, as well as to the banks, to accept a greater share of the burden of adjustment. The dramas of Argentina and Venezuela, both of which had deliberately chosen to go into arrears on their debt rather than submit to harsh austerity programs, attested to the decline of patience in the region. And other regional governments were also considering a reordering of their domestic and foreign priorities. As a report of the Americas Society pointed out, "In virtually every Latin American and Caribbean country, there are major pressures to turn inward. . . . to turn their backs on existing obligations, and to look to solutions which stress a higher degree of protection and greater state control."[56] Washington's initial foreign-policy dividends in the region seemed after two

years of crisis in danger of evaporating without a new investment of financial or trade concessions.

The Role of the IMF

One issue raised by the gradual erosion of Washington's early
gains in Latin America was whether the government's power
resources, in the context of the global debt problem, could be
supplemented through the intermediation of the International
Monetary Fund—in effect, by using the IMF as an instrument of
U.S. linkage strategy. The U.S. government's attitude toward
the IMF changed dramatically over the first years of Ronald
Reagan's presidency. Initially cool to any significant or rapid
enlargement of Fund resources, the Reagan administration eventually became one of its strongest advocates. This policy shift
appears to have reflected, at least in part, an altered perception
of how a strong IMF might serve U.S. interests. Yet here too, as
the crisis wore on, Washington's short-run gains in foreign policy
came to be significantly eroded.

During its first year and a half the administration actively
sought to discourage any early increase of Fund quotas (which
determine a member-country's borrowing privileges). The
Seventh General Review of Quotas, which raised quotas by half,
from approximately SDR 40 billion to SDR 59.6 billion (the
value of the SDR in recent years has ranged from $0.95 to $1.05),
had just been completed in November 1980, and another review
was not formally required before 1983. Yet it was clear that the
IMF's usable resources would soon be running low. Mostly as a
result of the second oil shock and the subsequent recession in the
industrial world, deficits of non-oil developing countries grew
enormously, from $41 billion in 1978 to $89 billion in 1980 and
$108 billion in 1981. Net borrowing from the Fund rose quickly,
from under SDR 1 billion in 1978 (new loan commitments less
repayments) to SDR 6.5 billion in 1980 and SDR 12 billion in
1981.[57] As early as the spring of 1981 the Fund's managing
director, Jacques de Larosière, was warning of an impending
threat to the Fund's own liquidity position. Without a new quota
increase, he insisted, the Fund itself would need to borrow as
much as SDR 6-7 billion annually to meet all of its prospective
commitments.[58]

Nonetheless, the Reagan administration remained adamant. Its opposition was to a large extent rooted in a critical view of IMF lending practices as they had developed during the presidency of Reagan's predecessor, Jimmy Carter, particularly after the second oil shock. In early 1979 the Fund's Executive Board had issued a revised set of guidelines on conditionality that put new emphasis on the presumed "structural" nature of many members' balance-of-payments difficulties. The traditional period for a Fund standby arrangement had been one year. But the revised guidelines extended standbys for up to three years if considered "necessary," confirming the trend toward longer adjustment periods already evident in programs financed through the Extended Fund Facility, first introduced in 1974, and the Supplementary Financing Facility (Witteveen Facility) established in 1979.[59] To the Reagan administration these changes smacked of development lending in disguise—totally inconsistent with the Fund's intended role as a limited revolving fund for strictly short-term assistance for balance-of-payments problems. The administration was especially critical of large, low-conditionality loans, such as the SDR 5 billion credit arranged for India in late 1981, and was not at all eager to facilitate more such loans in the future.[60] At most, the administration stated, it might be prepared to contemplate a quota increase of perhaps 25 percent, and even for that there was no particular hurry.

But then came the Mexican crisis—and with it the dramatic shift in U.S. policy. Suddenly the administration *was* in a hurry. Not only did it now pronounce itself in favor of an accelerated increase of quotas (and a more sizable one at that), it wanted to go even further. At the Fund's annual meeting in Toronto, in September 1982, Treasury Secretary Donald Regan suggested "establishment of an additional permanent borrowing arrangement, which would be available to the IMF on a contingency basis for use in extraordinary circumstances."[61] And in the following months the secretary pushed hard for formal consideration of such a proposal, surprising observers who had become accustomed to administration recalcitrance on the size and timing of any new IMF funding. Said one private banker, "Maybe there's a problem out there that we don't know about."[62]

With Washington no longer dragging its heels, the details did not take long to work out. In February 1983 the IMF announced agreement on an increase of quotas from approximately SDR 61 billion to SDR 90 billion—a rise of 47.5 percent. Furthermore, the Fund's General Arrangements to Borrow (GAB) were to be tripled, from approximately SDR 6.4 billion to SDR 17 billion, and for the first time made available to finance loans to countries outside the Group of Ten—thus converting the GAB into precisely the sort of emergency fund that Secretary Regan had earlier suggested.[63] The U.S. share of these increases, which at prevailing exchange rates came to a total of some $8.5 billion ($5.8 billion for a quota increase, $2.7 billion for the GAB expansion), was finally approved by Congress, after protracted lobbying by the administration, in November 1983. In the following month the enlargement of Fund resources formally came into effect.

A policy shift of this magnitude demands some explanation. At one level the explanation was simple: there really *was* a problem "out there"—the threat of a chain reaction of defaults in Latin America and elsewhere that could have plunged the whole world into the abyss of another Great Depression. The Reagan administration did not want to go down in history alongside the Hoover administration; in any event, there was a presidential election coming up in 1984. It had to do *something,* and the IMF was there. It seemed only natural to use what was already available.

At a deeper level, however, the explanation was more complex. Use of the IMF, some administration officials began to believe, might actually serve U.S. policy interests more effectively than attempts to deal with debt problems on a direct, bilateral basis. "A convenient conduit for U.S. influence," one high-level policymaker called it.[64] Any effort by Washington itself to impose unpopular policy conditions on troubled debtors would undoubtedly have fanned the flames of nationalism, if not revolution, in many countries. But what would be intolerable when demanded by a major foreign power might, it seemed, be rather more acceptable if administered by an impartial international agency with no ostensible interests other than the maintenance of international monetary stability. Likewise, the Fund could apply pressures to banks, to maintain or increase lending exposure in debtor countries, that the banks might have resisted had they come from national officials. As the country with the largest share of votes in the Fund (just under 20%), and as the source of the world's preeminent international currency, the United States still enjoys unparalleled influence over IMF decisionmaking—in effect, an implicit veto on all matters of substantive importance. Through its ability to shape attitudes at the Fund, therefore, Washington could hope to exercise more leverage over debtors and banks indirectly than seemed feasible directly, and at a lower political cost.

On the issue of policy conditions the Fund had begun to tighten its standards even before the Mexican crisis, owing in good part to the Reagan administration's active disapproval of earlier lending practices. By the summer of 1982 its institutional attitude had already shifted back toward more rigorous enforcement of domestic austerity measures. Thus once the storm hit, Fund officials needed no persuasion to take on the role, in effect, of the "cop on the beat"—setting policy conditions for new or renewed credits and ensuring strict compliance with their terms. Following the Mexican crisis nearly three dozen countries fell into arrears on their foreign loans; and over the next year nearly two dozen of them found it necessary to negotiate debt relief of some sort with private or official creditors, or both. In all of these negotiations the Fund became a central arbiter of access to, as well as of the terms of, new external financing. Creditors began to insist formally that a debtor country, as a precondition to their own financial assistance, first conclude a standby arrangement with the IMF subject to upper-credit-tranche conditionality. Many restructurings were also made conditional upon continued compliance with Fund performance criteria; and on occasion disbursements of new loans were even timed to coincide with drawings scheduled under Fund stabilization programs.[65] The IMF spelled financial relief and, as such, exercised considerable leverage over the policies of troubled debtors.

That leverage, however, was clearly resented. Throughout the Third World the IMF became a dirty word. And the hand of the United States behind the IMF was increasingly evident to many. In this respect, too, Washington's gains proved essentially transient. Initially, U.S. interests were served by letting the Fund get out in front. But as the crisis persisted the veil tended to wear thin, and criticism came to be focused more and more on the perceived power behind the throne—the United States. This criticism helped stimulate the widespread and growing dissatisfaction with what was viewed as Washington's miserliness and insensitivity toward the problems of debtor countries.

The story is similar in the IMF's relationship with the banks. Initially, it seemed, U.S. interests might also be served by the Fund's ability to apply effective pressure on banks. Washington's own exhortations to banks to resume lending in Latin America or elsewhere fell, as already indicated, largely on deaf ears. Not so, however, with the Fund, which in several key instances successfully demanded specific commercial commitments as a precondition for its own financial assistance. In connection with its $3.9 billion arrangement for Mexico, for instance, which took some four months to negotiate, the Fund refused to go ahead until each of the country's fourteen hundred creditor banks first agreed to extend additional credits amounting to 7 percent of their existing loan exposure (amounting overall to some $5 billion in new bank money for Mexico).[66] Likewise before approving a loan of $5.5 billion for Brazil, in February 1983, the IMF laid down a number of requirements for the banks: restoration of interbank credit lines to $7.5 billion; new loans of $4.4 billion; rollover for eight years of $4 billion in principal due in 1983; and maintenance of short-term trade credits at $8.8 billion.[67] Similar conditions were attached to agreements with other countries as well, most notably Argentina and Yugoslavia.[68]   The IMF's message to the banks was clear. In the words of de Larosière, "Banks will have to continue to increase their exposures . . . if widespread debt financing problems are to be avoided."[69]

Not that all the banks were eager to cooperate—not at first, at least. Many, pursuing their private interests, simply wanted to get their money out as quickly as possible. Managing Director de Larosière had to "knock heads together," as one official phrased it.[70] But eventually the banks themselves came to recognize the crucial public interest in such "involuntary" lending in critical cases. Said one prominent U.S. banker: "It was clear that somebody had to step in and play a leadership role."[71]   Said another: "The IMF sensed a vacuum and properly stepped into it."[72] Could anyone imagine the U.S. government taking such interventionist initiatives? In the first place, Washington had no jurisdiction over the banks of other countries (which accounted for well over half of total loan exposure). And second, even American banks would have been highly reluctant to take such direction straight from government officials. U.S. banks have traditionally paced great store in their arm's-length relationship with the authorities, insisting vehemently on their right as competitors in the marketplace to make their own commercial decisions. In this respect, too, U.S. interests seemed to be served by letting the Fund get out in front.

But this gain also proved to be essentially transient. What the banks were willing to tolerate in certain critical cases, they would not accept as a general rule. Certainly they might again be prepared, should similar emergencies arise in the future, to surrender temporarily some of their traditional operating autonomy. But they would not accept a permanent role for the IMF in the management of private international credit flows, and increasingly they reasserted their right to go their own way. Washington could not long rely on Fund intermediation with the banks either.

Conclusion

The limited selection of experiences that I have briefly examined suggest some interesting insights into the foreign-policy implications of international debt for the United States as a major creditor country.

In the first place, it is evident that America's foreign-policy capabilities are indeed affected, and that the influence is in fact significant. In Poland and Latin America alike, bank priorities turned out to be substantially at variance with the goals of public officials in Washington; and as a result the effectiveness of existing policy instruments in each region was to some extent compromised. For banks, the main goal was simply to avoid default while limiting the extent of any new loan expo-sure. In Poland this attitude made it more difficult for the Reagan administration to make its economic sanctions stick. In Latin America it undercut efforts to keep friendly governments financially secure without new concessions from Washington. In neither case could the negative impacts on policy effectiveness be described as trivial. In both cases money did indeed "talk"— but not to U.S. advantage.

Moreover, it is evident that in the complex intersection of high finance and high politics the government had at best only limited influence over the behavior of banks, given the tradi-tional arm's-length relationship of the public and private sectors in the United States. The limitation was most obvious in Latin America, where despite both carrots (e.g., new Export-Import Bank loan guarantees) and sticks (e.g., threatened closer scrutiny of books), banks could not be induced to resume signifi-cant new amounts of voluntary lending. Bank behavior in this instance was not difficult to understand: Why should bankers accept the risk of increasing exposure more than they themselves consider prudent? In fact, much more could have been expected only if bankers could have been persuaded that vital national interests were at stake.

Third, it is evident that policy linkages were indeed created, though their consequences for U.S. power differed in the two instances. In Poland debt acted marginally as a constraint limiting Washington's ability to influence the ultimate outcome of events. Despite its proclaimed opposition to martial law the Reagan administration felt compelled by its concern over default, when push came to shove, to make a key financial concession to Warsaw—namely, the unconditional decision to pay off CCC-guaranteed credits as they came due. As a result Washington's leverage over Poland was reduced. The United States may not have been "conquered," but it did not "win" either.

In Latin America, by contrast, foreign-policy capabilities were initially enhanced after the Reagan administration acted to help out some of the region's major debtors. The crises of Mexico and others offered Washington, at least for a time, an opportunity to gain considerable goodwill and influence for itself in return for only limited financial concessions. The difference between the two cases was that in one U.S. relations were nonconflictual while in the other they were adversarial. In both cases avoidance of default was treated as an important policy goal. When dealing with an enemy like the Jaruzelski regime, this goal tended to handicap the realization of U.S. foreign-policy preferences, since it undermined the credibility of other policy measures; when dealing with our friends in Latin America, on the other hand, it meant that we were able to help ourselves even as we helped others. The lesson seems clear. Linkage strategies bred by the debt issue are more apt to work when the interest we share with others in avoiding default is reinforced by other shared economic or political interests.

Even in Latin America, however, the initial foreign-policy gains proved essentially transient. As the region's debt crisis wore on, Washington's ability to determine the course of events there declined. Additional concessions, it appeared, would be necessary if the U.S. government wished to retain its newly won leverage. Power in such situations seems to be a wasting asset. Repeated investment is needed to avoid the depletion of goodwill and influence.

Finally, it is evident that any tendency toward power depletion in such situations can only for a time be countered by reliance on the intermediation of a multilateral agency. In the immediate aftermath of the Mexican and other Latin rescues, the IMF gained considerable leverage over the behavior of both debtor governments and banks; and insofar as Washington still retained paramount influence over IMF decisionmaking, U.S. interests, it seemed, could be served more effectively via the Fund than on a direct, bilateral basis. This realization helps to explain the sudden policy shift by the Reagan administration in mid-1982 in favor of a strong, well-endowed IMF. Money seemed to talk best indirectly. But this too, in time, proved to be an essentially transient opportunity.

All of these considerations have very serious implications for the politics of stabilization of the international financial system. The global debt problem appears to suggest an urgent need for some actor, or set of actors, to provide the "collective good" of stability. According to the popular "theory of hegemonic stability," that stabilizing role can be played only by a hegemonic power—meaning, in the contemporary era, the United States. But if my analysis is correct, America does not seem to have the capacity to play that role. Only at the outset of the series of crises in Latin America was the United States able to exercise significant influence over the course of events. The financial collapse of Mexico and others in effect threw those nations willy-nilly into the arms of the only country capable of organizing rescue packages on short notice (just as Poland's financial difficulties pushed it more under the influence of its patron, the Soviet Union). Emergency conditions gave Washington leverage. But once the emergency was past, even this gain was eroded. American power has been insufficient to stabilize the system.

In part, this insufficiency explains why Washington was prepared to try relying to the extent it did on the intermediation of the IMF. Why accept the constraints of operating indirectly through a multilateral agency unless power resources to act directly are inadequate? Unfortunately, even this tactic proved effective only in emergency conditions.

The key to the dilemma lies in the U.S. government's limited influence over the banks, which can best be understood in terms of the continuing dialectic between the "market" and the "state." At Bretton Woods, in 1944, an international monetary regime was designed that in principle excluded private markets from decisions affecting the creation of international liquidity. But the gradual emergence of the Eurocurrency market as a major source of balance-of-payments financing to a significant extent "privatized" the creation of liquidity.[73] In effect, the market moved beyond the influence of any one state, even that of the former hegemonic power. The pendulum can swing back only if the jurisdiction of states catches up once more with the domain of the market—which means *collective* action by governments in lieu of reliance on a single stabilizer. The United States, it would appear, can no longer win the game on its own.

Notes

1. Karin Lissakers, "Money and Manipulation," *Foreign Policy*, no. 44 (Autumn 1981), p. 123.

2. Meyer Rashish, "Bank Lending Overseas Has Become Intertwined with Politics," *American Banker*, 15 January 1982, pp. 4-5.

3. Robert O. Keohane and Josephy S. Nye, *Power and Interdependence: World Politics In Transition* (Boston: Little, Brown, 1977), p. 26.

4. Ibid., pp. 30-32.

5. Surprisingly, there have been few attempts by scholars to explore systematically, in a foreign-policy context, the question of reciprocal influences between governments and banks. But see Jonathan David Aronson, *Money and Power: Banks and the World Monetary System* (Beverly Hills: Sage, 1977); Janet Kelly, "International Capital markets: Power and Security in the International System," *Orbis* 21 (Winter 1978), pp. 843-74; and J. Andrew Spindler, *The Politics of International Credit* (Washington, D.C.: Brookings, 1984).

6. As quoted in *The New York Times*, 11 November 1982, p. D3.

7. "The Politics of Banking," *Banker*, September 1977, p. 21.

8. Jack Zwick and Richard K. Goeltz, "U.S. Banks are Making Foreign Policy," *The New York Times*, 18 March 1979.

9. U.S. Senate, Committee on Foreign Relations, *International Debt, the Banks, and U.S. Foreign Policy*, A Staff Report (Washington, D.C., 1977). p. 7.

10. *IMF Survey*, 18 May 1981, p. 162.

11. Rashish, "Banking Lending Overseas," p. 6.

12. Committee on Foreign Relations, *International Debt,* p. 7.

13. "State Department Calls in U.S. Bankers to Warn against Cutting off Yugoslavia," *The Wall Street Journal,* 22 April 1982, p. 33.

14. Zwick and Goeltz, "U.S. Banks Are Making."

15. Robert W. Russell, "Three Windows on LDC Debt: LDC's, the Banks, and the United States National Interest," in Lawrence G. Franko and Marilyn G. Seiber, eds., *Developing Country Debt* (Elmsford, NY: Pergamon, 1979), pp. 263-264.

16. Herbert Feis, *Europe, the World's Banker, 1870-1914* (1930: rpt. New York: Norton, 1965), p. 468.

17. U.S. Treasury and State Department Fact Sheet on Polish Debt, in U.S. Senate, Committee on Foreign Relations, Sub-committee on European Affairs, *The Polish Economy,* Hearings, 17 January 1982 (hereafter *Polish Economy Hearings*), p. 12.

18. *The New York Times,* 5 December 1981.

19. Interview, U.S. State Department, August 1984.

20. Robert Hormats, "Statement," *Polish Economy Hearings,* p. 4.

21. Treasury and State Department Fact Sheet, *Polish Economy Hearings,* p. 12.

22. Ibid., pp. 11-12. Bank capital is defined to include shareholders' equity, undistributed profits, and reserves for contingencies and other capital reserves—in essence, what a bank would have after paying off depositers and creditors.

23. See, for example, *The New York Times,* 26 May 1982, p. D1.

24. Interview, U.S. State Department, August 1984.

25. *The New York Times,* 1 February 1982, p. 1.

26. "Polish Default: Bankers' Perspectives on the Issues," 22 March 1982, p. 4.

27. As quoted in *The New York Times,* 1 February 1982, p. 1.

28. Marc Leland, "Statement," *Polish Economy Hearings,* p. 7.

29. See, for example, *The New York Times,* 8 June 1982, p. D1.

30. William Safire, "Payoff for Repression," *The New York Times,* 1 February 1982.

31. Interview, U.S. State Department, August 1984.

32. See, for example, *The New York Times*, 30 July 1983, p. 34.

33. Gary Clyde Hufbauer and Jeffrey J. Schott, *Economic Sanctions in Support of Foreign Policy Goals* (Washington: Institute for International Economics, 1983), pp. 73-75.

34. John Van Meer, "Banks, Tanks and Freedom," *Commentary*, December 1982, p. 17.

35. Jeff Frieden, "Third World Indebted Industrialization: International Finance and State Capitalism in Mexico, Brazil, Algeria and South Korea," *International Organization* 35 (Summer 1981), pp. 407-31.

36. Pedro-Pablo Kuczynski, "Latin American Debt," *Foreign Affairs* 61 (Winter 1982-83), p. 349.

37. Morgan Guaranty Trust Company, *World Financial Markets*, October 1982, p. 5.

38. For detail, see Paul A. Volcker, "Statement," in U.S. House Committee on Banking, Finance and Urban Affairs, *International Financial Markets and Related Problems*, Hearings, 2 February 1983, Appendix I, pp. 80-81.

39. Ibid., pp. 81-83.

40. Paul A. Volcker, "Sustainable Recovery: Setting the Stage," Remarks before the New England Council, Boston, 16 November 1982 (processed), p. 17.

41. *The New York Times*, 14 January 1983, p. D1.

42. Bank for International Settlements, *International Banking Developments, Fourth Quarter 1983* (Basle, April 1984).

43. Pedro-Pablo Kuczynski, "Latin American Debt: Act Two," *Foreign Affairs* 62 (Autumn 1983), p. 24.

44. *The New York Times*, 5 November 1983, p. 46.

45. As quoted in ibid., 13 May 1984, p. 1.

46. Ibid., 11 May 1984, p. D2.

47. As quoted in ibid., 18 August 1983, p. 1.

48. *The Economist*, 21 August 1982, p. 11.

49. William R. Cline, *International Debt and the Stability of the World Economy*, Policy Analyses in International Economics no. 4 (Washington, D.C.: Institute for International Economics, September 1983), p. 34.

50. *The New York Times*, 6 December 1982, p. D9.

51. As quoted in ibid., 4 June 1983, p. 29.

52. Interviews, U.S. Treasury, November 1983 and January 1984.

53. *The New York Times*, 15 November 1982, p. D1.

54. *Miami Herald,* 30 August 1982.

55. *The New York Times,* 21 May 1984, p. D1.

56. Western Hemisphere Commission on Public Policy Implications of Foreign Debt, *Report* (New York: Americas Society, February 1984), pp. 19-20.

57. *IMF Survey,* 6 February 1984, p. 40.

58. See, for example, ibid., 18 May 1981, p. 152.

59. Ibid., 19 March 1979, pp. 82-83.

60. Ibid., 23 November 1981, p. 365; for the India loan.

61. As quoted in ibid., 4 October 1982, p. 327.

62. As quoted in *The New York Times,* 12 December 1982, sec. 3, p. 1.

63. The United States for a time held out for a slightly smaller quota increase, to only SDR 85 billion, but was unsuccessful. It *was* successful in preventing expansion of the General Arrangements to Borrow to the figure of SDR 20 billion favored by European governments. See *The Economist,* 22 January 1983, pp. 62-62.

64. Interview, U.S. Treasury, January 1984.

65. *Recent Multilateral Debt Restructurings with Official and Bank Creditors,* IMF Occasional Paper no. 25 (Washington, D.C., December 1983), pp. 10, 26.

66. *The Economist,* 19 February 1983, p. 89.

67. *The New York Times,* 1 March 1983, p. D1.

68. Ibid., 22 January 1983.

69. As quoted in *The New York Times,* 9 January 1983, sec. 3, p. 10.

70. Ibid.

71. Ibid.

72. Ibid.

73. Benjamin J. Cohen, "Balance-of-Payments Financing: Evolution of a Regime," in Stephen D. Krasner, ed., *International Regimes* (Ithaca: Cornell University Press, 1983), pp. 315-36.

4
The Revolution in Atlantic Economic Relations: A Bargain Comes Unstuck*

A revolution has occurred in the foreign policy of the United States. The international provisions of President Nixon's New Economic Policy, announced on August 15, 1971, signaled a fundamental transformation in economic relations between the United States and the rest of the world—and, in particular, in U.S. relations with Europe.

For 25 years the United States and Europe had dealt with one another as allies. Within a framework of partnership, relations had been conducted on a basis that was essentially cooperative rather than antagonistic. The alliance was not always placid, to be sure. Yet even in its stormiest days it was generally understood that what the two sides of the Atlantic shared in common was more important than what divided them. Repeatedly, the United States emphasized its willingness to sacrifice short-term economic benefits for the longer-term advantages of partnership with a united Europe. Its attitude was that what was good for Europe was also good for the United States.

Now, however, the atmosphere has changed. The president's New Economic Policy has launched the United States on a trade and monetary offensive the outcome of which is still uncertain but the message of which is already abundantly clear: henceforth, the United States intends to put its own economic interests first. What divides the United States from Europe is now what receives most emphasis in official Washington. According to one of the president's former chief advisers on international

*From Wolfram Hanreider (ed.), *The United States and Western Europe: Political, Economic and Strategic Perspectives* (Cambridge, MA: Winthrop , 1974), ch. 6.

economic policy: "President Nixon's New Economic Policy announced August 15, 1971, marked the beginning of a new era in international economic relationships."[1] Or as another former top Administration official put it, rather more pithily: "It's a new ball game with new rules."[2] What worries the Europeans is whether the new ball game means the end of the old alliance.

This essay addresses itself to the impact of the president's New Economic Policy on the future of the Atlantic alliance. The first section briefly outlines the major international provisions of the new policy. The next two sections attempt to place the policy in its proper perspective, in order to demonstrate just how radical the transformation in relations has been. Possible explanations for the revolution in policy are considered in the remaining sections of the essay. In my opinion, the reversal cannot be explained either by bureaucratic confusion or by a revival of protectionist sentiment in the United States, although both factors undoubtedly have contributed to the current difficulties. The explanation in fact runs much deeper, and has to do with the changing balance of power in international economic relations and with U.S. efforts to redress that balance of power.

The New Economic Policy

When President Nixon outlined his New Economic Policy in August 1971, he made it "perfectly clear" that he was concerned about more than just the unsatisfactory state of the domestic economy. He was at least as much concerned about the deteriorating state of the U.S. balance of payments. To combat that deterioration, he included two major international provisions in his package of economic policy measures.

First, he announced that he was suspending the convertibility of the dollar into gold. "I have directed (Treasury) Secretary Connally to suspend temporarily the convertibility of the dollar into gold or other reserve assets." The purpose of this step was plain—to persuade the governments of other industrial nations to accept an upward revaluation of their currencies relative to our own. The Japanese yen and the German mark were prominently mentioned in this connection. The idea was to achieve an effective devaluation of the dollar—to cheapen U.S. exports in foreign markets and make imports into the United States more expensive, and thereby lead to a net improvement of our trade balance and balance of payments.

Second, the president imposed a surcharge of 10 percent on all imports into the United States not already subject to quota restriction. (Also exempt were imports not already subject to duty of any kind, mainly raw materials and foodstuffs.)   Much was made of the fact that the surcharge was intended to be temporary. Its function, apparently, was to provide some transitory relief to U.S. import-competing industries pending the desired realignment of exchange rates. Obviously it could also provide useful leverage in convincing other governments to accept the appreciation of their currencies relative to the dollar.

Both of these provisions were aimed directly at our industrial trading partners in Europe and Japan. Both also violated the letter as well as the spirit of international law. Suspension of convertibility was clearly inconsistent with our obligations under the Articles of Agreement of the International Monetary Fund (IMF); and as the United States was repeatedly reminded at a special meeting in Geneva of the General Agreement on Tariffs and Trade (GATT) called a week after President Nixon's announcement, the Administration's import surcharge clearly clashed with our obligations under GATT. The surcharge was criticized for undoing virtually all of the trade liberalization negotiated under the auspices of GATT throughout the whole of the postwar period. Nevertheless, Washington apparently considered both steps justified by the state of the balance of payments. The U.S. delegate to the special meeting in Geneva insisted that the problem of the dollar "transcended any particular article of GATT."[3]

In fact, Washington seemed prepared to transcend any particular article of *anything* in order to get its way on these matters. Traditionally, the United States had been the leader in efforts to extend and strengthen the rules of international economic conduct. But as the weeks and months passed after August 15, it became increasingly clear that the New Economic Policy was by no means a temporary aberration of behavior. The United States had thrown the rule book to the winds. Its objective was a massive improvement in its trade balance and balance of payments— and Washington seemed willing to risk even open economic warfare in order to achieve that goal. The two steps announced by President Nixon turned out to be only the opening shots. Very soon the administration began to escalate its offensive.

At first, Washington had not indicated just how much of an improvement of the balance of payments it was seeking. However, in mid-September, at a meeting of the Group of Ten,[4] Secretary Connally announced that our objective was a net "turn-around" of $13 billion—from a trade deficit (at full employment) of $5 billion to a surplus of $8 billion. The ten percent surcharge on imports would not be removed, he said, until this turnaround was achieved. Our trading partners were stunned. This was a much larger figure than had ever previously been mentioned, and would have required a weighted revaluation of the other currencies relative to the dollar on the order of 16 to 18 percent.[5]   Moreover, the secretary indicated that this was now only *part* of the price being sought by the administration for removal of the surcharge. In addition, Washington expected "tangible progress" toward relaxation of European and Japanese tariff and non-tariff barriers to American exports, and also a more "equitable" sharing of the burden of defense costs in Europe and Asia. These same demands were repeated by secretary Connally at the annual meeting of the IMF in Washington at the end of September.

In October, the U.S. offensive was escalated even further. Japan was warned that unless "voluntary" restraints were imposed on exports of synthetic-fiber and woolen textiles and clothing to the United States, the administration would invoke the half-century-old Trading With the Enemy Act to impose quotas unilaterally. *The Washington Post* called this the "crudest coercion"[6]—but it worked. After some hard bargaining, the Japanese finally acquiesced in an accord setting a ceiling of five percent on the growth rate of sales of synthetics to this country, and a ceiling of one percent on woolens. (Parallel agreements signed simultaneously by Korea, Taiwan, and Hong Kong provided a growth rate of seven and one-half percent for synthetics.)   As a sop, Washington excluded all textile imports from the ten percent surcharge.

In November and December, the administration began to spell out the specifics of its demands on foreign trade barriers. The list of concessions being sought could by no means be described as a short one. Japan was asked to relax restrictions on 40 separate items, including citrus fruit and juices, soybeans, coal, leather, computers, refrigerators, air conditioners, and automobiles. The Japanese were also asked to consider "voluntary" restraints on sales to this country of automobiles, color television sets, tape recorders, and cameras, and to extend and tighten the existing "voluntary" agreement on steel. In Europe the focus was on the Common Market. Immediate concessions were sought on a variety of U.S. agricultural exports, including especially citrus fruits, tobacco, and wheat. For the longer term, Washington demanded a wholesale revision of the European Community's common farm policy, in order to reduce the protectionist impact of its high support-price structure. In addition, Washington demanded an end to the Community's proliferating network of preferential trading agreements around the Mediterranean and throughout Africa.

When the Community was set up in 1958, it had immediately negotiated preferential arrangements with eighteen African countries and Madagascar (all former colonies of the Six); later, similar deals were worked out with three East African countries (Kenya, Uganda, and Tanzania) and with such Mediterranean countries as Greece, Turkey, Tunisia, Morocco, Spain, Yugoslavia, Lebanon, Israel, Cyprus, and Malta. And finally, in 1971, with impending enlargement of the Community to include Britain, Ireland, and Denmark, plans were being made to extend preferences to the remaining non-applicant members of the European Free Trade Association as well. Washington indicated that it now intended to claim compensation for diversion of U.S. export trade caused by the discriminatory features of these arrangements. (Ironically, the claim was based on a right available to the United States under GATT.) The United States even claimed compensation for trade diversion caused by the enlargement of the Community itself.

In mid-December, at another of the series of meetings of the Group of Ten, a temporary pause was reached in the U.S. offensive with agreement on a new global pattern of exchange rates. The administration pledged to ask Congress to raise the price of gold formally from $35 to $38 per ounce, effectively devaluing the dollar by 8.57 percent. Simultaneously, other countries realigned their rates upward in coordination with the dollar devaluation to achieve a total net weighted revaluation of other currencies relative to the dollar of approximately 12 percent. In return, the United States removed the ten percent surcharge on imports. Washington stipulated, however, that at any time the surcharge might be reimposed at the president's discretion. Furthermore, the suspension of the dollar's convertibility remained fully in effect, and still continues in effect despite the dollar's second devaluation in February 1973 (by an additional ten percent, to $42.22 per ounce of gold) and the subsequent global movement a month later to a new system of freely floating exchange rates.

Thus, the pause in December 1971 was not the end of the story. Quite the opposite, in fact. Washington's economic offensive still continued. As 1971 ended, the White House published a report on the international economic situation of the United States written by Peter G. Peterson, then the President's special assistant for international economic affairs.[7] The report had originally been submitted to Mr. Nixon in April in the form of a confidential memorandum; reliable sources later indicated that it provided "the underpinning" for the New Economic Policy eventually announced in August.[8] Released to the public in updated form in late December indicated that it continued to be representative of the administration's official attitude on economic policy. The report said that the United States still expected Japan and the Common Market to make tangible progress toward relaxation of their barriers to U.S. exports: "our intention will be to construct a new trading system to take the place of the old."[9] In fact, the first devaluation of the dollar was made conditional on these commercial concessions by our partners. At the Group of Ten meeting in December, administration spokesmen had made clear that they would insist on such progress before submitting a bill to Congress to authorize formally the rise of the official price of gold.[10] Moreover, Washington continued in the background to brandish a variety of weapons useful to promoting U.S. commercial interests—including both the dollar's inconvertibility and the option to reimpose the ten percent surcharge on imports.

In February 1972 the requisite concessions were forthcoming. Japan agreed to relax restrictions on virtually all of the items specified by the United States, and the Common Market agreed to liberalize imports of citrus fruits, tobacco, and wheat. Furthermore, in public statements, both the Japanese and the Europeans acceded to the U.S. demand for a complete review and reconstruction of the world trading system. It was agreed that a new round of global negotiations under the auspices of GATT, involving all aspects of trade relations, would begin in September 1973.

As far as the United States is concerned, there is no question that the main subject of this review should be the European

Economic Community. As the Peterson Report made clear, and subsequent Washington statements have reaffirmed, the Common Market has always been the main target of the administration's international economic offensive. For example, the annual report of the president's Council of Economic Advisers in January 1973, singled out "the accelerated liberalization of trade within the enlarged European Community and countries associated with it" as the principal reason why the United States is insisting on the need for the new round of GATT negotiations.[11]   The point was further underscored after President Nixon submitted his proposed new "Trade Reform Act" to Congress in April 1973, designed to provide him with the bargaining authority he needs to participate effectively in the forthcoming negotiations. When Congressional hearings on the bill opened in May, John Connally's successor as secretary of the treasury, George Shultz, asserted that these negotiations were not intended to be "reciprocal."   "There may have to be more giving than taking as far as other people are concerned."[12]   Shultz left no doubt that the "other people" he had in mind were the Europeans.

In short, the administration remains as determined as ever to pursue its grievances against the Europeans, in particular against their farm policy and preferential arrangements—even, apparently, if it means open economic warfare. In the words of one former EEC trade official, the United States is demanding "fundamental changes in all policies."[13]   Yet for a number of reasons it simply may not be possible for the Common Market to make such changes and still preserve its fragile cohesion. Consequently, what worries the Europeans is that Washington seems in effect to be forcing them into a most unwelcome choice—either unity in Europe or cooperation with the United States.[14]   And the fear is that ultimately it will be the Atlantic alliance that will suffer. As the foreign minister of West Germany has warned: "By its decisions on trade policy, the United States may bring about the disintegration of the Western world."[15]

Policy in the Postwar Period

Clearly, this is a revolution in the United States' policy. Since 1945 integration in the Western world has been a prime objective of the foreign policy of the United States. This was considered an indispensable condition toward ensuring its national security—its independence and way of life—against what, once the Cold War began, was viewed as an ominous threat from expansionist world communism. Such an objective is not dispensed with lightly.

From the point of view of analysis, it does not matter whether in fact the perceived threat from world communism after World War II was "real": what matters is simply that the *fear* of a threat was real. That much suffices to explain why Americans considered it so important during the 1950s and 1960s to become involved in so many "entangling" alliances, spheres of influence, and even wars in various areas of the globe. In the western hemisphere Americans considered it in their national interest to maintain their traditional position of hegemony. In the eastern hemisphere they considered it in their national interest to maintain the balance of power against the pressure of expansion from the Soviet Union and its allies; in other words, to "contain" communism. In one-half of the world the U.S. design was to keep Canada and the Latin American republics as closely associated with the United States as possible; in the other half, it was to buttress the nations of Western Europe and Japan, counter-balancing, respectively, the Soviet bloc in Europe and mainland China in Asia, while at the same time competing against the attempts of communist states to extend their influence in the non-aligned Third World of South Asia, the Middle East and Africa. For twenty-five years these were the principal goals of U.S. foreign policy.

In pursuing these goals the U.S. government showed itself ready to use any or all of the instruments of foreign economic policy at its disposal—commercial policy, foreign-investment policy, foreign-aid policy, balance-of-payments policy. Economic programs were continuously subordinated to the broader considerations of its general foreign policy; commercial and financial interests were frequently sacrificed for purposes of national security. As it happened, this represented a significant departure from the pattern that had prevailed historically up to World War II. Then it was more often the diplomats—and even the Marines—that were called in to promote economic objectives overseas, rather than the reverse. After 1945, the objectives of an activist foreign policy were usually given first priority.

Geographically, U.S. foreign economic policy was divided into three primary components that correspond roughly to the three broad economic divisions in which the world found itself at the end of World War II: the noncommunist industrial nations of Europe, Canada and Japan; the communist bloc; and the less developed Third World of Africa, Asia and Latin America. U.S. policy regarding the noncommunist industrial nations was unmistakably clear. From the start of the Cold War, official Washington's chief objective was to reconstruct the war-ravaged economies of Western Europe and Japan, and maintain the vigor of the undamaged Canadian economy, so that these countries could all serve as effective barriers to communist expansion. Toward this end the United States disbursed aid to the former war zones in the form of grants and loans, most spectacularly under the European Recovery Program (Marshall Plan), which lasted from 1948 to 1952. Toward this end, also, the United States later encouraged an outflow of private investments from the United States, particularly to Canada but also to Europe, and it promoted through GATT a broad program of worldwide liberalization of industrial trade that frequently benefited its allies directly at its own expense. Japan, for instance, starting in the early 1950s was granted privileged access to the U.S. home market for a wide variety of industrial exports. And in Europe various schemes of regional cooperation and integration were encouraged despite the potential threat to U.S. economic interests, on the grounds that these would cement ties and substitute cohesion for fragmentation in the face of external communist pressures. These included the European Payments Union, the European Coal and Steel Community, the European Free Trade Association, and, in particular, the Common Market (European Economic Community). Any cost of these arrangements was regarded as a small enough price for pre-serving the power balance in Europe and Asia as well as the united strength of the North American continent.

With respect to the communist bloc, the postwar foreign economic policy of the United States was equally plain. The United States' main objective was the economic equivalent of political "containment": to minimize its own and its allies' trade contacts with the bloc in order to deny the Soviet Union and its client states the major benefits of an international division of labor. East-West trade, the United States reasoned, was far more important to the communists than to it. Hence, correct or not, it seemed possible for the United States to enhance its national security at relatively little cost in terms of income forgone. Its policy began in 1948, after the Berlin blockade, with the initiation of mandatory export licensing controls. It was later extended in several major pieces of legislation, including in particular the Export Control Act of 1949, which withdrew most-favored-nation tariff treatment from communist states and established a list of "strategic" goods for which no U.S. export licenses would be issued.

Finally, with respect to the underdeveloped Third World, the main objective of U.S. foreign economic policy was to cooperate in the aspiration for economic development in order to maximize its own net influence in the area and to protect its existing commercial and financial interests. The main U.S. instrument of policy in this connection was the foreign-aid program, beginning in 1949 with Point Four technical assistance and later expanding to include grants and loans by a succession of such alphabetical agencies as MSA, FOA, DLF, ICA, and AID. Trade policy was not used much for this purpose, and private investors received only modest encouragement to seek out investment opportunities in the less developed countries. Even the foreign-aid program was never large relative to U.S. potential. Apparently the United States, as a political community, did not feel compelled to pay a great deal for this aspect of national power and security.

Underlying its foreign economic policy in all these areas was its policy regarding the balance of international payments. This category of policy had no geographical limitations, because it influenced and regulated U.S. actions in every part of the globe. After World War II the international monetary system was reconstructed in the form of a gold-exchange standard based on the dollar. The United States found itself functioning as central banker for the world: its liabilities circulated widely both as the principal "vehicle" currency for international trade and investment—even the communist states tend to use dollars when trading outside their bloc—and as the principal reserve currency for governments and international institutions. In practice, this meant that the amount of new "international" money placed in circulation depended mainly on the magnitude of the annual deficits in U.S. balance of payments. When the world's demand for new money exceeded the available supply, the United States, the central bank, could run deficits of almost any conceivable magnitude. This happened during the period of the "dollar shortage," which lasted from the end of World War II until about 1958. During those years the United States was effectively freed from balance-of-payments constraints to pursue whatever policies it considered appropriate and to spend as freely as it thought necessary to promote objectives believed to be in the national interest. From the foreign-exchange point of view, the United States could afford to forgo potentially profit-able trade with the communist bloc, it could afford to revive Europe and Japan with aid, investments and trade advantages, it could afford to promote development in the Third World with substantial grants and loans, and it could afford to maintain hundreds of thousands of U.S. military personnel abroad. In effect, although a payments balance, by definition, is a mutual experience, the U.S. position as international central banker enabled it to adopt a unilateral balance-of-payments policy: it issued the world's principal vehicle and reserve currency in amounts presumed to be consistent with its priorities—not with those of its depositors.

After about 1958 that situation changed dramatically. A deterioration of the U.S. balance of payments showed that the world's demand for new money no longer greatly exceeded the then available supply. Indeed, according to many observers, the dollar shortage by the late 1950s had become a "dollar glut." As a result, the United States could no longer continue ignoring the priorities of its depositors as it had until then: the balance of international payments now constrained its policies overseas. Yet U.S. foreign policy objectives remained essentially un-changed. Accordingly, much of the 1960s was spent devising policies and programs that would minimize the impact of this payments constraint on U.S. ability to act as it saw fit in world affairs. That was the purpose of such schemes as the "gold pool" and the network of foreign-exchange swaps arranged with various foreign central banks. The ambition of the United States was to preserve the political privileges accorded it, as inter-national central banker, to act abroad unilaterally in promoting its perceived national interest.

The Bargain Comes Unstuck

Within this elaborate edifice of foreign economic policies, the keystone undoubtedly lay in the U.S. alliance with Europe. A prosperous and united Europe was considered vital to the achievement of all other U.S. postwar overseas objectives—the *sine qua non* of the United States overall foreign economic policy design. Rehabilitation of Japan, for instance, would have been much more difficult—and surely would have been much more costly for the United States—had the Europeans remained economically weak and fragmented. Japanese recovery depended absolutely on access to foreign markets. But Japan suffered from discrimination by the Europeans both in their home markets and in their former colonial areas in South and Southeast Asia. Had their own recovery been incomplete, the Europeans would never have tolerated the penetration of Japanese commercial interests into their privileged trading areas. (American persuasion was instrumental in this regard.) And they certainly would never have accepted Japanese membership in international economic organizations such as the IMF and GATT, despite the sponsorship of the United States. Japan's reentry into the global system of multilateral trade and payments would have been indefinitely delayed. As a result, Japan's rehabilitation would have had to rely even more heavily than it did on privileged access to the U.S. market. The cost to U.S. industry would have been even greater than it was.

Reconstruction in Europe was vital also to the U.S. policy on East-West trade. The Europeans were never in complete agreement with the U.S. policy of economic "containment" of the Soviet bloc, in part owing simply to the fact of their geographic proximity. Nevertheless, they effectively complied with its overall policy by withdrawing most-favored-nation treatment and by maintaining their own lists of "strategic" items (albeit usually shorter than that of the United States). It is clear, however, that they would never have done this at all had their own recovery after the war been delayed: they would have been too busy scrambling for whatever trading crumbs might have been offered them by the bloc to the East. Likewise, the U.S. policy of promoting development in the Third World would have required a much higher level of economic commitment had it not been able to rely on complementary efforts by the European allies of the United States in their own traditional spheres of interest. Such complementary programs would have been impossible had the Europeans remained weak and fragmented after the war.

Most importantly, it is questionable whether the United States could have operated as freely as it did as central banker for the world if European reconstruction had been any less successful than it was. Europe, of course, was in no position to challenge the central role of the United States in the gold-exchange standard. No European currency could possibly have replaced the dollar as the system's principal vehicle currency or reserve currency. But the Europeans were in a position to challenge the United States' *use* of its role as world central banker. Furthermore, there is no doubt that the Europeans would have been so inclined had the system not contributed so dramatically to their own economic revival by helping them to replenish their reserves and to rebuild their industries. Implicitly, a bargain was struck. The Europeans acquiesced in a system which accorded the United States special privileges to act abroad unilaterally to promote U.S. interests. The United States, in turn, condoned Europe's use of the system to promote its own regional economic prosperity, even if this happened to come largely at the expense of the United States.

In particular, the United States condoned the creation of those preferential trade and payments arrangements already referred to (EPU, ECSC, EFTA, EEC) despite their inherent—and obvious—discrimination against U.S. export sales. The prime case in point is the Common Market, which was always expected to result in a certain amount of diversion of trade from American to European sources. On the basis of straightforward commercial calculations, the United States ought to have been expected to oppose the Community as soon as it was conceived back in 1958. Yet in fact the United States not only tolerated but actively promoted the integration of the Six. The Community was viewed as a particularly useful device to promote European prosperity and unity. The potential cost to the United States was considered by official Washington to be a quite tolerable trade-off for the broader advantages to be gained for the overall U.S. foreign policy design. In any event, it was felt that the United States could bear the cost because presumably it was freed from any significant constraint due to the balance of payments. Its role as world central banker was supposed to mean that it would not need to worry about any deficit pressures generated by trade diversion in Europe. It would still be able to pursue whatever policies overseas it considered to be in its national interest as a political community.

It is significant that already in the 1960s the implicit bargain between the United States and Europe was beginning to come unstuck. In the United States there had always been some concern about the competitive threat of the Common Market to U.S. commercial interests. This concern rapidly increased as integration among the Six proceeded. Very soon official Washington felt compelled to respond. The response took the form of the Trade Expansion Act of 1962, granting the president sweeping new powers to negotiate reciprocal tariff reductions of up to 50 percent in all categories—and of up to 100 percent in those categories for which the United States and the European Economic Community together accounted for 80 percent or more of world exports. This latter provision, promising free trade for a wide range of goods, was intended to nullify most of the potential for trade diversion generated by the emergence of the Common Market. It was also intended to spur the movement toward general European integration which had been revived that year by Great Britain's decision to seek membership in the Community. Everyone understood that without the British the provision was meaningless. In other words, everyone understood that the United States was still trying to pursue its postwar goal of regional cooperation and integration in Europe. The only difference was that perhaps for the first time it was also taking more explicit account of the potential cost to itself.

As it happened, the free trade provision of the Trade Expansion Act became a dead letter when President de Gaulle vetoed British membership in January 1963. Thus, for all its success over the next four and one-half years in reducing tariffs across the board by as much as 35 to 40 percent on average, the Kennedy Round of trade negotiations did not eliminate the competitive threat from the Community. If anything, the threat seemed to loom greater than ever as the Common Market grew to become the world's largest trading unit. As the 1960s ended, the United States was becoming increasingly uncomfortable about the economic costs of European regionalism.

The bargain was also coming unstuck on the other side of the Atlantic. In Europe there had always been some concern about the special role of the dollar in the international monetary system, and as early as the mid-1960s there was already an inclination to challenge the United States' use of that role. France, in particular, under President de Gaulle, was resentful of the freedom the dollar's pre-eminence gave the U.S. government to pursue policies the French considered abhorrent—such as the U.S. involvement in Vietnam. Essentially, this explains the difficulties the United States experienced in managing its balance of payments during the 1960s. France and other countries expressed their displeasure with U.S. policies by threatening a "run on the bank"—that is, by threatening to bring about a depletion of the U.S. gold stock, either directly—by means of massive conversions of their own reserve dollar holdings—or indirectly, by withholding assistance in the event of speculative drains through the private gold market. (The United States had assumed the role of residual supplier of gold to the private market, first unilaterally, and then, after 1961, as the principal member of the so-called gold pool.) As indicated earlier, the U.S. response consisted of policies and programs designed to minimize the impact of this constraint on its ability to act as it saw fit in world affairs. Tension and uncertainty—to say nothing of drama—resulted.

The first act of the drama ended suddenly during the great "gold rush" of March 1968. Without prior warning the United States, in accord with other major financial powers, announced that it was ending support of the private market for gold. Henceforth, the international system would be characterized by a two-tier gold price—one price for the private market, determined by supply and demand; and another price for central banks, to remain at the previous fixed level of $35 per ounce. This effectively ended any danger of a run on the bank due to private speculation against the dollar.

The danger of *official* speculation against the dollar, however, remained. Technically, the U.S. currency remained convertible at the central bank level. Foreign governments still retained the legal right to exchange their reserve holdings of dollars for U.S. gold. But that right was clearly a limited one, *de jure* rather than *de facto*. Dollar liabilities far exceeded the amount of gold in Fort Knox. The U.S. government made it quite plain that if a serious depletion of its gold stock were threatened, it would be prepared to close the window and refuse further sales—in effect declaring the dollar inconvertible. Other countries would then be faced with a choice of one of two alternatives: either they could keep accumulating dollars indefinitely, or they could sell them in the foreign exchange market for whatever price they would bring. The first choice would represent acquiescence in a world dollar standard; the second would transform the economic order into a system of currency blocs or flexible exchange rates. Neither choice represented an especially attractive option from the European point of view.

And thus the stage was set for Act II of the drama. The question was: Would the bargain hold? Would the United States continue to condone European regionalism with its attendant high costs to U.S. commercial interests? Would Europe continue to acquiesce in a monetary system which gave special privileges to the Americans?

Bureaucratic Confusion?

The major development came in August 1971 and raised the question "Why was the bargain scuttled?" Why is the United States now insistent on putting its own commercial interests first—even if it means jeopardizing the unity of Europe or the cohesion of the Atlantic alliance, or both?

Conceivably, the explanation might lie in bureaucratic confusion. Within the machinery of the United States government, there are more than sixty separate departments, agencies, and commissions involved in one way or another in the conduct of foreign economic policy—each with its own viewpoint, its own specialization, its own vested constituency. Operational authority in the area is extremely fragmented.[16] Consequently, coordination of economic policy with other aspects of foreign policy has always been quite difficult. It is altogether possible that this fact alone can account for the apparent reversal of the U.S. European policy. It may not really be a reversal of policy at all: it may be merely a mistake—the product of disarray or inconsistency among the bureaucrats. This conclusion, although possible, is not probable.

Historically, leadership in the area of U.S. foreign economic policy was vested in the departments of State and Treasury, with State concentrating mainly on commercial policy and the international trading system, and Treasury on balance-of-payments policy and the international monetary system. However, over time, as the United States became increasingly integrated into the world economic structure, this simple division of responsibility gradually broke down. Other departments began to develop distinct international interests of their own, including especially Commerce, Labor, Agriculture, and more recently Defense. Both the Federal Reserve Board of Governors and Federal Reserve Bank of New York developed a distinct international interest in the area of finance and exchange rates. And, since World War II, various more specialized agencies were created or broadened, each also logically concerned with some aspect or other of foreign economic relations, such as the Council of Economic Advisers, the Office of Management and Budget, the National Security Council, the Agency for International Development, the Federal Maritime Commission, the International Trade Commission, and the Office of the U.S. Trade Representative. The division of responsibility for policy grew increasingly complex and overlapping. The result was fragmentation of authority and dispersion of control.

Within this complex mosaic, there has been only one governmental unit (other than the White House) with a direct responsibility for coordinating economic policy with other aspects of foreign policy. That of course has been the State department. Its viewpoint is by definition the national interest, broadly conceived—the entire range of the country's political, diplomatic, and military relations around the world. The perspective of most other actors is narrower and more specialized—oriented toward the interests of particular domestic constituencies. But because of the fragmentation of authority in the area, the Department of State has never been able to guarantee overall consistency in the conduct of its economic relations. State has been just one more voice added to the many within the councils of government. And as students of bureaucratic politics are well aware, the voice that will catch the ear of the man at the top is an arbitrary business at best, depending as much on the personalities who are speaking as on anything else. Moreover, as students of the U.S. bureaucracy are well aware, the influence of the State department in official Washington has declined sharply in recent years. Other agencies with other interests have impinged increasingly on State's prerogatives in foreign relations. Some observers have suggested that this fact alone may suffice to account for the reversal in the government's policy toward Europe since the summer of 1971.

Certainly some inconsistency among the bureaucrats has been evident. Conflicts between former Treasury Secretary John Connally and Federal Reserve Board Chairman Arthur Burns over the gold-price issue, for instance, were reported in the press throughout the summer and fall of 1971. And some State Department spokesmen expressed considerable reservations about the priority being accorded the economic interests of the United States in its relations with Europe and Japan. Nevertheless, it is difficult to believe that bureaucratic confusion alone explains the origin of the economic offensive. When President Nixon first entered office, he was determined to end this inherited disorder enveloping foreign economic policy.[17] His solution was the Council on International Economic Policy, a special office established in January 1971 within the Executive Office of the president to provide organizational leadership in the formulation of foreign economic policy—in Mr. Nixon's own words, to "provide a clear, top-level focus on international economic issues."[18] Moreover, Mr. Nixon himself takes a strong interest in all aspects of foreign affairs, which, as is well known, he considers his special forte. It is highly unlikely that he would allow inconsistency at the lower echelons of government to interfere with his overall "game plan" for international relations. In fact, he has not. Rather, he has used the planning mechanism provided by the new council to impose his own signature on policy.

Of course, the council did not remove the various departments and agencies from their individual responsibilities. Each still has its own specialized operational authority; each still competes on behalf of its own distinct vested constituency. (At the moment Secretary Shultz's Treasury seems to dominate the competition.) But the council does provide a framework of strategy within which all of these units must try to function. To some extent this simply substitutes formality for informality; earlier presidents also had means for developing a framework of strategy for economic relations. But Mr. Nixon has an aversion to unorganized decisionmaking. What the existence of the council indicates is that the New Economic Policy is no accident of organization. Like it or not, the policy is the product of a deliberate analysis and design. It represents a coherent vision of the world.

Revival of Protectionism?

An alternative explanation of the New Economic Policy might lie in a revival of protectionist sentiment in the United States. Political pressures for new trade measures to aid American industry have been gathering for some time. In 1971 imports were up, production and employment were down, an election year was in the offing. It is altogether possible that these facts alone suffice to account for the change of direction in policy. Again, I would suggest: possible—but not probable.

Certainly, it is true that protectionist sentiment has revived in the United States. There has been a fundamental shift in the balance of domestic political forces affecting policy on foreign trade.[19] Support for the traditionally liberal trade posture of the United States has gradually dwindled across the country. Support for protection of domestic commercial interests, meanwhile, has been growing by leaps and bounds. Organized labor, for instance, has reversed its attitude completely on the issue of international trade. Once the unions were among the strongest advocates of trade liberalization. Free trade, they stressed, offered many advantages—new jobs, higher incomes, lower prices for consumers. Support from labor was crucial to the Kennedy administration in obtaining passage of the Trade Expansion Act in 1962. More recently, however, organized labor has turned against trade liberalization, especially as unemployment has risen since 1969. What the unions now stress are the disadvantages of free trade—the painful occupational and personal dislocations that workers are forced to suffer when imports are more competitive than domestic products. Increasingly, workers are expressing a reluctance to accept the costs of adjustment to imports. They would much rather simply keep the foreign goods out.

In part, this change of attitude is particularist, reflecting the difficulties of specific unions in individual industries. The rising protectionism of such unions is quite understandable in view of the dramatic improvements of foreign competitiveness that have occurred in their particular lines of work (e.g., textiles, shoes, and rubber products). But this is by no means the entire explanation. There are also more general reasons for labor's reversal on trade. Lawrence Krause has pointed out how, as U.S. economic activity has become increasingly oriented toward the provision of services of various kinds, the comparative advantage of the United States has gradually shifted away from many of its traditional goods-producing industries.[20] Yet these are precisely the industries in which the unions tend to be most heavily concentrated. The labor movement has not been particularly successful in organizing workers in the services sector. Nor, for that matter, has it moved very quickly to organize the newer, science-based goods-producing industries where rapidly changing technology still does give the United

States some comparative advantage. For the most part, it has continued to identify its interests with a sector of the economy that is rapidly declining in relative importance and competitiveness. No wonder labor now seems concerned more about the costs of adjustment than about trade gains.

These general changes in the economy also help to explain other shifts in the balance of domestic forces on trade. The rising importance of services in the economy has meant a declining interest among businessmen in the export of goods—and, consequently, a declining interest in general in any further liberalization of trade. There are exceptions, of course. The agricultural sector remains vitally concerned about access to foreign markets. And many smaller industrial corporations that sell some share of their output abroad can also be expected to continue supporting a liberal posture on trade. The same cannot be expected, however, of the larger industrial corporations which have managed to develop a multinational base for the production and sale of their output. These corporations are more concerned about maintaining freedom for their international investments than for their export trade. And these happen to be the corporations with the most political clout in the United States.

The shift in the balance of forces has been reflected in Washington. On Capitol Hill the high point of trade liberalism was reached in the early 1960s, with the passage of the Trade Expansion Act of 1962 by the largest majority in the history of the trade agreements program (begun by Cordell Hull in 1934). Since then, Congress has grown increasingly protectionist in outlook. In 1968, the modest trade bill submitted by the Johnson administration never even got reported out of the House Ways and Means Committee. In 1970 the so-called Mills bill, which would have imposed quotas on imports of textiles and shoes (as well as a host of other items at the discretion of the president), came within a hairbreadth of passage. And in the current Congress numerous bills have been submitted to protect various U.S. industries. The most prominent of these, by far, is the Burke-Hartke bill, which would (among other things) put quota restraints on every single product imported into the United States. (Organized labor is a strong supporter of the Burke-Hartke bill.) In response to this change of attitude, successive administrations have made an effort to tighten up the range of restrictions on imports. In fact, apart from the tariff reductions negotiated during the Kennedy Round, the trend of U.S. trade barriers has been distinctly upward, rather than downward. From 1962 to 1970 the number of U.S. industrial imports subject to quota control, including "voluntary" restraint by foreign suppliers, rose from seven to 67. And during the same years anti-dumping and border-tax rules,[21] among other restrictions, were also toughened up significantly.

Is the New Economic Policy merely a continuation of this trend—a capitulation to protectionist forces? Undoubtedly the rising tide of protectionism in the country has been a factor in the administration's thinking. No one has ever accused Richard Nixon of ignoring domestic political considerations when framing policy. And it is certainly true that administration spokesmen keep talking about the need to appease the forces of protectionism in the United States lest Congress resort to even more extreme forms of action.[22] (It is significant that Mr. Nixon's proposed new "Trade Reform Act" contains authority for the president to increase, not just to decrease, any U.S. trade barriers now in existence.)   However, it is difficult not to see a certain amount of diplomatic opportunism in assertions of this kind. Protectionist forces may be strong in this country—but not that strong. If appeasement is considered politically necessary, it could nevertheless be achieved at levels of escalation far short of the total economic offensive currently being waged against the Europeans. It is not necessary to break up the Common Market or the Atlantic alliance in order to sell more lemons. The president is too consummate a politician to risk the general design of his foreign policy if he does not have to. If he insists on forcing the Europeans to choose between unity and alliance, it is because that choice itself must be part of his general design. Protectionism alone cannot suffice as an explanation.

The Changing Balance of Power

What, then, is the explanation?   In my opinion, the answer is to be found in the changing balance of power in international economic relations and in U.S. efforts to redress that balance of power.

When World War II ended, the balance of power in international economic relations was, of course, heavily weighted in favor of the United States. The U.S. economy was the only major industrial economy to emerge from the global hostilities undamaged and fully employed. The U.S. competitive advantage in the system was unchallenged—indeed, unchallengeable. Its goods and capital were in demand everywhere; the dollar reigned supreme in international finance. Under the circumstances, there seemed little risk in subordinating economic programs to the broader considerations of the U.S. general foreign economic policy. The United States could afford it. The implicit bargain struck with the Europeans was therefore a natural one—marginal economic sacrifices in return for special political privileges.

The circumstances, however, were bound to change. Europe was bound to recover from the war—and it has. As a result, the relative positions in the system of the United States and Europe (especially the EEC's Six) have shifted quite dramatically. All through the postwar period, growth rates of gross national production in Europe (with the exception of Britain's) have far exceeded that of the United States. The U.S. share of the world GNP has fallen sharply, from nearly 40 percent in 1950 to just over 30 percent 20 years later.[23] The share of the Common Market countries, meanwhile, has risen from 11 percent to almost 15 percent. European competitiveness in world markets has increased enormously as well, and European currencies have now begun to challenge the supremacy of the dollar. The U.S. share of global exports has shrunk from 16.7 percent in 1950 to 13.7 percent in 1970, while the Common Market share has soared from 15.4 percent to 28.6 percent (almost half of which, though, is intra-EEC trade). And the U.S. share of international reserves has dwindled from 49.8 percent to 15.7 percent, while the Common Market share has increased from 6.1 percent to 32.5 percent. Clearly, the abnormal disparity of power prevailing in 1945 has long since disappeared. And as Robert Gilpin has reminded us, when a basic pattern of interstate relations changes so profoundly, alterations in the framework of economic activity can usually be expected:

> Politics determines the framework of economic activity and channels it in directions which tend to serve the political objectives of dominant political groups and organizations. Throughout history each successive hegemonic power has organized economic space in terms of its own interests and purposes. . . .

The Corollary of this argument is, of course, that just as a particular array of political interests and relations permitted this system of transnational economic relations to come into being, so changes in these political factors can profoundly alter the system and even bring it to an end.[24]

The United States was the hegemonic power in 1945; the bargain with Europe was its way of organizing economic space in terms of its own interests and purposes. Since 1945 the U.S. hegemony has declined. It was only to be expected that as a result the bargain itself would eventually be called into question. Essentially this explains the gradual weakening of the bargain through the course of the 1960s. As their relative position improved, the Europeans became increasingly restless about the special privileges accorded the United States. As its relative position deteriorated, the United States became increasingly concerned about the cost of sacrifices to Europe. It was only a matter of time before the framework of economic activity would be altered in some more or less fundamental way. This is the basic explanation for President Nixon's New Economic Policy. Administration spokesmen have made clear that the change of policy stemmed directly from their dissatisfaction with the old postwar arrangement with Europe (and Japan). The United States, they insisted, can no longer afford to subordinate its own economic interests: the cost has grown too high. Europe and Japan have recovered from World War II: they are no longer weaklings dependent on concessions from the United States. "They are big boys now," said the President's trade representative. "They can support themselves."[25] Now it is time for them to begin reciprocating with equivalent concessions of their own. According to the Presidential Commission on International Trade and Investment Policy:

The European Community and Japan have become major centers of economic power and strong competitors of the U.S. in world markets. Western Europe and Japan have been slow to assume the responsibilities that come with power and strength.[26]

In his original confidential memorandum to the president, Peter Peterson spoke of the need to adjust to "new realities":

> One of the new realities of the 1970s is that our partners no longer need special crutches. In fact, as is sometimes the case, the patients may be inclined to throw the crutches at the doctor . . . .
>
> Has not the time come in our international economic policy for a doctrine of equivalence, of true reciprocity, of discarding handicaps and abiding by a common set of rules?[27]

Here in a nutshell is Washington's argument for its economic offensive. The thesis has been repeated by administration spokesmen, both formally and informally. It has also been echoed in the President's annual Economic Reports and even in his Reports on the State of the World. As George Shultz put it: "Santa Claus is dead."[28] The United States cannot and will not continue to play the role of benefactor of the Western world. Its responsibilities to its allies will now be conceived in narrower and more self-interested terms. According to Shultz: "We don't think present arrangements are quite fair."[29] Consequently, the United States intends henceforth to push much harder for its own interests in international negotiations. Fred Bergsten has called this "neonationalism" in trade policy.[30] Peter Peterson calls it the new reality:

> To meet the new realities, not only our policies but our methods of diplomacy will have to be changed. Our international negotiating stance will have to meet our trading partners with a clearer, more assertive version of new national interest. This will make us more predictable in the eyes of our trading partners. I believe we must dispel any "Marshal Plan psychology" or relatively unconstrained generosity that may remain . . . this is not just a matter of choice but of necessity.[31]

But is it a matter of necessity? Must the United States now conceive its responsibilities in such narrow and self-interested terms? Certainly one can be in sympathy with the basic rationale of administration policy. The balance of power in economic relations has changed; it is necessary to adjust to the new reality. Nevertheless, one can be critical of the extraordinarily assertive approach adopted by the United States. Europeans have their own trading grievances, after all. Indeed, these may be considered a fair match for the administration's current list of complaints against the Common Market. In a sense, Santa Claus is not dead at all: he has never existed—at least not since the days of the Marshal Plan, anyway. In fact, the United States is at least as guilty of trade discrimination and protectionism as the Europeans are, if not more so.

Although average U.S. tariffs are no lower than those of the Common Market, quotas in the United States apply to 17 percent of industrial imports, in contrast to just four percent in the Community. Moreover, benzene-based chemical imports into the United States are virtually completely excluded by the American Selling Price system of tariff valuation (despite the U.S. pledge in the Kennedy Round to eliminate ASP). In addition, "Buy American" rules are applied by the federal government that give a preference to domestic suppliers to government agencies of six percent, or 12 percent in areas of high unemployment, or 50 percent for defense contracts; and Washington's anti-dumping regulations have become the tightest in the world. Europeans wonder what this talk of "relatively unconstrained generosity" is all about. In fact, the value of European trade that is deflected by U.S. import barriers is probably at least equal to the diversion of U.S. exports resulting from the discriminatory features of the Common Market.[32]

For the United States to demand unilateral trade concessions from the EEC, therefore, really is highly inequitable—virtually a "Marshall Plan in reverse," to use the words of one French journalist.[33] Many Europeans view the administration's new policy as an exercise in pure mercantilism—a straightforward attempt to export unemployment at Europe's expense. The Europeans appreciate that Washington faces an employment problem at the moment, particularly in certain industries especially exposed to competition from abroad; they are aware as well of the revival of protectionist sentiment on the U.S. side of the Atlantic. But they, too, face employment problems; they also have their protectionists to deal with. Moreover, foreign trade accounts for a much larger proportion of economic activity on the European side of the Atlantic than it ever has in the United States. Europe fears, quite realistically, that it simply could not bear the burden of what the Nixon administration is trying to obtain. The industrial dislocations and unemployment costs would be too great to accept.

Moreover, the fragile structure of European integration could suffer irrevocably as a result. Europe feels it must be permitted to maintain its preferential arrangements around the Mediterranean and throughout Africa. Otherwise, its collective influence in these areas would in all likelihood rapidly diminish. This influence is regarded as an important contribution to the overall effectiveness of the Atlantic alliance: "We do more with our preferences than six, seven or even eight fleets in the Mediterranean," one Community official has said.[34] Similarly, Europe must be permitted to extend trade preferences to all the EFTA non-applicants, as it has pledged to do. Otherwise, the expansion of the Six to Nine could prove to be short-lived. Denmark would probably not be able to remain a member if an accommodation with the rest of Scandinavia were to be prevented; and if the Danes were to back out, it might not be feasible for the British or the Irish to remain members either.[35] Most importantly, Europe must be permitted to continue operating its common farm policy. Otherwise, survival of the Community itself could prove to be impossible. The agricultural agreement is the key to French participation in the Market[36]— and without France the EEC would not be much more than a rump. That this may be precisely the objective of the Nixon administration's new policy is worrisome. It has long been obvious that U.S. political support for the EEC was dwindling. Now the United States may have turned actively hostile, and may be trying to break up the Common Market—at a minimum, to weaken it enough so that it will no longer pose a significant competitive threat to U.S. commercial interests.[37]   This is not a declining hegemonic power attempting to adjust to a new reality of equivalence and reciprocity; talk along these lines by the administration may be dismissed as so much diplomatic rhetoric. What is apparent is a still powerful United States attempting to preserve its traditional position of hegemony in the Western world. This seems to be Washington's true perception of the new reality.

One may point to the other side of the old postwar bargain as evidence. Has Washington shown any inclination to give up the special political privileges accorded it by the dollar's preeminence in international finance?   Again, talk along these lines by the United States may be dismissed as so much rhetoric. One must look not to what the United States has said but to what it has done—in effect, to consolidate a genuine world dollar standard. Although exchange rates are presently floating, the dollar's inconvertibility remains suspended, meaning that other countries now have no means left to challenge Washington's global use of its central-banking role. Unless they prefer to move to a system of controlled currency blocs or permanently flexible exchange rates, they have nothing to do but accumulate dollars indefinitely. The United States is effectively freed from all constraints of the balance of payments. The ability of the United States to act abroad unilaterally to promote the national interest has, if anything, actually been enhanced by President Nixon's New Economic Policy.

Furthermore, it should not escape notice that the New Economic Policy concentrates exclusively on the current account of the overall balance of payments of the United States. The "turn-around" that the administration says it is seeking is intended only in merchandise trade. Little is mentioned about a reduction of U.S. investments overseas, or about controls over military expenditures. Washington apparently has no plans to constrain either of these kinds of foreign activities. Quite the contrary, in fact. Its objective seems to be a trade surplus sufficient to support their continued expansion. This only tends to confirm the worst possible interpretation of U.S. economic policy. The United States is not adjusting to weakness. Rather, it is still trying to lead from strength.

At an Impasse

Thus, the New Economic Policy has created a genuine impasse in Atlantic relations. In its public rhetoric Washington keeps insisting that the United States is a diminished giant, deserving of gratitude and concessions from the Europeans. But in its diplomatic actions Washington seems to be trying to use its remaining power to regain a position of supremacy in the Western world, even if this means breaking up the Common Market in the process. The risk in this kind of situation, of course, is that actions will speak louder than words. In that case the Atlantic alliance itself could prove to be the victim, for if the administration perseveres in its current economic offensive, the Europeans, in turn, may feel that they have no choice but to take countervailing discriminatory measures of their own in order to preserve their fragile cohesion. And this in turn could force the United States to resort to even more massive forms of retaliation. The New Economic Policy has made economic warfare respectable again, for the first time since the "beggar-thy-neighbor" days of the 1930s. Furthermore, each side has an arsenal of weapons at its disposal which is certainly more than adequate to the purpose. A process of disintegration in the Western world, therefore, could easily be set in motion.

In view of the size of the main protagonists, a disintegrating alliance would most probably be succeeded by a system of large trading and currency blocs—one centered in Europe, another around America (and perhaps a third around Japan). In fact, in official Washington today the idea of a world bloc system seems to have gained considerable favor at policy-making levels. If the United States cannot maintain its supremacy globally, then at least it might perhaps be able to do so on a somewhat more limited scale. However, this would be a distinctly second-best resolution of the current impasse in Atlantic relations. Separate economic blocs could hardly be expected to be anything other than antagonistic, each narrowly concerned with protection of its own parochial interests. At the least, this would mean an end to the postwar atmosphere of cooperation across the Atlantic—less give-and-take on specific negotiating issues. One Common Market official has said: "I cannot conceive of the European Economic Community ever being anti-American, but I can conceive of it being more independent of decisionmaking by Washington."[38] At the worst, it could mean open economic hostilities.

A far more preferable resolution of the current impasse in Atlantic relations would preserve the postwar atmosphere of cooperation between the United States and Europe. To accomplish this, Washington must acknowledge that the United States is no longer the dominant economic power in the world. Deeds must speak as loud as words: the United States must demonstrate that it is in fact prepared to adjust to the new reality in reorganizing economic space—not assertively or in excessively self-interested terms, but on the basis of a genuine reciprocity of interests and purposes. And this must encompass the issue of the balance of payments and the status of the dollar as well as outstanding commercial problems. The old bargain has come unstuck. A new one, signifying real equivalence, is needed.

Notes

1. Peter G. Peterson, *A Foreign Economic Perspective*, (The Peterson Report, December 27, 1971), p. 1

2. John R. Petty, former Assistant Secretary of the Treasury for International Affairs, as quoted by Dom Bonafede, "White House Report," *National Journal* (November 13, 1971), p. 2248.

3. GATT, *Press Release* (August 26, 1971).

4. The Group of Ten is an informal club of the most important financial powers which meets periodically to discuss international monetary questions. It includes Belgium, Canada, France, Germany, Italy, Japan, the Netherlands, Sweden, the United Kingdom, and the United States (plus Switzerland, which usually participates in meetings on an *ex officio* basis).

5. "Weighting" refers to the relative importance of each country in the foreign trade of the United States. According to calculations used in the discussions of the Group of Ten, every one percent of weighted revaluation of other currencies relative to the dollar would produce on average an improvement of $750-800 million in the US balance of payments.

6. *The Washington Post* (October 18, 1971).

7. Cf. footnote 1. Peterson was later appointed Secretary of Commerce.

8. See Bonafede, "White House Report," p. 2212.

9. Cf. footnote 1, The Peterson Report, *Summary*, p. v.

10. Group of Ten, *Press Communique (December 18, 1971)*.

11. *Council of Economic Advisers, Annual Report* (1973), p. 132.

12. Quoted in *The New York Times* (May 10, 1973), p. 65.

13. Ralf Dahrendorf, as quoted in *The New York Times* (December 10, 1971), p. 72.

14. See e.g. *The New York Times* (December 16, 1971), p. 8; (December 31, 1971), p. 27; (November 10, 1972), p. 53.

15. Walter Scheel, as quoted in *The New York Times* (December 8, 1971), p. 107.

16. See Harold B. Malmgren, "Managing Foreign Economic Policy," *Foreign Policy*, no. 6 (Spring 1972), pp. 42-68.

17. See Bonafede, "White House Report," pp. 2241-2243.

18. Quoted by Bonafede, "White House Report," p. 2241. The Council is intended to function parallel to the National Security and Domestic Councils. Its Executive Director (who is also the President's Assistant for International Economic

Affairs) is currently Peter Flanigan, succeeding Peter Peterson.

19. Cf. Harold B. Malmgren, "Coming Trade Wars (Neo-Mercantilism and Foreign Policy)" *Foreign Policy*, no. 1 (Winter 1970-71), pp. 115-143; and C. Fred Bergsten, "Crisis in U.S. Trade Policy," *Foreign Affairs*, vol. XL, no. 4 (July, 1971), pp. 619-635.

20. Lawrence B. Krause, "Trade Policy for the Seventies," *Columbia Journal of World Business*, vol. VI, no. 1 (January-February, 1971), pp. 5-14.

21. Anti-dumping rules are designed to prevent "dumping" by foreign exporters, that is, sales of goods at prices lower than in a producer's own home market. Border-tax rules are designed to adjust for price differences between home and foreign products that are due solely to international discrepencies in the level of indirect taxation. Both types of rule are sanctioned under GATT.

22. Cf. *The New York Times* (December 9, 1971), p. 77; (December 16, 1971), p. 8; (January 12, 1972), p. 55.

23. The data in this paragraph are derived from Annex 3 of *United States International Economic Policy in an Interdependent World*. Report to the President submitted by the Commission on International Trade and Investment Policy, (The Williams Report, July 1971), and from the statistical background material provided with The Peterson Report: Cf. footnote 1.

24. Robert Gilpin, "The Politics of Transnational Economic Relations," *International Organization*, vol. XXV, no. 3 (Summer 1971), pp. 403, 443.

25. Willian Eberle, as quoted in *The New York Times*, Europe Mideast Economic Survey (January 21, 1972), p. 52.

26. Cf. footnote 23, The Williams Report, p. 7.

27. Quoted by Bonafede, "White House Report," pp. 2239-2241.

28. Quoted by Bonafede, "White House Report," p. 2238.

29. Quoted in *The New York Times* (May 10, 1973), p. 65.

30. Bergsten, "Crisis in U.S. Trade Policy," pp. 625-626. See also Bergsten's "The New Economics and U.S. Foreign Policy," *Foreign Affairs*, vol. L, no. 2 (January 1972), pp. 199-222.

31. Cf. footnote 1, The Peterson Report, p. 49.

32. See *The Economist* (December 18, 1971), p. 78.

33. Alain Vernay of *Le Figaro*, as quoted in *The New York Times*, Europe-Mideast Economic Survey (January 21, 1972), p. 52.

34. Quoted in *The New York Times* (December 17, 1971), p. 63.

35. Cf. *The Economist* (November 27, 1971), p. 92.

36. Cf. *The New York Times* (December 23, 1971), p. 37; (December 31, 1971), p. 27.

37. Cf. *The New York Times* (December 10, 1971), p. 12; (December 16, 1971), p. 8; (December 31, 1971), p. 27; (January 6, 1972), p. 53.

38. Quoted in *The New York Times* (December 31, 1971), p. 27.

5

An Explosion in the Kitchen?
U.S. Economic Relations
with Other Advanced
Industrial States*

In the 1980s, the United States will continue to be subject
to adverse foreign economic pressures. These pressures . . .
will lead to conflict. American foreign economic policy
under President Carter and his successors will be judged
according to its success in keeping international conflict
manageable while retaining domestic political support and
maintaining U.S. influence as well as fostering prosperity
at home and abroad. The foreign economic policy kitchen
will be hot; success will come to those who can turn out the
goodies without setting off an explosion.

—Robert O. Keohane

Robert Keohane's closing words in his contribution to *Eagle
Entangled*[1] provide a useful starting point for an analysis of
the foreign economic policy of the Reagan administration during
its first five years in office. The test, as Keohane stressed, is not
whether conflict has been absent—conflict is virtually
inevitable in international economic relations—but rather
whether conflict has been kept manageable. Has the United
States used its resources wisely, given existing policy constraints, to promote national interests and objectives? Has
prosperity been promoted? Have domestic support and foreign
influence been retained?

*From Kenneth A. Oye, Robert J. Lieber and Donald Rothchild
(eds.), *Eagle Resurgent? The Reagan Era in American Foreign
Policy* (Boston: Little, Brown, 1987), ch. 4. Copyright by
Kenneth A. Oye, Robert J. Lieber and Donald Rothchild.
Reprinted by permission of Scott, Foresman and Company.

We know that the Reagan administration has so far avoided an outright explosion. But that is no more than a *de minimus* test of success. Judged by the more discriminate criteria suggested by Keohane, the administration's record can be described as dismal at best. The purpose of this essay is to evaluate that record in greater detail, focusing on America's relations with other advanced industrial states.

Traditional   Objectives   of   Policy

Analysis of decisionmaking in foreign economic policy may be approached in a variety of ways. For an economist, the most congenial approach views policy as a problem of "maximization under constraint." Conventional economic analysis begins with the assumption of scarcity: the things that people and societies value are limited in supply; Tin Pan Alley notwithstanding, the best things in life are *not* all free. Choices therefore are necessary. The task for economic decisionmakers (assuming they are rational) is to do the best they can to maximize some value or other—or several values simultaneously—under the constraint of scarcity. The task for the analyst seeking insight into such behavior is to focus on this problem of choice, to understand the trade-offs among objectives. As Walter Heller has written of the political economist: "Problems of choice are his meat and drink. His method is to factor out the costs, the benefits and the net advantage or disadvantage of alternative courses of action."[2]

In United States foreign economic policy, the choices of decisionmakers have traditionally focused on four main objectives: (1) national economic welfare, (2) distribution, (3) national security, and (4) system preservation. All four "target variables" reflect fundamental political and economic interests.

The first target, national economic welfare, stands for real income, the quantity of real goods and services available to the nation for final use. Although this is the traditional objective identified in conventional economic analysis, it is not a simple concept. Indeed, despite more than two centuries of development of modern economic theory, we still do not know precisely how to go about maximizing economic welfare, in good part because the target is decomposable—at the micro level, identified with efficiency of resource allocation; at the macro level, with both full employment and price stability. As these three dimensions may not always be mutually compatible, policy choices necessarily involve value judgments regarding the relative weights to be attached to each and the trade-offs to be made among them. On such matters, clearly, reasonable people may reasonably disagree.

The second target variable, distribution, stands as a proxy for the set of relevant domestic political goals of policy. Being politicians and not disinterested statesmen or philosopher-kings, policymakers may be assumed to concern themselves not only (if at all) with the general interests of the nation as a whole, but also with the specific interests of certain narrower constituencies within the nation and to seek, through policy decisions, to maximize the gains of such domestic groups or to minimize their losses. In other words, they may be assumed to aim at some particular distribution of the costs and benefits of policy. This of course is the traditional objective identified in political analysis, the meat and drink of the political scientist: Whose ox is gored if one policy is chosen rather than another? It is also, like economic welfare, not a simple concept. As with economic welfare, we still do not know precisely how to go about achieving some particular distribution of the costs and benefits of policy, again in good part because the objective is decomposable. Distribution implies not only gains or losses of real income but also of relative rank, prestige, privileges, and the like; and since here too value judgments and trade-offs are necessarily involved, here too disagreements among reasonable people are possible.

The two remaining variables, national security and system preservation, embody the principal objectives that must be added when the foreign dimension, and not only the purely domestic dimensions of economic policy, are considered. National security is mainly concerned with such issues as political independence and territorial integrity, and it can logically be translated into an imperative to maximize, insofar as possible, influence abroad and autonomy of decisionmaking at home. System preservation reflects the interest that the United States has in common with other countries to avoid disruption of the international economic relations from which everyone presumably benefits, even if unevenly. Many observers have called attention to the similarity of the system of international economic relations to a "nonzero-sum game," in which, because the interests of the players are neither entirely harmonious nor

completely irreconcilable, state policies inevitably mix elements of competition and cooperation.[3] The targets of national
security and system preservation express, respectively, these two
elements of policy (although they may, of course, receive quite
different relative weights in the policies of different
governments).

Of the four objectives of American policy, national economic
welfare always seems to take precedence at the level of rhetoric. On assuming office, every new administration declares
America's prosperity to be its fundamental goal, defined in terms
of such desiderata as full employment, price stability, and rapid
growth. But then, at the level of action, every administration
eventually compromises its welfare objective in some degree for
the sake of the other three. Ultimately all four targets come
into play in practice. Successive administrations differ only in
the nature of the compromises they regard as acceptable or are
willing to admit.

Thus, every American administration since World War II has
emphasized this nation's commitment to an open and liberal
(that is, market-oriented and nondiscriminatory) world trading
system. Yet repeatedly, administrations undertake to protect
specific domestic constituencies against "injury" from foreign
imports, even at the expense of perpetuating an inefficient
resource allocation and potentially retarding domestic growth.
Similarly, all administrations have seemed prepared to pay an
economic price for the sake of extending American influence
overseas or preserving the international system that we were so
instrumental in constructing after 1945. In postwar Europe the
United States tolerated, even promoted, preferential regional
trade and payments arrangements despite their inherent and
obvious discrimination against American export sales, because
such arrangements were thought essential to restore the health
of key economic allies; similarly, America's internal market was
opened to Japanese exports even when markets elsewhere
remained tightly closed to goods labeled "Made in Japan." It
must be assumed that policymakers are not unaware of the
potential welfare costs of the compromises they make.

The reasons for such compromises are familiar. Measures to
protect the interests of specific domestic constituencies have
their roots in America's internal politics—our fragmented and
pluralistic federal system in which disproportionate influence
can be wielded by relatively narrow pressure groups. Similarly,

measures to extend American influence abroad or the autonomy of decisionmaking have their roots in America's external politics— the anarchic and insecure international system in which national interests are never entirely safe from overt or covert threat. As a major power, the United States has long enjoyed a high degree of influence over global economic events, as well as comparative freedom from external constraint on internal decisionmaking—for so long, in fact, that what in other countries would be regarded as a privilege has come to be treated here, by many, as a right. One need only think of Washington's continued reluctance to give up the international reserve-asset role of the dollar, which grants the United States the extraordinary privilege (what Charles de Gaulle used to call the "exorbitant privilege") to finance balance-of-payments deficits, in effect, with IOUs rather than with reserve assets of its own. Few other countries enjoy a similar privilege, and none, certainly, to the same extent.

System preservation has also long figured prominently among American policy targets because of America's continuing position of leadership in international economic affairs. The story of this "hegemonic" role in shaping the institutions and structures of the postwar world economy needs no retelling here.[4] Once having fashioned an external environment largely favorable to American objectives, the United States thereby gained a vested interest in maintaining it. Other countries might act as "free riders," enjoying the benefits of a system of growing economic interdependence without contributing significantly to its preservation, but not the United States, whose support continued to be a necessary (even if now no longer a sufficient) condition of systemic survival. American policymakers have often felt obliged to make concessions to keep the system functioning without undue discord or disruption.

Thus, although national prosperity may be described as the most enduring interest served by American foreign economic policy, it is by no means either exclusive or absolute. It is not exclusive because other interests are also felt to be vital, most notably the compulsion of a great power to maintain a maximum of influence abroad and autonomy of decisionmaking at home. It is not absolute because in order to promote economic welfare in the long term, concessions in the short term have often been felt to be necessary, most notably to safeguard the interdependent international system, the coherence and viability of which continued to be identified with America's own national self-interest. In addition, since every administration feels the need to cultivate and retain domestic political support, the particular interests of key domestic constituencies are also factored into policy calculations of the interests of the nation as a whole.

For the purposes of this essay, what is most significant about these compromises is the extent to which, over time, their costs in terms of welfare have risen as a result of the evolution of objective conditions, both domestically and internationally. In the United States, our political system has grown ever more fragmented and stalemated as a result of the historic ebb of power in recent years from the "Imperial Presidency" toward Congress, where particular regional or sectorial interests can more easily exercise effective influence over policy. Today even relatively small private groups, if well organized, can have a significant impact on public decisionmaking. Accordingly, the price required to accommodate them seems to have steadily increased.

Abroad, too, the system has grown ever more fragmented and stalemated, as a result of the historic ebb of power away from the "imperial" United States. At the end of World War II, America could truly be described as a hegemonic world power. In international trade and finance our dominance was unquestioned; the United States could well afford the cost of aid programs and trade concessions designed to maintain its foreign influence and shore up the newly erected international economic order. But as time has passed, and, as is well known, our economic position has declined relative to that of our allies in Europe and Japan and, more recently, in relation to others as well, our leadership role has been increasingly challenged by other countries. Still preeminent but no longer predominant, the United States is no longer able to determine the course of events alone, at a comparatively low cost to itself. As in the domestic arena, power has become more diffused. Hence in the international arena, too, the price of accommodation has increased.

Finally, the costs of compromise have risen as the result of the sheer complexity of international economic relations today. The proliferation of issues and multiplying linkages among them have greatly magnified the uncertainties inherent in the decisionmaking process and limited even further the government's ability to develop an effective and coherent set of policies.

Not that the United States has therefore become a pitiful,

helpless giant. Quite the contrary. As is also well known, the United States still commands impressive resources in international economic relations, based on an economy that is still the largest, most diversified, and most technologically advanced in the world. Our foreign trade is still greater than that of any other single country, our overseas investment the most extensive, our financial markets the most attractive, our currency the most widely used for international purposes. But conditions *have* changed, and as a result our ability to achieve traditional policy goals, while still considerable, is no longer what it used to be. Decisionmakers find their range of choice increasingly hemmed in by pressures of interest groups at home, by the growing assertiveness of governments abroad, and by the ever-greater complexity of the issues with which they have to deal. The constraints are real. How to come to terms with them has been the central dilemma of foreign economic policymaking for all recent administrations.

From Carter to Reagan

How have successive administrations tried to cope with this dilemma? At first glance, little continuity seems apparent in the historical record. As the constraints on American policy have grown, decisionmakers have veered often, and sharply, between efforts to adjust to the new limits of power and efforts to reassert the primacy of American interests. When Richard Nixon became president, for instance, the first inclination of his administration seemed to be to accommodate our economic allies in Europe and Japan with macroeconomic policies that would help bring the burgeoning American balance-of-payments deficit under control. But when appeals for complementary initiatives from the Europeans and Japanese, particularly with respect to exchange rates, seemed to fall on deaf ears, policy was soon shifted to a more confrontational stance, culminating in August 1971 with a 10 percent import surcharge and suspension of the dollar's convertibility into gold. The purpose of these moves, Washington made clear, was to pressure other countries into accepting an exchange-rate realignment that would improve America's competitive position, whether others liked it or not: this was "economic gunboat diplomacy" at its most naked. Under the influence of his blunt and impatient Treasury Secretary, John

Connally, President Nixon was not above destroying one of the key foundations of the postwar Bretton Woods system for the sake of promoting American exports.

Not that such policy swings were anything new. One need only recall the Smoot-Hawley tariff of 1930, followed four years later by the first Reciprocal Trade Agreements Act; or the generosity of our early postwar policies in Europe and Japan, followed shortly by a reversion to the narrowest sort of protection of domestic clothespin manufacturers and the like. Nor are such swings confined only to economic policy. Other dimensions of foreign policy manifest the same "oscillations," as Robert Osgood has called them, "between assertion and retrenchment, between the affirmation and restraint of national power."[5] These oscillations have deep roots in America's historical approach to the outside world, which has always reflected an uncertain tension between pretensions to America's leadership in international affairs and a gut urge to be rid of all foreign entanglements, with policy preferences switching frequently between the two. The apparent discontinuities in the historical record really constitute one of the more notable continuities in the rhythm of our external relations, political no less than economic. It is hardly surprising that other countries often accuse the United States of "incoherence" in our foreign policies, of "insensitivity," "indifference," or "lack of finesse."

In this respect, the administration of Jimmy Carter was no exception. Initially inclined toward an activist reaffirmation of America's influence over economic events, it ended by stressing the advantages of compromise and collaboration with our key allies in Europe and Japan. This trend, despite criticisms of inconsistency (or worse), was evident in both of the main dimensions of our economic relations with the other industrial states, macroeconomics and trade.

In macroeconomic relations, the administration began by promoting a grand strategy of reflation by the strongest industrial states—quickly dubbed the *locomotive* strategy—to pull the world economy out of recession. When the other main locomotives, Germany and Japan, balked at introducing new expansionary measures, primarily for fear of renewing rampant inflationary pressures, the United States pressed ahead anyway. The new administration felt a heavy responsibility for renewed growth not only at home but also in the world economy as a whole, which seemed gravely threatened by slow growth, rising unemployment, and severe balance-of-payments problems; and it was determined to take the lead in fostering global recovery, on its own, if need be.[6]

The outcome is well known.[7] Inflation began to accelerate again in the United States. In addition, because of the absence of parallel stimulus elsewhere, very large deficits reemerged in the American balance of payments which, in turn, led to severe selling pressures on the dollar and uncertainty in the exchange markets. At first Washington tended to view the dollar's decline with equanimity: "[T]he administration does not believe it is appropriate to maintain any particular value for the dollar," President Carter's Council of Economic Advisors asserted in its first Annual Report.[8] But as exchange-market conditions became more chaotic, criticisms of American policy mounted, and in Europe, plans began for the construction of a new "zone of monetary stability"—the European Monetary System—to insulate currencies on the other side of the Atlantic from the vagaries of the dollar.[9] Increasingly isolated, the administration eventually shifted toward greater demand restraint at home, more active exchange intervention abroad, and closer coordination of both macroeconomic and intervention policies with other major industrial countries. The turning point came with the Bonn economic summit in July 1978, when the United States pledged to ease up on its domestic expansionary policies, and it was confirmed on November 1, 1978, when the administration announced a decisive new commitment to support the dollar in exchange markets (backed by a $30 billion "rescue package" arranged with allied governments and the International Monetary Fund). By mid-1979 it could accurately be said that "[t]he Carter administration had conceded defeat."[10] In its last two years, the administration's emphasis was not on unilateral initiatives but rather on the need for greater international collaboration and cooperation to sustain macroeconomic and intervention policies consistent with both internal and external balance. In its last Annual Report, the very same Council of Economic Advisors could now speak of the merits of "consistency in economic policy objectives and cooperation in exchange-market policies . . . to ensure the smooth functioning of the international monetary system."[11]

Similarly, in the trade area the administration began—ritual declarations of adherence to traditional liberal principles notwithstanding—by reasserting the primacy of American commercial interests. Our policy was now to be "free but fair trade," according to President Carter's Special Trade Representative, Robert Strauss. In practice, this translated into a series of measures designed to protect sensitive domestic industries from the competition of lower-cost imports. During 1977 so-called orderly marketing agreements (negotiated quotas) were established to restrict, *inter alia*, imports of footwear from Korea and Taiwan and color television sets from Japan. An in early 1978, the so-called trigger-price mechanism was instituted to discourage steel imports by assuring that any shipments below the specified reference price (based on the production costs of the most efficient producer, Japan) would trigger an accelerated antidumping investigation. In effect, the device fixed a minimum price for imported steel. In addition, the administration significantly tightened the application of provisions of the 1974 Trade Act involving countervailing duties (intended to offset the price-reducing effects of foreign export subsidies) and escape-clause actions.[12]

Here, too, the tide shifted in 1978, again in good part because of mounting criticisms from abroad. The Carter administration was never mercantilist in an ideological sense. Most of its protectionist initiatives were apparently taken reluctantly and only under strong domestic pressures. Not surprisingly, therefore, when similar tendencies toward increased restrictiveness became manifest in Europe and Japan,[13] threatening a snowballing of retaliatory measures that could bring down the whole edifice of international trade, the thrust of policy eventually became more conciliatory, shifting toward mutual accommodation with America's principal trading partners. In late 1978 a new National Export Policy was announced; it switched the emphasis in trade relations from import restraint to export promotion. And in April 1979 the so-called Tokyo Round of multilateral trade negotiations was brought to a conclusion, with the United States making crucial concessions on such matters as countervailing duties, agricultural subsidies, and customs valuation procedures.[14] During the administration's last two years, not one single new restriction was imposed on imports from other industrial countries, despite persistent protectionist sentiment at home (aggravated, especially, by the recession of 1980).

In effect, in both macroeconomics and trade, the Carter administration went through a kind of difficult learning process, first reasserting traditional policy goals and then gradually becoming educated to the new limits of American power. To its credit, the administration seemed to learn the lesson well. In the administration's second two years, unilateral foreign economic policy initiatives were infrequent and then taken only in response to what seemed extreme provocation—for example, the 1979 freeze of Iranian assets following the seizure of American hostages in Teheran or the 1980 grain embargo on the Soviet Union following the Russian invasion of Afghanistan.[15] For the most part, policy emphasis shifted instead to closer collaboration with our allies, in a groping attempt to find some way to manage jointly what, it was now recognized, the United States could no longer control entirely on its own. Given the evolution of objective conditions, there seemed few realistic alternatives to a stance of mutual accommodation and compromise. But to a nation long accustomed to a high degree of autonomy and influence in international economic affairs, it was a frustrating if not alarming experience; and it no doubt contributed to Jimmy Carter's defeat in November 1980.

With the arrival of Ronald Reagan the pendulum swiftly swung back, almost as if the Carter learning process had never occurred. For the new Republican administration, elected in part precisely because of the frustrations and alarms of the preceding years, it was simply inconceivable that the United States could not reclaim its accustomed autonomy and influence over economic events. President Reagan's reading of history was far different: Objective conditions had *not* fundamentally changed; American power *could* be reaffirmed. All that was needed was renewed vigor and incisive action in support of American interests. At home a new macroeconomic policy had to be initiated unencumbered by troublesome accommodation of governments elsewhere. Abroad trade policy had to be used forcefully to promote the market position of American producers. In such initiatives, it was felt, lay the real alternative to the compromises of the Carter years.

The key, according to the Reagan administration, was to be found in the "magic of the marketplace." If markets would be allowed to work, America's natural leadership would swiftly reemerge. In this respect there was no distinction at all between the administration's faith in private economic activity and its faith in the country: The two were intertwined. In the words of President Reagan's Council of Economic Advisors[16]:

The successful implementation of policies to control inflation and restore vigorous real growth in the United States
will have a profound and favorable impact on the rest of
the world. . . . More generally, the administration's
approach to international economic issues is based on the
same principles which underlie its domestic programs: a
belief in the superiority of market solutions to economic
problems and an emphasis on private economic activity as
the engine of non-inflationary growth.

How well did this market-oriented approach fare during the
administration's first five years?

Macroeconomic Policy: Reaganomics Rampant

Like so many administrations before it, the Reagan administration came to office proclaiming America's prosperity to be
its fundamental goal. The country was to have a "New Beginning." The first order of business was to be a "Program for
Economic Recovery," announced with great fanfare by President
Reagan himself before Congress and a prime-time television
audience on February 18, 1981, less than a month after his inau-
guration. The program embodied the four main pillars of Reaganomics: (1) noninflationary (tight) monetary policy, (2) slower
growth of government spending, (3) reduction of federal tax
rates, and (4) regulatory reform. Together, the president
promised, these four steps would achieve "a full and vigorous
recovery of our economy... and a brighter future for all our
citizens."[17]

Of course, neither monetary nor fiscal policy was entirely under
the president's control. Monetary policy was still the province
of the independent Federal Reserve System; tax and spending
policies still had to be reviewed and approved by the Congress.
Yet to a remarkable degree, President Reagan was able to work
his will with both institutions. Monetary growth was slowed by
a willing Federal Reserve from an annual rate of 13 percent in
the last quarter of 1980 to under 4 percent in the second half of
1981. In the summer, the president got his tax cuts, reducing personal income tax rates by a full 25 percent over three years. And
in the fall, Congress voted his spending cuts as well, eliminating
overall $95 billion from the next two fiscal years (as measured
against previous spending trends) while greatly increasing mil-

itary expenditures. At the year's end the president was satisfied, looking back on what he called a "substantial beginning."[18]

But what a beginning! In his February program, President Reagan predicted that economic growth would recover from the 1980 recession to a steady 4 to 5 percent annual growth path through 1986; whereas the Federal budget deficit, which had approached $60 billion in each of the last two Carter years, would gradually shrink to near balance by Fiscal Year (FY) 1984.[19] Instead, with the initiation of Reaganomics, America's economy set off on the most pronounced roller-coaster ride of the postwar period, and the budget deficit soared to heights never before seen in the United States. First came a sharp new recession, with the gross national product (GNP) dropping at an annual rate in excess of 5 percent in late 1981 and early 1982 before leveling off at midyear. Only then came the recovery promised by President Reagan, starting in late 1982 and taking the GNP to growth rates near 4 percent in 1983 and over 6 1/2 percent in 1984. But the boom did not last long, and it was soon followed by yet another period of sluggishness, with growth in 1985 barely topping 2 percent, unemployment still hovering near 7 percent (where it had been when Mr. Reagan took office), and with little prospect for renewed buoyancy in 1986 or beyond. The recovery turned out to be neither "full" nor "vigorous," whereas the budget deficit, far from shrinking, exploded past $110 billion in FY 1982 and some $180 billion in the next two years to reach a record $211 billion in FY 1985. Reaganomics, it seemed, had not, in fact, achieved a "brighter future for all our citizens" after all.

How could the administration have been so wrong? The best answer, ironically, was provided by President Reagan's own director of the Office of Management and Budget, David Stockman, in his celebrated *Atlantic Monthly* interviews in 1981: "The whole thing is premised on faith . . . on a belief about how the world works."[20] The belief was supply-side economics, the new religion of the Grand Old Party. Administration supply-siders, above all the president himself, assumed that the key to national prosperity lay in increasing incentives for saving and investment. If taxes could be cut, the role of the government rolled back, and money kept tight, investor confidence in the future value of money would be restored, leading to a rise of productive employment that would, in turn, help balance the Federal budget. Of little concern were charges of "voodoo economics." Disciples of the new faith were confident that taxes could be shrunk, military expenditures raised, and the budget balanced all at the same time. It took years of depressing fiscal returns to demonstrate what a false doctrine this really was. As one commentator put, "Reaganomics proves only one thing—you *can't* do it with mirrors."[21]

In 1985, the chickens came home to roost. Hoisted on the petard of his own policies, President Reagan felt obliged to accept a congressional initiative—the so-called Gramm-Rudman amendment—designed to eliminate the Federal budget deficit entirely over a period of five years, even though this might possibly require either raising taxes once again or substantially cutting back the president's cherished defense buildup. Supply-side economics was effectively discredited. Significantly, Mr. Reagan chose to sign the new legislation in seclusion, eschewing the usual pomp and circumstance of an open White House ceremony.[22]

From an international perspective, what was most striking during this period was the way in which policy was determined in almost total disregard for the outside world. At no time during the administration's first term was there any serious attempt to moderate the external impacts of America's fiscal dilemma, either by way of collaboration with our industrial allies or by intervention in the exchange market. On the contrary, being convinced of its own rectitude, the administration accepted no responsibility at all for problems that might crop up elsewhere. Early in 1981, consistent with its belief in the superiority of market solutions, the Treasury scaled back foreign-exchange operations dramatically. Henceforth, according to administration spokesmen, the United States would intervene in the exchange market only at times of extreme disturbance (such as in the event of an attempted presidential assassination). Otherwise the dollar would remain free to seek its own value. The best way to stabilize exchange rates, it was said, was for each country to restore price stability domestically. America was doing its part. If others were experiencing difficulties, they might profitably follow America's example. No compromises were called for so long as markets were free to work their magic. This unilateral approach, authoritatively labeled "domesticism" by Henry Nau (for two years a senior staff member of President Reagan's National Security Council), was contrasted

with the presumed "globalism" of the previous Carter administration.[23] The globalist view, according to Nau, traced
economic problems "largely to the malfunctioning of the international economic system itself. . . . The alternative approach
reverses the globalist logic and places national policymaking at
the foundation of the world economy. . . . The administration's
policy has consistently emphasized the primary importance and
role of domestic economic policies as the key to stable and
prosperous international economic relations."[24] As the president himself said at the 1981 annual meeting of the International Monetary Fund and World Bank: "The most important
contribution any country can make to world development is to
pursue sound economic policies at home."[25]

But would this approach *ensure* "stable and prosperous international economic relations?" No responsible official was ever
likely to question the importance of "sound economic policies at
home"; certainly no official of the previous administration was
on record as having done so. As President Carter's former
assistant secretary of the Treasury, C. Fred Bergsten, pointed
out, Nau's "domesticist-globalist" dichotomy is in fact a straw
man.[26] The real question was not whether there should be
"proper" domestic policies—of course there should be—but rather
whether such policies would be *enough* to promote world
economic development. In Bergsten's words: "Sound national
policies remain a *necessary* condition for global stability, but
they are highly unlikely to be *sufficient*."[27] The reason,
simply put, is that effective national policies in an interdependent world cannot be formulated without regard for their international consequences, including the feedbacks of those consequences into the domestic economy itself. By that standard, the
Reagan administration's "domesticism" could be severely
criticized, and was.

Criticism focused in particular on the administration's fiscal-
monetary "mix"—its combination of tight money and large fiscal
deficits—that was bound to keep American interest rates high,
which in turn acted as a powerful magnet for liquid savings
elsewhere. After 1980, vast amounts of capital were attracted
from abroad, pushing the dollar to heights not seen since the
start of generalized floating in 1973. In the first four years of
the Reagan administration, the average value of the dollar in
terms of the currencies of other major industrial countries, as
measured by the International Monetary Fund, rose by some 60

percent before peaking in the spring of 1985. Few observers doubted that this represented a sizable overvaluation of America's money in international markets.

For our industrial allies, these developments compounded an already unpleasant policy dilemma.[28] Following the run-up of oil prices in 1978-1979, inflation had once again accelerated even as growth slowed and unemployment continued to rise. In most of the industrial countries, the desire to reverse price trends kept central banks from easing up on monetary policy, despite the sluggishness of domestic output and employment. The appreciation of the dollar, which meant, of course, depreciation of their own currencies, only added to the inflationary pressures in their economies by raising import costs, while the drainage of savings attracted by America's high rates meant lost opportunities for productive investment at home. Europeans, in particular, grew increasingly vocal in their criticism of American policy, resurrecting charges of benign neglect not heard since the first two years of the Carter administration. America, they knew, was not the sole—or perhaps not even the principal—cause of their troubles. But they were understandably aggrieved by the Reagan administration's unwillingness to do anything at all to help, either in terms of domestic policy or in the exchange market. As Flora Lewis perceptively explained[29]:

> Successive U.S. governments have insisted on their sovereign right to run the economy as they think best. But it adds to Europe's sense of impotence, and resentment, when changes of policy it cannot influence aggravate its own less than satisfying attempts at economic management.

Indeed it was not very long before European officials began talking openly of a "complete breakdown" in monetary cooperation between America and Europe, describing Atlantic economic relations as now at their lowest point since President Nixon's suspension of the dollar's convertibility into gold in 1971. According to one senior official, "We have simply never before seen a United States administration that displayed this degree of indifference to the effects of its actions on its allies."[30] This was not benign neglect, wrote a British commentator: This was "an almost malign rejection of the need for a good neighbor policy."[31] At the Williamsburg economic summit in 1983, according to Chancellor Helmut Kohl of West Germany, the administration's policies were "clearly opposed by everyone from the Japanese to the Canadians to us Europeans." Yet when asked if any shift of direction could be expected, he admitted ruefully "I wouldn't say I was optimistic."[32] At the London summit in 1984, Britain's' chancellor of the exchequer labeled Reaganomics "simple-minded."[33] Yet the administration remained impervious to criticism.

Nor was the criticism exclusively foreign. At home too, questions increasingly were raised about the administration's neglect of the external dimension of its domestic policies. Exporters and import-sensitive industries, in particular, had reason to complain as they found their sales more and more severely disrupted by the dollar's unprecedented appreciation. In 1980 the United States had a trade deficit of $25 billion. Four years later, the deficit was up to $110 billion (another historic high) and still climbing; and with the resulting accumulation of foreign liabilities, America—long the greatest creditor in international finance—was on its way to becoming a net debtor for the first time since World War I. It was realized only gradually that the administration's attitude of benign neglect in the exchange markets was only adding to the difficulty of achieving a truly durable economic recovery. At least two million American jobs were estimated to have been lost during President Reagan's first term as a result of the dollar's over-valuation.[34] As Lawrence Krause of the Brookings Institution commented pointedly: "The dollar is one of the elements in our international competitiveness, but we ignore it as a matter of principle."[35] The situation was aptly summarized by investment banker Jeffrey Garten at the end of 1984[36]:

> Over the last four years America's foreign economic policy jumped its traditional track. . . . America's foreign economic policy showed little regard for the impact of U.S. fiscal and monetary policies on the rest of the world. Moreover, it was a policy which ignored the erosion of America's international competitive position. . . .
>
> The administration should have been acutely sensitive to the open and interrelated nature of the world economy and the sophistication of the policies required to deal with it effectively. Instead it embraced a naive optimism that the unfettered marketplace would handle all.

Only in 1985, after the president's triumphant reelection, did this "naive optimism" finally begin to yield to a more realistic appraisal of the costs of "domesticism." Having effectively placed autonomy of decisionmaking above all other objectives of policy, the administration now found that it had succeeded neither in promoting a sustained economic prosperity nor in fully retaining domestic political support, while managing only to alienate most of the other industrial states. At home, the economy once again was faltering, after two years of boom, even as the budget and trade deficits continued to climb to record heights. (The trade deficit was projected to reach a new high of $148 billion in 1985.) Supply-side economics, it was evident, had been no more successful in increasing domestic savings than it had been in decreasing the federal deficit. Instead, the United States had seemingly become addicted to foreign borrowing to help finance both government and import expenditures and was fast becoming a net debtor nation in the process. (By the year's end, America's net debt approached $100 billion—more than even Mexico's or Brazil's.) Abroad an unnecessary—and potentially perilous—strain had been placed on the Western alliance by the administration's exercise in unilateralism. Prospects for macro-economic relations with our economic allies were the bleakest in years. Something, clearly, would have to be done to repair the damage.

What could be done? Manifestly, what was needed was a renewal of the spirit of mutual accommodation and compromise that had characterized the Carter administration in its later years—a greater sensitivity to constraints and an increased willingness to cooperate in the pursuit of common objectives. In concrete terms, this would mean (1) a revised fiscal-monetary "mix" (smaller budget deficits and somewhat less restrictive monetary policy) to permit a gradual reduction of American interest rates and (2) a resumption of coordinated currency interventions to achieve an alignment of exchange rates more consistent with both internal and external balance. In effect the Reagan administration, too, would have to acknowledge the limits of American power (*pace* all its ideological instincts to the contrary). The pendulum, after its sharp swing toward laissez-faire in Ronald Reagan's first term, would once again have to return to a degree of multilateral management of macroeconomic relations.

The turning point came with the appointment of James Baker as Treasury secretary in January 1985, replacing Donald Regan (who took Baker's old job as White House chief of staff). Far more pragmatic than his predecessor, Secretary Baker lost no time in moving toward closer collaboration with the other industrial states on fiscal and monetary matters. In April, at a meeting of the Organization of Economic Cooperation and Development in Paris, he raised the possibility that the United States might be willing to host an international conference to review the functioning of the floating exchange-rate regime, which he noted was "not without weaknesses."[37] In May, at the annual economic summit in Bonn, he persuaded President Reagan, for the first time ever in this series of get-togethers, to make a formal commitment to our allies "to achieve a substantial reduction in the [U.S.] budget deficit."[38] Even more dramatically in September, he joined the finance ministers of Britain, France, West Germany, and Japan (along with the United States, the Group of Five) in announcing a major new initiative to realign and manage currency values. "Exchange rates should better reflect fundamental economic conditions than has been the case," the ministers declared, and they "stand ready to cooperate more closely to encourage this."[39] And this in turn was followed, most dramatically of all, by a call from President Reagan in his State of the Union address in January 1986 for a study to determine "if the nations of the world should convene to discuss the role and relationship of our currencies." Said the president: "Never again" should the United States permit "wild currency swings." Nothing could have been further from the "domesticism" of Mr. Reagan's first term. In the words of one New York banker: "In terms of philosophy, these are major changes."[40] Like its predecessors, the Reagan administration, too, was ultimately forced to concede defeat for a policy of assertive unilateralism.

Trade Policy: Reciprocity Redolent

The story was only a little different in the area of trade relations with our allies. Here too, as in monetary relations, unnecessary and potentially perilous strains were produced by the Reagan administration's own policies and priorities. Once again a presidency began—ritual declarations of adherence to traditional liberal principles notwithstanding—by reasserting the primacy of American commercial interests. A shift away from the generally conciliatory attitude of the later Carter years effectively placed domestic distributional goals above all other objectives of policy. Not only did this lead, once again, to a threat of snowballing retaliatory measures by our major trading partners; worse, it helped to unleash—along with the dollar's unprecedented appreciation—a veritable tidal wave of protectionist sentiment in the United States that appeared to place the whole edifice of international trade in jeopardy. Here too, therefore, by the end of President Reagan's first term, it was clear that something would have to be done to repair or contain the damage. But there was also a difference. In contrast to the area of macroeconomic policy, administration officials were less prepared to concede defeat openly for their unilateralist trade policies. The possible need for greater accommodation was acknowledged, but not for any basic change of principle. Hence the outlook for trade relations with our allies still remained uncertain as the president's fifth year in office drew to a close. The pendulum in this area still had some distance to travel.

The administration's initial attitude was best summarized by President Reagan's first Trade Representative, William Brock, in a carefully crafted white paper on American trade policy released in July 1981.[41] Although free trade was pronounced essential, the white paper also contained warnings that free trade must be a two-way street and that the American market would not necessarily remain open to countries that, in the administration's view, failed to observe commonly agreed rules. "We will *insist* that our trading partners live up to the spirit and the letter of international trade agreements, and that they recognize that trade is a two-way street . . . and we *will make full use of all available channels for assuring compliance*" [italics added]. These would include both (1) strict enforcement of existing import regulations (for example, antidumping and countervailing-duty laws) designed to neutralize or eliminate "trade distortive practices which injure U.S. industry and agriculture" and (2) active pursuit of satisfactory market access for American business abroad "in a manner consistent with the goal of reducing trade barriers and trade-distorting measures." The guiding light for our policy would be the principle of reciprocity. The objective would be to "promote positive adjustment of economies by permitting market forces to operate."

Underlying the administration's policy was a perception, common in Washington, that the United States was not getting a fair shake in international trade. In part this was, supposedly, because in past multilateral bargaining, including the Tokyo Round, the United States had failed to negotiate trade rules that adequately served American interests. The American market, it was thought, had been opened up to a far greater extent than had markets elsewhere. And in part this was because other industrial states were believed to ignore systematically or to violate the framework of understanding historically championed by this country in the General Agreement on Tariffs and Trade (GATT). American industrial and agricultural trade was handicapped by a myriad of foreign nontariff distortions; service industries and direct investments fell victim to subsidized competition or trade-related performance requirements. Hence the spotlight on reciprocity, which was generally understood to stand for "substantially equivalent market access." From now on it would be necessary not only to monitor foreign access here but also to seek unilateral concessions from other governments to provide American business with "fair and equitable" opportunities abroad. Otherwise retaliatory measures would have to be contemplated.

This was not simply protectionism in disguise. Most officials of the administration, from President Reagan on down, genuinely believed in the desirability of free trade. But it was, as *The Economist* suggested, "free-trade-tempered-by-nationalism,"[42] reminiscent of the assertiveness of Robert Strauss's "free-but-fair-trade" campaign of the early Carter years. Why, Reagan officials demanded, should the United States be forced to pay the highest price for preserving a system that seemed to them to have become increasingly discriminatory against American industry and agriculture? The time had come, they declared defiantly, to end the "free ride" of others. As Trade Representative Brock explained in a 1982 speech, "I am confident that, under this president, reciprocity will not become a code word for protectionism, but it will be used to state clearly our insistence on equity."[43]

Unfortunately the administration's policy involved two rather substantial risks. First was the danger that, in adopting such a belligerent tone, Reagan officials might actually provoke the very trade-distorting measures they were pledged to reduce. Equity, after all, is subjective: what looks to some like getting a fair shake may well appear as protectionism in the eyes of others. Many foreign governments questioned the perception that in trade relations, the United States was more sinned against than sinning. What about America's own unfair trading practices, they asked, such as "Buy American" regulations at federal or state levels or import restrictions on such agricultural commodities as sugar, meat, and dairy products? Most governments seemed prepared to resist the Reagan administration's efforts to wring unilateral concessions from them, and some made it quite clear that they would respond in kind to retaliatory measures from the United States.

Furthermore, many complained, the very concept of reciprocity could signal a retreat from the postwar system of multilateral trade relationships, a step toward bilateralism. The charge was denied by the administration, which lost no opportunity to reaffirm this country's commitment to the fundamental rule of the GATT, embodied in the most-favored-nation clause, that trade should be conducted on the basis of nondiscrimination. Critics warned, however, that in practice the concept could easily degenerate into a rigid insistence on "equivalence," market by market and product by product. Barrier would be matched for barrier, concession for concession, trade balance for trade balance—all bilaterally. Nothing could be more threatening for system preservation.

The second risk was that additional protectionist pressures would be ignited at home by the administration's tough new attitude abroad. Domestic constituencies might be emboldened to think that now, after the Carter administration, they at last had friends in Washington who would move decisively to help them sustain their profits and market shares in the face of rising foreign competition. Protectionist sentiment, which was already running strong when President Reagan first took office (in particular, because of the recession of 1980), continued to build even after the end of the new 1981-82 recession and was further aggravated by the remorseless climb of the dollar in exchange markets (itself, as indicated a by-product of the administration's own economic policies). By the end of the president's first term, with America's trade deficit soaring to record heights, the trickle of petitions for import relief had become a flood; in 1985, more than 300 bills intended to provide some form of trade protection for American producers were filed in Congress.[44] In effect, the administration had created a Frankenstein monster.

Could the monster be controlled? At the outset of President Reagan's second term, it was evident to even the most dogmatic trade officials that the open and liberal world trading system was now seriously threatened. Gradually, therefore, the administration's initial policy stance was broadened in an effort to keep home-grown protectionist pressures in check. One new element was the Group of Five exchange-rate initiative announced in September 1985, quietly orchestrated by the administration and explicitly intended to engineer a depreciation of the dollar to help ease competitive strains on American manufacturing and agriculture. A second element was a determined American campaign for a new round of multilateral negotiations in the GATT aimed, in particular, at liberalizing the movement of services such as banking, insurance, data processing, and telecommunications—all fields in which the United States, as the world's leading service-industry economy, could be expected to benefit disproportionately. Administration calls for a new trade round actually began as early as 1982. But it was only in October 1985 that the President's new trade representative, Clayton Yeutter (who had replaced William Brock the previous April), finally won formal assent from the other members of GATT.[45] Talks were expected to get under way sometime in late 1986.

For all their usefulness, however, from the point of view of system preservation, these additional elements remained subordinate to the main thrust of administration policy, which continued to assert the primacy of American commercial interests and to seek unilateral concessions from our major trading partners. Despite the risks of "free-trade-tempered-by-nationalism," Reagan officials were determined to pursue their own conception of economic equity. Tactically, they felt, the best way to stem the protectionist tide at home would be to keep up the pressures for fairer trade practices abroad. Strategically, the guiding light for policy must continue to be the principle of reciprocity as interpreted by the administration. This was evident as late as September 1985, when President Reagan announced new proceedings against the European Economic Community (EEC) and Japan for "unfair" barriers to American sales of such items as canned fruit, tobacco, and leather products. "We hope that . . . we will be able to convince our trading partners to stop their unfair trading practices and open those markets that are now closed to American exports," Reagan said. Otherwise, he warned, "We will take countermeasures [though] only as a last resort."[46] And later the same month, in a similar vein, the administration proposed a $300 million special fund to combat what officials described as "predatory" export financing by some foreign governments.[47] In addition, more covertly, the administration seemed almost to welcome the swelling threat of congressional action on imports as yet another form of leverage on our trading partners to coerce them into concessions—a traditional tactic of the Executive Branch in international trade negotiations. The basic belligerence of the administration's tone remained essentially unchanged.

After five years, then, it was not clear whether the damage being done by this defiant trade policy would be contained or not. What *was* clear was that the administration was playing a risky game, skating on very thin ice. Either its approach would have to produce results, in its home market as well as in opportunities to trade elsewhere, or its hand might be forced by a disappointed Congress. Ultimately reciprocity must either succeed or trigger American retaliation. Yet at the same time the United States did not want to provoke its allies into a trade war by seeming to bully them. A few examples illustrate how dangerously thin the ice really was.

Japan

Of all our allies, Japan is regarded in Washington as the most guilty of unfair trading practices. Provoked by Japan's huge and growing surplus in our bilateral trade—approaching $50 billion in 1985, more than five times the figure for 1980—complaints address both sides of the mutual balance. On the export side, the Japanese are criticized for their habitual strategy of massive penetration of export markets in relatively narrow product lines, which severely injures local competitors. In addition, Japan's exporters are said to benefit improperly from generous government support, especially at the research and development stage. On the import side, the Japanese are criticized for a whole range of formal and informal nontariff barriers, from special product standards to time-consuming and expensive customs procedures, that limit access to their internal market. If there is any single country that is the implied target of reciprocity, it is Japan.

In many instances, the grievances against Japan appear justified—as the Japanese themselves, when pressed, have often implicitly conceded by acting selectively to restrain exports or liberalize imports. What was remarkable after the Reagan administration arrived in Washington, however, was the sharp rise in the level of acrimony in American accusations. Neither the administration nor the Congress had any tolerance for past piecemeal approaches, which, it was thought, had resulted at best in only tactical retreats by the Japanese. The feeling was that only by means of a broad, blunt assault could really significant concessions be obtained. "We needed to get their attention," one administration official said privately. "We had to use the proverbial two-by-four."[48]

The assault began on the export side, under pressure from domestic interests, with negotiation in May 1981 of a "voluntary" agreement, on the model of earlier negotiated quotas, restraining Japanese automobile sales in the United States. Having lost on a petition for escape-clause relief before the International Trade Commission in December 1980, the American automobile industry had turned instead to Congress, where supporters introduced highly restrictive quota legislation. In turn, the administration made use of this threat to persuade Japan to accept an export limit of 1.68 million units in the year beginning April 1, down from 1.82 million units the previous year, and to continue restraint each year thereafter (although with the ceiling rising to 1.85 million units in 1984 and 2.3 million units in 1985).[49] There is no question that the Japanese acceded reluctantly to these limits. Calling them "voluntary," however, allowed the administration to claim no responsibility for a protectionist agreement that it had, in fact, actively negotiated, thus ostensibly maintaining its free-trade credentials. Later those credentials were more tarnished when President Reagan, in April 1983, ordered a tenfold increase in the tariff on Japanese motorcycles—the strongest protectionist action by any administration in years—and again, in December 1984, when a fixed quota was agreed on sales of Japanese finished steel in the United States.[50]

The major focus of policy, however, was on Japanese imports. As a result of its many nontariff barriers, administration spokesmen repeatedly noted, Japan imported fewer manufactured goods as a proportion of its GNP than any other industrial country (about 1 1/2 percent, as against 3 1/2 percent or more in the United States and Europe); indeed the share of manufactured imports in GNP had actually declined over the previous two decades, while that of other industrial states had risen rapidly.

And Japan also maintained strict controls on imports of agricultural commodities of interest to the United States, such as rice, citrus, tobacco, and beef. The Japanese furthermore were criticized for their strong "Buy Japan" ethic and their complex distribution system, which was highly dependent on long-standing social relationships; both also inhibited imports.

The assault on Japanese import practices was continued throughout the administration's first five years. In response, Japan announced no less than eight liberalization programs between December 1981 and December 1985, cutting tariffs and easing nontariff barriers on a wide array of products of interest to the United States. In April 1985, Prime Minister Yasuhiro Nakasone even went on Japan's national television to make an extraordinary appeal to the Japanese people to buy more "foreign" goods. "If we do not solve the existing trade frictions today," he said, "there is a possibility that there will arise a very serious situation affecting the life and death of our country."[51] Yet the administration was hardly mollified. In fact criticisms grew ever harsher, despite such concessions. "The mood is very strong . . . to hit the Japanese," observed a trade specialist on the Senate Foreign Relations Committee.[52] The head of a Japanese government advisory committee on trade said: "The sentiment in the United States is like that before the outbreak of a war."[53] Just one week before Prime Minister Nakasone's television appeal, President Reagan's cabinet publicly declared "equivalent access" to be its goal in trade relations with Japan—the first time that reciprocity had been formally made such a high policy goal by the entire government.[54]

In turn the Japanese, gradually abandoning their customary deference, began to lash back, citing their own grievances against this country, such as discriminatory government procurement programs, restrictions on the sale of Alaskan oil, and alleged dumping of petrochemical products. They also cited the overvaluation of the dollar, caused by the Reagan administration's fiscal-monetary "mix," as well as the lack of effort by most American businessmen to penetrate the Japanese market. "They expect to just walk in and talk to a distributor and say, 'Here's my product,' the way they do in the U.S.," said a member of the Japan Economic Institute. "It doesn't work that way in Japan."[55] Frustration was particularly strong over Washington's threat of unilateral retaliatory measures. "If the United

States does not want to trade with Japan, politics here would change," warned one high trade official in Tokyo as early as 1982. "There would be no benefit for Japan to remain a member of the free world."[56] Though perhaps an extreme example, such a statement was symptomatic of the frictions generated by the Reagan administration's demands.

Europe

In commercial relations with Europe, three issues, in particular, stood out during the administration's first five years: steel, agriculture, and trade with the Soviet bloc. Each contributed to what *The Economist* called the "rockiest patch for 30 years"[57] in the Atlantic trading relationship.

The steel issue was inherited from the Carter years. Despite the trigger-price mechanism instituted in 1978, steel imports had continued to increase their penetration of the American market (19 percent in 1981, up from 16 percent in 1980 and only 14 percent as recently as 1976), intensifying industry pressures for relief. The major culprits, the industry charged, were members of the EEC, who were accused of illegal subsidies as well as outright dumping. Reviving a tactic that had been used successfully during the Carter administration, companies such as U.S. Steel again began threatening antidumping and countervailing-duty suits against the Europeans. "The target price is simply out of control," argued the chairman of U.S. Steel in November 1981. "It is being blatantly ignored by most of the European producers. The time for patience is past. It is time for action."[58] Action finally came in early 1982, when U.S. Steel and six other companies filed more than 1900 complaints against seven EEC countries, as well as Brazil, Rumania, South Africa, and Spain.

The Reagan administration was caught in the middle, between the protectionist demands of the industry and its own free-trade pretensions. Unfortunately, its instincts seemed to place the highest priority on the interests of a powerful domestic constituency. Although there seemed much truth in industry charges against the Europeans, American companies had by no means helped their case by repeatedly raising prices in previous years, despite weak market conditions. In addition, the EEC could legitimately claim that at least some of its subsidies were legal, being tied to plans for rationalization of its own industry, and in

any event were being gradually phased out. Yet the administration never hesitated to put pressure on the Europeans to
restrain their sales in the United States. In October 1982, four
months after Washington threatened countervailing duties
ranging up to 40 percent on European steel, the EEC felt obliged
to accept a three-year "voluntary" export agreement, similar to
the earlier Japanese automobile pact, limiting basic steel shipments to approximately 5.5 percent of the American domestic
market (reduced from 6.3 percent in 1981). In July 1983, quotas
and tariffs were unilaterally imposed on European specialty
steels. In early 1985, the EEC was persuaded to restrict sales of
pipes and tubes. And in November 1985, after painful negotiations, the 1982 agreement was succeeded by a new four-year
pact holding European shipments to roughly the same share of
the American market but covering a wider range of products.
"Happily we were able to maintain peace," said the EEC's
commissioner for external relations after the new pact was
signed.[59] But the bitterness on the European side over the
Reagan administration's strong-arm tactics was palpable.

Another major irritant was agriculture. For the Reagan
administration, one of the most unfair of all trading practices
was the EEC's common farm policy which, with its high prices
and open-ended guarantees, had turned the EEC from a net
importer of food into a net exporter of such items as dairy
products, beef, poultry, sugar, and wheat—thereby threatening
some of the traditional overseas markets of the United States.
The issue, as the administration saw it, was the EEC's aggressive use of export subsidies to gain competitive advantage. For
the Europeans, however, this was a case of the pot calling the
kettle black, since the United States, they pointed out, also
provides broad government support for its farmers. Objecting to
the administration's contentious tone, EEC officials warned that
any action against European farmers would provoke countermeasures endangering America's historical markets in Europe
and elsewhere. When Washington announced in early 1983 a
large, heavily subsidized sale of wheat flour to Egypt, long one
of the EEC's best markets, the EEC retaliated with a shipment
of cheap wheat to China, where America had been the biggest
outside supplier. When Washington acted in mid-1985 to restrict
imports of European pasta as part of a campaign to open the EEC
market to American citrus fruit, the EEC responded with higher
tariffs on American exports of walnuts and lemons. The Reagan

administration's attitude on farm policy "smacks of a trade war," said France's minister of agriculture in June 1985, and could lead to "a spread of protectionist measures."[60]

Finally, there was the issue of trade relations with the Soviet bloc, where early tensions developed as a result of the economic sanctions imposed by the Reagan administration on Poland and the Soviet Union following the Polish government's declaration of martial law in December 1981. Administration spokesmen criticized the Europeans for their failure to match America's actions, charging that Europe seemed more interested in markets than in the security of the Western alliance. The Europeans, in turn, criticized Washington for overreacting, suggesting pointedly that they might be more willing to cut their trade with the Soviet bloc if the United States were to make an equivalent sacrifice by reinstating the grain embargo that President Reagan had lifted in 1981. Throughout most of 1982, the dispute was raised to what *The Economist* described as the "hair-pulling level"[61] by administration efforts to persuade the Europeans to cancel their planned natural gas pipeline from Siberia and to restrict government-subsidized export credits to the Soviet Union, before a cooling-off was finally negotiated by Secretary of State George Shultz in November 1982. Subsequently, new tensions arose over the issue of high-technology exports to the Soviet Union, exports that Reagan hard-liners wanted to persuade European governments to restrict to the maximum extent possible. Representative was the reaction of West Germany's economics minister, who warned that Bonn would "not tolerate" further administration attempts to curb technology transfers to the East.[62]   After five years, differences over Soviet-bloc trade remained a continuing source of strain on the Atlantic alliance.

Canada

Like Japan and Europe, Canada initially was attacked by the Reagan administration for practices viewed as unfair to American commercial interests—in particular for "nationalistic" investment rules that both limited opportunities for foreign investors in Canada and imposed trade-related performance requirements on them. Such rules were anathema to Reagan officials, not only because they interfered with market forces but also because they were inherently discriminatory, contravening international undertakings regarding "national treatment" (the same treatment of foreign and domestic enterprise). For the government of Prime Minister Pierre Elliot Trudeau, restriction of foreign investment seemed essential if Canada was to preserve an independent national identity in the face of the pervasive influence of its giant neighbor, whose companies already controlled one-third of Canadian manufacturing and whose economy accounted for better than two-thirds of Canadian foreign trade. When confronted with threats of retaliation from Washington, however, Canada had few options, especially at a time of deep recession and high unemployment at home. Even before the landslide election victory of Conservative Brian Mulroney in September 1984, it was evident that Ottawa had reluctantly begun to relax enforcement of its investment rules and to retreat on other issues of bilateral commercial interest. Canada's sense of grievance could not stand up easily to American pressures. As one Canadian writer commented: "You would expect the more powerful nation to get what it wants."[63] Washington's belligerent tactics, in this case, paid off.

Indeed, under the pro-business government of Prime Minister Mulroney, the Reagan administration not only won legislation in Ottawa, in early 1985, which formally abolished many of Canada's controversial investment restrictions; Washington was even offered, in September, a commitment to begin negotiating a liberalized trade agreement between the two nations. The move was welcomed by Reagan officials still eager to demonstrate whenever possible the magic of the marketplace. What motivated Ottawa, however, was less principle than national self-interest—in particular, concern about the rising tide of protectionism in the United States. Trade talks offered a way to ensure that concessions in the future would not be all one-way. "We need a better, a fairer and a more predictable trade relationship with the United States," Prime Minister Mulroney said in proposing the talks. "At stake are more than two million jobs which depend on Canadian access to the United States market."[64] Given Canadian sensibilities about national identity, it was clear that, once begun, negotiations would be long and arduous and could end up producing more trade frictions than they might resolve. For the Reagan administration, the ice still remained dangerously thin.

Conclusion

It can hardly be said that the Reagan administration's approach to international economic relations fared well during its first five years. Quite the contrary, the combination of Reaganomics at home and reciprocity abroad proved no solution at all to the central dilemma of foreign economic policy—the growing constraints on policymakers. In effect the administration tried to ignore the new limits of American power, disregarding the lesson learned by the Carter administration, and thus was forced to repeat the difficult learning process of its predecessor. The return swing of the pendulum was most evident in the management of macroeconomic relations, especially after the appointment of James Baker as Treasury secretary; it was more gradual in the trade field. America's accustomed autonomy and influence over economic events, President Reagan first believed, could simply be reasserted. The results, predictably, were disappointing. Not only was a "full and vigorous" prosperity not promoted, but relations with most other industrial states were brought to a new post-World War II low, endangering the very foundations of the Western alliance. The administration's trade-offs among policy objectives threatened to be highly costly for the nation as a whole.

Domestically the costs were evident in our exploding fiscal and trade deficits, rising protectionist pressures, and persistently long unemployment lines. Abroad the costs were potentially even more severe. By reasserting as forcefully as it did the primacy of American interests, defined in the narrowest possible terms, the administration effectively served notice that it no longer felt any special responsibility for preserving the economic system as a whole. America, too, would act as a "free rider," extracting gains where we could. In the short run, such a policy might indeed succeed in wringing concessions from our allies. But the risk was that the more often this was done, the more likely it was that these same allies would feel driven to insulate themselves from the United States in their trade and monetary relations, just as they felt driven by the chaos of the dollar in 1978 to form the European Monetary System. And this, in turn, would most certainly deprive the United States of much of the benefit of global economic interdependence. In the long run, we too would be losers. Like it or not, America still has a vested interest in avoiding undue discord or disruption in the system, and this the Reagan administration clearly failed to do, particularly in the trade area. Conflict was not kept manageable. After five years, it seemed that there could yet be an explosion in the kitchen.

Notes

1. Robert O. Keohane, "U.S. Foreign Economic Policy Toward Other Advanced Capitalist States," in *Eagle Entangled: U.S. Foreign Policy in a Complex World,* Kenneth A. Oye, Donald Rothchild, and Robert J. Lieber, eds. (New York and London: Longman, 1979), pp. 118-119.

2. Walter W. Heller, *New Dimensions of Political Economy* (New York: Norton, 1967), p. 5.

3. See, for example, Richard N. Cooper, "Prolegomena to the Choice of an International Monetary System"; and Lawrence B. Krause and Joseph S. Nye, "Reflections on the Economics and Politics of International Economic Organizations"—both in *World Politics and International Economics,* C. Fred Bergsten and Lawrence B. Krause, eds. (Washington, D.C.; The Brookings Institution, 1975); and Benjamin J. Cohen, *Organizing the World's Money* (New York: Basic Books, 1977), Ch. 2.

4. But see, for example, Benjamin J. Cohen, "U.S. Foreign Economic Policy," *Orbis* (Spring 1971), vol. 15, no. 1, pp. 232-246; and Benjamin J. Cohen, "The Revolution in Atlantic Economic Relations: A Bargain Comes Unstuck," in *The United States and Western Europe,* Wolfram Hanrieder, ed. (Cambridge, MA: Winthrop, 1974).

5. Robert E. Osgood, "The Revitalization of Containment," *Foreign Affairs* (1982), vol. 60, no. 3, p. 465.

6. For an authoritative statement of the administration's thinking at the time, see Richard N. Cooper, "Global Economic Policy in a World of Energy Shortage," in *Economics in the Public Service,* J. Pechman and J. Simler, eds. (New York: Norton, 1981). Cooper was President Carter's Under Secretary of State for Economic Affairs.

7. See, for example, Keohane, "U.S. Foreign Economic Policy," pp. 102-109.

8. Council of Economic Advisors, *Annual Report, 1978* (Washington, D.C.: U.S. Government Printing Office, 1978), p. 124.

9. Benjamin J. Cohen, "Europe's Money, America's Problem," *Foreign Policy* (Summer 1979), no. 35, pp. 31-47.

10. Andrew Shonfield, "The World Economy in 1979," *Foreign Affairs* (1980), vol. 58, no. 3, p. 607.

11. Council of Economic Advisers, *Annual Report, 1981* (Washington, D.C.: U.S. Government Printing Office, 1981), p. 199.

12. See, for example, Marina Whitman, "A Year of Travail: The United States and the International Economy," *Foreign Affairs* (1979), vol. 57, no. 3, pp. 543-544.

13. Ibid., p. 545.

14. See, for example, Shonfield, "World Economy," pp. 616-617; and Thomas R. Graham, "Revolution in Trade Politics," *Foreign Policy* (Fall 1979), vol. 36, p. 55.

15. For evaluations of these two policy measures, see Robert Carswell, "Economic Sanctions and the Iran Experience," *Foreign Affairs* (Winter 1981-82), no. 60, pp. 247-265; and Robert L. Paarlberg, "Lessons of the Grain Embargo," *Foreign Affairs* (Fall 1980), vol. 59, no. 1, pp. 144-162.

16. Council of Economic Advisors, *Annual Report, 1982* (Washington, D.C.: U.S. Government Printing Office, 1982), p. 167.

17. Presidential Message to the Congress accompanying his Program for Economic Recovery, February 18, 1981.

18. *Economic Report of the President* (Washington, D.C.: U.S. Government Printing Office, 1982), p. 4.

19. *America's New Beginning: A Program for Economic Recovery* (Washington, D.C.: U.S. Government Printing Office, 1981), pp. 12, 25.

20. As quoted in William Greider, "The Education of David Stockman," *The Atlantic Monthly*, December 1981, p. 29.

21. Tom Wicker, "Mr. Reagan's Mirrors," *The New York Times*, December 11, 1981, p. A35.

22. *The New York Times*, December 13, 1985, p. 13.

23. Henry R. Nau, "Where Reaganomics Works," *Foreign Policy* (Winter 1984-85), no. 57, pp. 14-37.

24. Ibid., pp. 15,23.

25. September 29, 1981, as quoted in *IMF Survey*, October 12, 1981, p. 317.

26. C. Fred Bergsten, "Reaganomics: The Problem?" *Foreign Policy* (Summer 1985), no. 59, pp. 132-144.

27. Ibid., pp. 134. (Italics added.)

28. See, for example, Robert Solomon, "The Elephant in the Boat?: The United States and the World Economy," *Foreign*

Affairs (1982), vol. 60, no. 3, pp. 557-581.

29. Flora Lewis, "Alarm Bells in the West," *Foreign Affairs* (1982), vol. 60, no. 3, p. 556.

30. *The New York Times*, February 12, 1982, p. 1.

31. John Wyles, "Europe: At the Mercy of Outside Forces," *Financial Times* Supplement, December 7, 1981, p. 1.

32. As quoted in *The New York Times*, May 31, 1983, p. D15.

33. As quoted in *The New York Times*, June 11, 1984, p. D4.

34. The estimate was by Data Resources Inc., a private economic forecasting firm, in a report released by the Joint Economic Committee in March 1985. See *The New York Times*, March 13, 1985, p. D17.

35. As quoted in *The New York Times*, April 26, 1982, p. D10.

36. Jeffrey E. Garten, "Gunboat Economics," *Foreign Affairs* (1985), vol. 63, no. 3, pp. 538, 545.

37. *The New York Times*, April 16, 1985, p. 24.

38. Joint Declaration, as reprinted in *The New York Times*, May 5, 1985, p. 16.

39. Statement, as reprinted in *The New York Times*, September 23, 1985, p. D11.

40. As quoted in *The New York Times*, September 29, 1985, Section 3, p. F1.

41. Office of the United States Trade Representative, "Statement of U.S. Trade Policy," July 8, 1981.

42. *The Economist*, July 4, 1981, p. 21.

43. Address before the European Management Forum, Davos, Switzerland, February 1, 1982.

44. See, for example, *The Economist*, September 28, 1985, p. 24.

45. *The New York Times*, October 3, 1985, p. D1.

46. As quoted in *The New York Times*, September 8, 1985, p. 1.

47. *The New York Times*, September 24, 1985, p. 1.

48. Interview with the author, January 1982.

49. For an evaluation of these restraints, see Robert W. Crandall, "What Have Auto-Import Quotas Wrought?," *Challenge* (January-February 1985), pp. 40-47.

50. *The New York Times*, April 2, 1983, p. 1; and December 7, 1984, p. D2.

51. As quoted in *The New York Times*, April 10, 1985, p. D10.

52. As quoted in *The New York Times*, April 4, 1985, p. D5.

53. As quoted in *The New York Times*, March 14, 1985, p. A4.

54. *The New York Times*, April 4, 1985, p. D5.

55. As quoted in *The New York Times*, April 4, 1985, p. D5.

56. Kazuo Wakasugi, director of the trade policy bureau of the Ministry of International Trade and Industry, as quoted in *The New York Times*, March 27, 1982, Business Section, p. 32.

57. *The Economist*, February 27, 1982, p. 20.

58. As quoted in *Financial Times*, November 4, 1981.

59. As quoted in *The New York Times*, November 2, 1985, p. 36.

60. As quoted in *The New York Times*, June 5, 1985, p. D1.

61. *The Economist*, February 27, 1982, p. 22.

62. As quoted in *The New York Times*, August 11, 1984, p. 29.

63. Stephen Clarkson, author of a book entitled "Canada and the Reagan Challenge," as quoted in *The New York Times*, July 18, 1983, p. D4.

64. As quoted in *The New York Times*, September 27, 1985, p. D5.

6

Britain's Decision to Join the Common Market*

Britain's 1971 decision to join the Common Market was an event of the first magnitude in British economic history. Only twice before in the last century and a half had the country's foreign economic policy undergone a comparable transformation—once in 1846 when the repeal of the Corn Laws ushered in an era of free trade, and a second time in 1932 when free trade was abandoned in favor of the system known as Imperial Preference. At least until the early 1960s Britain still regarded itself as a major economic power—not the world's leading power certainly, but a force of some importance nonetheless, with widespread commercial and financial interests, particularly in the Commonwealth. But by the middle and late 1960s this conception had begun to fade. In place of the global and Commonwealth perspectives that had previously guided Britain's foreign economic policy, a new "European" orientation gradually emerged, culminating in Parliament's formal approval of British membership in the European Community in October 1971, and surviving even the Labor Party's pledge to renegotiate the terms of membership after Labor's return to power in 1974 and the referendum debate of 1975.

This essay will discuss this dramatic transformation of British foreign economic policy, commenting on how it came about and suggesting some insights into the decisionmaking process that

*From Wilfrid Kohl (ed.), *Economic Foreign Policies of Industrial States* (Lexington, MA: D.C. Heath, 1977), ch. 3.

was involved. The first section develops, in a rather cursory fashion, an abstract analytical framework that can be used generally to gain an understanding of the decisionmaking process in foreign economic policy. The second section gives content to the framework of analysis by applying it to the specific instance of Great Britain in the decade of the 1960s.

The final section considers briefly some of the implications of the 1971 decision for the substance and direction of the decision-making process in British foreign economic policy in the future.

Analytical Framework

The analysis of the decisionmaking process in foreign economic policy generally may be approached in a variety of ways. For an economist, the most congenial approach views policy as a problem of "maximization under constraint."[1] Conventional economic analysis always begins with the assumption of scarcity: the things that people and societies value are limited in supply; the best things in life (Tin Pan Alley not-withstanding) are not all free. Choices therefore are necessary. The task for economic decisionmakers (assuming they are rational) is to do the best they can to maximize some value or other—or several values simultaneously—under the constraint of scarcity. The task for the economic analyst seeking insight into such behavior is to focus on this problem of choice. As Walter Heller has written of the political economist: "Problems of choice are his meat and drink. His method is to factor out the costs, the benefits, and the net advantage or disadvantage of alternative courses of action."[2]

The traditional analytic mode of economics concentrates attention on three sets of interrelated variables: (1) independent variables, which are the instruments available to decisionmakers; (2) dependent variables, which are the targets of decisionmakers; and (3) parameters, which are the constraints on decisionmakers. For analytical purposes these three sets of variables are combined, implicitly or explicitly, to form "models," in which the dependent variables are assumed to be functionally related to the independent variables, and the nature of each functional relationship (in mathematical terms, the magnitude and sign of each partial derivative) is assumed to be determined by the parametric constraints. For any given problem, specifying a model (implicit or explicit) enables the economist to analyze how he or she can use available instruments, subject to the constraints imposed by objective circumstances, to maximize a certain target. When the model incorporates multiple targets, the problem becomes one of joint maximization, with analysis focusing as well on the trade-offs at the margin among the several targets.

This mode of analysis has always lent itself quite readily to explaining the behavior of private economic units. Economic theory speaks of the firm, for example, rationally maximizing the target of profit by making use of the instruments at its disposal—principally, its price and quantity of output—subject to such constraints as input costs, demand for output, and the prices of related goods. Or theory speaks of the consumer, rationally maximizing the target of personal utility by varying purchases subject to the constraints of income and tastes. Analysis of this sort has proved to be highly relevant and rich in practical insights. It is also relatively straightforward, because in dealing with private economic units discussion can usually proceed in terms of a single dependent variable, and also because the specified targets of private economic units normally, though not always, can be quantified.

On the other hand, when it comes to explaining the behavior of public (political) economic units, analysis of this sort becomes a bit more complex. In the first place, governmental decisionmakers usually have multiple rather than single policy targets. Specifically, political variables enter alongside economic variables as separate and independent objectives of action, which means that realistically, public economic policy must be viewed as a problem of *joint* maximization with much of the focus of analysis thus being trained directly on the marginal trade-offs among objectives. Furthermore, since political variables usually cannot be easily quantified, analysis also must necessarily be rather more qualitative than quantitative. For both these reasons, the economist's traditional analytic mode does not lend itself quite so readily to the study of public economic policy as it does to the study of private economic units. And the analysis becomes even more complex yet as we move from domestic economic policymaking to foreign economic policy, where foreign political targets must be added to the already crowded array of economic and domestic political variables. Nevertheless, I would maintain that the mode of analysis can be highly relevant and useful. Even though our actual knowledge of all the complex functional relationships involved may be quite limited, organizing thinking in these terms at least has the virtue of adding clarity to discussions. So long as policymakers can be assumed to be rational, significant insights can be gained by approaching the problem of foreign economic policy in this way, as will become apparent later.

What specific variables should be included in a realistic model of rational decisionmaking in foreign economic policy? In my opinion, at least the following dozen variables should be considered for analytical purposes:

1. Independent variables
   a. trade policy
   b. investment policy
   c. aid policy
   d. financial policy
2. Dependent variables
   a. economic welfare
   b. distribution
   c. national security
   d. national prestige
3. Parameters
   a. geography
   b. demography
   c. development
   d. history

No explanation ought to be necessary of the four independent variables listed, for they are the familiar instruments of governmental action in international economics.[3] Trade policy is concerned with the international movement of goods and services; investment policy, with the movement of money, both short-term and long-term; aid policy, with the movement of either goods, services, or money on concessional terms; and financial policy, with the balance of payments and exchange rate of the country as well as with the international status (if any) of the national currency.

The four dependent variables listed constitute, I believe, the principal independent targets of governmental action in international economics. Economic welfare stands for real income—that is, the real volume of goods and services available for final use by the nation's consumers, businesses, and government sector.

This is the traditional objective identified in economic analysis. It is not a simple concept; despite more than two centuries of development of modern economic theory, we still do not know precisely how to go about maximizing economic welfare. One reason is the existence of competing economic theories. Economists disagree among themselves, in large part because of the impossibility of testing competing theories against one another. In the physical sciences, more often than not, it is possible to test one theory against another by means of a controlled experiment in a laboratory. In the social sciences, controlled experiments are out of the question: the laboratory is the real world, and all the samples are samples of one. Accordingly, honest people can honestly disagree on such matters as how to maximize economic welfare.

A second reason for such disagreements is that economic welfare is decomposable. At the micro level, welfare may be identified with efficiency of resource allocation; at the macro level, with both full employment and relative price stability. These three dimensions may not always be mutually compatible. The famous Phillips curve, for instance, defines a tradeoff between employment and price stability. Likewise, situations may arise when policymakers must choose between promoting either employment or efficiency (e.g., when a balance-of-payments deficit forces the government to choose between domestic deflation or import controls). Since such choices necessarily involve value judgments regarding the relative weights to be attached to each of the three dimensions of economic welfare, normative differences can also cause disagreements about how this objective may be maximized.

The second dependent variable, distribution, stands as a proxy for the set of relevant domestic political goals of policy. I take for granted that policymakers do have political goals in mind. Being politicians and not disinterested statesmen or philosopher-kings, they may be assumed to concern themselves not only (if at all) with the general interests of the national society as a whole, but also with the specific interests of certain narrower constituencies within the national society, and to seek through policy to maximize the gains of such domestic groups or to minimize their losses. In other words, they may be assumed to aim at some particular distribution of the costs and benefits of policy. This of course is the traditional objective identified in political analysis, the meat and drink of the political scientist:

Whose ox is gored if one policy is chosen rather than another? It is also, like economic welfare, not at all a simple concept. As in the case of economic welfare, we still do not know precisely how to go about achieving some particular distribution of the costs and benefits of policy, again in part because of competing theories, but even more importantly because this objective too is decomposable. Distribution implies not only gains or losses of real income, but also of relative rank, prestige, privileges, and so forth, and since here too value judgments are necessarily involved in weighing the trade-offs between the pecuniary and nonpecuniary costs and benefits of policy, honest disagreements among honest people are possible with respect to this objective also.

Analogous points may be made regarding the remaining two dependent variables, national security and national prestige, which embody the two most important foreign political targets that must be added when remove from domestic policymaking to foreign economic policy. These concepts are hardly simple either. National security is mainly concerned with issues of territorial integrity and political independence and can be logically translated into an imperative to maximize national power.[4] National prestige is listed separately because it appears to operate with considerable force as an independent influence on the foreign economic policies of many states. The problem here is to know just what constitutes power or prestige, and to understand precisely how in fact either may be enhanced.

Turning lastly to the parameters, geography stands for the whole variety of physical attributes of a country—its size, location (is it maritime or landlocked? is it near major transportation routes?), natural resources, topography, arability, and climate. Demography refers to both the size and the composition of a country's population. Development represents the variety of economic characteristics of a country—e.g., its degree of industrialization and urbanization, its overall and per capita levels of income, the depth and breadth of its financial markets, and so on. And history stands for the entire cultural, social, political, and economic background that is embodied in the structure of the contemporary national society. These four multivariate factors are, I believe, the most important of the many constraints operating on the decisionmaking process in foreign economic policy. All are influential in determining the nature of the functional relationships between independent and dependent variables.

For example, consider the functional relationship between trade policy and economic welfare. Some countries may be able to use protectionist commercial regulations (e.g., export quotas, import tariffs) to gain an improvement of their terms of trade if their geography gives them some degree of monopoly power in the sale of their principal export commodities, or if their population size, level of development, or historical commercial ties give them some degree of monopsony power in the purchase of their imports. Countries less favorably endowed geographically and historically and with lower populations and levels of development, on the other hand, are apt conversely to find that a protectionist trade policy produces only a negative impact on the nation's real income. Similar differences may be noted with respect to all the other functional relationships between instruments and targets as well. The point is that in every country foreign economic policy must be conducted under the constraint of objective circumstances, and these circumstances will vary greatly from country to country. The essential task for policymakers is to take account of these constraints in deciding how to use the several instruments at their disposal to achieve their preferred objectives. The "maximization under constraint" approach can give a useful insight into how this decisionmaking process works.

In particular, the approach can give a useful insight into how *changes* in foreign economic policy come about. The fact that there is at least a quartet of independent targets of governmental action in international economics means that policymakers are continually obliged to make decisions about tradeoffs among objectives at the margin. When a substantial shift of foreign economic policy does occur, it must be because of a decision to modify these marginal trade-offs. The "maximization under constraint" approach suggests that such a decision could be attributed either to a change of objective circumstances that has altered the functional relationships between instruments and targets of policy; or to a change of the government's "utility function," reflecting altered preferences in policymaking circles. The usefulness of the approach lies in the framework of analysis that it provides. But the framework itself is nothing more than a set of "empty boxes." It is the individual analyst's responsibility to give the boxes some actual content, as is attempted for one specific case in the next section of this essay.

The Transformation of Policy

What explains the dramatic transformation that occurred in British foreign economic policy in the 1960s? I have already suggested that this shift compares with only two others in the last century and a half. Britain's transition in the 1840s and 1850s from mercantilism to free trade was associated mainly with a redistribution of domestic political power from the Tory landed gentry and aristocracy to the rising Whig bourgeoisie (and hence may be attributed largely to altered preferences in policymaking circles). The adoption of Imperial Preference in the 1930s may be interpreted primarily, though not exclusively, in terms of a concern for assuring national economic welfare in the midst of the Great Depression (and hence it may be attributed largely to changed objective circumstances). What factors account for the current European orientation of British foreign economic policy?

To begin with, Britain is a small, crowded island archipelago that has always been relatively poorly endowed with natural resources or arable land. As Table 6-1 indicates, mining and agriculture tend to account for very little of the country's gross domestic output or employment. Britain's structure of production is heavily skewed in favor of manufacturing and service activities, reflecting the fact that this is a country that has learned to trade to survive. Quite early in the Industrial Revolution, the British people seem to have realized that if they were to achieve anything significantly above an uncomfortable subsistence standard of living, they would have to obtain considerable amounts of food, fuel, and raw materials from abroad; and in order to pay for the imports they required, they would have to promote a high level of exports. Britain therefore became a trading nation—for many years, the world's leading trading nation. The movement toward free trade in the middle of the nineteenth century was an entirely rational act from the British economy's point of view, and so was the effort in the uncertain atmosphere of the 1930s to secure the country's export markets and sources of supply by formalizing the Imperial Preference system.

The structure of Britain's domestic economy is reflected in the volume and composition of its foreign trade. Foreign trade accounts for approximately one-sixth of the country's gross domestic product; fully half of all exports are finished manu-

Table 6-1
Sectoral Structure of the British Economy
(In Percentages)

	Share of each sector in:	
	Gross Domestic Product[a]	Employment
Mining and quarrying	1.5	1.5
Agriculture, forestry, and fishing	3.0	1.5
Manufacturing	32.0	34.0
Services	63.5	63.0

Source: Central Statistical Office
Note: Data are for 1971.
[a] Gross domestic product equals gross national product less net overseas investment earnings.

factures, as can be seen in Table 6-2. Imports, on the other hand, consist primarily of foods, fuels, raw materials, and semi-manufactured industrial inputs. Britain trades to promote its own economic welfare. Of course, in principle the British could eschew foreign trade if they wanted to—but only if they were willing to trade off almost totally the goal of economic welfare for other policy objectives, and to tolerate not much more than a Stone Age standard of living. Such forbearance is hard to imagine, even given the long-suffering imperturbability for which the British people are justifiably noted. In practice, therefore, autarky (self-sufficiency) cannot be considered a feasible policy option for Britain. Objective circumstances constrain the country to accept a relatively high degree of involvement in the international economy.

But the international economy is not a homogeneous entity. It consists rather of a multitude of partially overlapping congeries of nations—some tightly organized into different types of economic blocs, others related more loosely through varying degrees and modes of economic intercourse—and in such a fragmented, differentiated world, states like Britain must make choices not just about the degree of their involvement in the international economy but also about the orientation of their commercial and financial relations. For the British from at least the 1930s onward, the preferred choice was an orientation toward the remnants of the old empire—that is, toward the

Table 6-2
Composition of British Foreign Trade
(In Percentages)

Imports		100.0
Foodstuffs		22.0
Fuels		12.5
Raw Materials		13.0
Manufactured goods		51.0
Semimanufactures	26.5	
Finished manufactures	24.5	
Unclassified		1.5
Exports		100.0
Foodstuffs		6.5
Fuels		2.5
Raw materials		3.0
Manufactured goods		85.0
Semimanufactures	35.0	
Finished manufactures	50.0	
Unclassified	3.0	

Source: Central Statistical Office.
Note: Data are for 1971.

disparate, widely scattered group of nations, dominions, and dependencies that has since come to be known simply as the Commonwealth. Until recently the fundamental *leitmotif* of Britain's foreign economic policy was this Commonwealth's "connection." The twin pillars of the connection were Imperial Preference and the Sterling Area.

Imperial Preference, first instituted at the Ottawa conference of Commonwealth nations in 1932, consisted simply of a set of mutual tariff preferences arranged between Britain and the other members of the Commonwealth. British duties on imports from the Commonwealth were reduced relative to the tariffs on goods originating elsewhere; and likewise Commonwealth members levied relatively lower duties on products originating in Britain. From the British point of view, the advantages of the system were twofold. First, an extra incentive was provided to Commonwealth countries to supply Britain with the foods, fuels, and raw materials it needed. And second, Britain obtained extra leverage in valuable export markets required to earn the wherewithal with which to pay for imports. Imperial Preference promised both a continuity of supply of imports and a "captive" demand for exports. (The advantages offered to overseas Commonwealth members were of course complementary.)

The Sterling Area consisted of a parallel set of financial relationships arranged between Britain and the other members of the Commonwealth (with the exception of Canada, which has always been more closely linked financially with the United States than with Britain). The system first emerged in 1931, following the suspension of sterling convertibility, when a number of countries that had customarily relied on the pound for private and official international monetary uses—including a variety of non-Commonwealth countries—elected informally to peg their currency rates to sterling and to hold the bulk of their official monetary reserves in the form of sterling balances in London. After 1939, the initiation of a common regime of exchange-control regulations applying to the group as a whole gave formal definition to Sterling Area membership; subsequently, most non-Commonwealth countries chose to exclude themselves from this more formal arrangement. From the end of World War II, therefore, membership of the Sterling Area was practically conterminous with the borders of the Commonwealth. The principal features of the group were (1) freedom of monetary transfers between members; and (2) continued reliance on sterling as the currency for both private transfers and official reserve holdings.

The advantages offered to overseas members by the Sterling Area derived mainly from the first of these two features. Freedom of monetary transfers between members meant above all freedom of access to the British capital market. In effect, it meant that British investment policy would be biased in favor of the Commonwealth. Sterling Area arrangements assured Commonwealth countries first claim on British capital resources. Likewise, these arrangements (to say nothing of historical ties) assured a Commonwealth bias in British aid policy as well.

Although the British of course also benefited (economically or otherwise) from these biases, the main advantage the Sterling Area offered Britain derived from the second of the group's two principal features—the continued use of sterling for private and official international monetary purposes. The major thrust of Britain's financial policy, at least until the late 1960s, was to sustain and promote the pound's status as an international currency, in the belief that such status was essential to a continued high level of so-called invisible earnings in the country's balance of payments. Historically, Britain's visible trade balance has always tended toward deficit: only rarely have the country's merchandise exports ever exceeded imports. Consequently, the British have always had to rely on a high level of income from services—"invisibles"—to make up the difference on trade balance and in addition to provide some surplus for capital export. Most such services, including banking, insurance, merchanting, and brokerage, have traditionally centered on the "City of London" (Britain's equivalent of Wall Street). And until recently it was a cardinal tenet of faith in the City of London that the foreign income from these services was highly dependent on the international use of sterling. The status of the City as an international financial center had grown from the middle of the nineteenth century onward *pari passu* with the status of sterling as an international currency: as foreign use of the pound for private and official monetary purposes had prospered, so too had the City's overseas earnings. It was only natural, therefore, to believe that without the support of a great international currency much of that business would be taken elsewhere, and the City's earnings would begin to crumble away. Accordingly, it was only natural that British financial policy would be directed toward preserving the pound's international roles to the extent possible through continuation and reinforcement of Sterling Area arrangements.

Thus all four instruments of British foreign economic policy were orchestrated in support of the Commonwealth connection—trade policy through the system of Imperial Preference; and investment, aid, and financial policy through the customary practices and formal regulations of the Sterling Area. This orientation reflected Britain's historic conception of itself as a major economic power, a conception that survived World War II and in a sense may even have been strengthened by that experience. In the 1940s and 1950s the British still viewed their role in the international economy largely in global rather than in regional terms. Britain was the leader of the Commonwealth and enjoyed a "special relationship" with the United States. Britain's commercial and financial interests were worldwide. Britain's industrial output put the country among the world's leaders. It was difficult for a majority of the British people at the time even to conceive of any alternative orientation for the nation's foreign economic policy.

Still, a few lonely voices could be heard raising the possibility of alternatives, and these voices grew progressively louder following the failure of negotiations for a Europe-wide free trade area in 1958. In 1955 the six original members of the European Community initiated planning for the Common Market; by the time the Rome Treaty was signed in 1957, the remaining countries of Europe, Britain included, were feeling seriously threatened by exclusion from such a rich export area. Negotiations were therefore begun to establish a broader free trade zone in Europe to include the Six, but these talks foundered in 1958, most crucially over the issue of Britain's Imperial Preference system. While the Six, led by France, insisted on a common external tariff for all European countries, the British were as yet unprepared to abandon their Commonwealth connection. As a result, Western Europe became divided into two economic camps—the Common Market (the "Inner Six") and the European Free Trade Association (the "Outer Seven"). In Britain, the failure of the talks with the Six led some people to raise basic questions about the underlying value of the Commonwealth connection, and to consider possible alternative options for British foreign economic policy. Two diametrically opposed reactions predominated.

One of these reactions was like that of a rejected lover: "If the Common Market doesn't want us, then we don't want them." Some Britons thus advocated turning away from Europe completely, hoping instead to formalize the "special relationship" with the United States in a broad free trade area encompassing both sides of the Atlantic Ocean (but excluding the Six). By the middle of the 1960s the proposal for a North Atlantic Free Trade Area (NAFTA) was receiving serious consideration in several quarters.[5] Membership of NAFTA was projected to include not just the United States and Britain but also the other Outer Seven and Canada, and perhaps also even Japan, Australia, and New Zealand—effectively isolating the Six from the rest of the non-communist industrial world. Parallel proposals were made for bringing sterling and the Sterling Area under the aegis of the U.S. dollar.[6] The opposite of the two reactions was more like that of a resigned loser: "If you can't lick them, join them." These Britons preferred to apply for formal membership in the Common Market more or less on the

Community's own terms, with the Sterling Area eventually to be either dissolved or else absorbed into a European monetary system. This European alternative began to receive attention almost immediately after the breakdown of talks with the Six in 1958.[7]

By the beginning of the 1960s, therefore, three quite different conceptions of British foreign economic policy were competing for official acceptance—the traditional Commonwealth connection, an "American connection," and a "European connection." As we know, in the grand national debate that followed, the European connection ultimately prevailed. The framework of analysis outlined earlier can help in explaining why.

First of all, recalling the four dependent variables included in that analytical framework, it should immediately be evident why the option of an American connection never managed to gain widespread popular support. Essentially it was because the British people were manifestly unwilling to trade off the goal of national prestige for other policy objectives. Historical preferences could not be easily altered. To join with the United States in NAFTA would have meant giving up the country's cherished conception of itself as a major economic power. Compared to the United States, Britain was a decidedly second-ranking economy. At the start of the 1960s, British gross national output amounted to just 15 percent of the U.S.'s GNP. Britain had only a fraction of the U.S. population or natural resources, and its currency had long since yielded the place of honor to the dollar in international finance. In short, Britain would have had to resign itself to being a relatively small fish in a relatively big pond—in effect, the U.S.'s fifty-first state. This was an eventuality British policymakers were clearly reluctant to accept, despite the apparent benefits of the course.

Britain certainly would have benefited from the course in the area of national security. Closer economic ties formalizing Britain's "special relationship" with the United States would undoubtedly have reinforced America's existing commitments to protect British territorial and political interests. Likewise, the objective of economic welfare would in all likelihood have been promoted by a free trade zone spanning the Atlantic, giving Britain access to what was by far the richest export market in the world. Any risk that the British economy might be depressed by superior U.S. competitiveness could easily have been forestalled by an adequate system of safeguards. In any event, with assurance of access to America's technologies and capital resources, Britain—as economic fifty-first state—quite probably would have turned out to be more of a California than a West Virginia inside NAFTA. Yet British policymakers were unimpressed. They were simply unwilling to surrender their remaining global presence and their residual leadership role in world affairs to retreat under the American shadow. Historical attitudes proved too enduring.

On the other hand, historical attitudes could not rule out considering the alternative option of a European connection. The prospect of membership in the Common Market represented nothing like the same threat to Britain's great-power pretensions as did the American connection. Compared to France or Germany, Britain was then still an economy of the first rank: along with the French and Germans, the British stood to become part of a triumvirate managing the affairs of the new Europe. For many Britons this possibility carried with it at least as much national prestige as the country's traditional leadership role in the old Commonwealth. Indeed, it was clear that in either pond, Europe or Commonwealth, Britain would continue to be a relatively big fish.

The real contest, therefore, was between the Commonwealth connection and the alternative of a European connection. During the 1960s the relative merits of these two policy options were debated publicly at great length and in exhaustive—and exhausting—detail.[8] The focus of the debate was on the trade-offs among the three objectives of economic welfare, distribution, and national prestige. (Interestingly, comparatively little attention was paid to the remaining objective of foreign economic policy, national security.) The key question for analysis is: Was the decision to choose the European connection dictated by altered preferences in policymaking circles or by changed objective circumstances?

The answer to this question, in my opinion, is clear: the choice was dictated by changed objective circumstances. Despite recurrent shifts of electoral sentiment in Britain during the 1960s, underlying preferences in policymaking circles remained remarkably stable (as we shall see below). What did change were the constraints on British policymakers, the parameters of foreign economic policy. As the decade progressed, it became increasingly evident that Britain's economic world had altered—that the old Commonwealth connection no longer served to maximize important national objectives, and that the continued isolation from Europe was blocking effective use of economic policy instruments. Gradually, dominant elites in Britain became educated to the real gains and losses accruing from the Commonwealth connection; they learned what potential gains and losses were in fact likely to result from shifting instead to the alternative of a European orientation. Assumptions and perceptions underwent a significant modification, reflecting (albeit with a lag) the substantial changes that had actually occurred, and were continuing to occur, in the functional relationships between independent and dependent variables of policy.

British industrialists, for example, began to perceive that there were considerable costs entailed in continued reliance on Imperial Preference in trade policy. Through the 1950s and 1960s, Britain's trade grew at a far slower rate with the Commonwealth than with the European Community. Indeed, as Table 6-3 shows, by 1971 the Commonwealth was actually taking a smaller share of Britain's exports than was the Common Market—despite tariff discrimination by the Six—and was supplying virtually an equal share of Britain's imports. There were two main reasons for this marked change of trade patterns. In the first place, the economies of the Commonwealth (many of them less developed) were expanding much less rapidly than were the economies of the Six. "Captive" or not, demand in the Commonwealth was simply too weak to ensure a high level of exports for Britain; demand in the rich and dynamic European market, on the other hand, was strong enough to draw in goods even over the wall of the Community's common external tariff. And second, much of the Commonwealth for its part was deliberately diminishing its economic ties with Britain (an inevitable part of the process of decolonization). One of the first things most of Britain's former colonies sought following attainment , of political independence was to reduce their remaining economic dependence on the British by diversifying export markets and sources of supply of imports. The result was a sharp drop during this period in Britain's share of both the Commonwealth's exports and imports, as can also be seen in Table 6-3.

The lesson of these developments was not lost on British industrialists. Gradually they came to recognize just how unpromising the Commonwealth really was as a long-term market for exports or source of import supply—even given Imperial Preference. The traditional trade policy simply was incapable of yielding the same economic gains as before, either for the national society as a whole or for many specific trading sectors. The truly fertile fields for commerce in the future, industrialists saw, lay rather in the European Community, particularly if mutual barriers to trade with the Six could be eliminated. During the 1960s, therefore, most of this influential constituency became solidly converted to the idea of a European connection.

So too did most of the British farming establishment, attracted principally by the prospect of high support prices embodied in the Community's common agricultural policy. Under Britain's traditional trade policy, the bulk of food imports entered the country duty-free; the only help British farmers received from the government to sustain their competitive position took the form of limited production subsidies ("deficiency payments"). Higher agricultural prices were universally expected to lead to expanded food production and farm incomes in Britain.

A third elite whose assumptions and perceptions changed during this period consisted of the leadership of the City of London—the officers and managers of the major banks, insurance companies, commodity exchanges, brokerage houses, and other financial institutions whose overseas earnings were such an important element in Britain's balance of payments. Throughout the 1950s and 1960s, Britain's external payments and currency were almost continually in trouble. There were sterling crises in 1951-1952, 1955, 1956-1957, 1959, 1961, and 1964-1967, culminating in the formal devaluation of the pound in November 1967. (Further crises in the early 1970s eventually resulted in a floating of the pound in June 1972.) Yet in spite of these recurrent difficulties the City's invisible earnings grew at a singularly healthy pace, topping 300 million pounds annually in the middle and late 1960s.[9] This led at least some financial interests to question whether the pound really was so important to the City's fortunes after all.

Gradually it became clear that London could actually get along quite satisfactorily without the support of an international currency, and that in fact only a small fraction of the City's overseas income was directly or indirectly dependent on the international use of sterling—not more than one-fifth according to one estimate.[10] By the early 1960s, London had already

Table 6-3
Changing Shares in British and Commonwealth Trade, 1951-1971
(In Percentages)

	Exports					Imports				
	1951	1956	1961	1966	1971	1951	1956	1961	1966	1971
Share of British trade accounted for by: Commonwealth	50.5	46	35	25	18	40	44	37	27	22
European Economic Community	9	11.5	16.5	20	21	11.5	12.5	15	18.5	21.5
Share of Commonwealth trade accounted for by Britain	25	28	22	17	12	25	24	21	15	12

Sources: Central Statistical Office, Board of Trade, and Commonwealth Economic Committee.

become the focal point of the vast and expanding Eurocurrency market: the City's banks no longer needed sterling and the Sterling Area to ensure a high level of earnings from foreign-exchange operations or other services provided to foreigners. Likewise, most of London's other financial activities had grown independent of the pound. City interests began to realize therefore that they did not really have a need for sterling—indeed, that official efforts to preserve the international status of the pound could actually prove to be counter-productive as far as London was concerned. A financial policy directed toward preserving Sterling Area arrangements, requiring ever-stricter exchange controls and other regulations, could result only in irreparable damage to the City's position as an international financial center. Continued isolation from Europe, where London stood the best chance of becoming the principal axis of the Community's money and capital markets, could only retard future growth of the City's invisible earnings. Thus by the end of the 1960s, most of this influential constituency too was solidly converted to the idea of a European connection.

One final elite to be considered in this connection was the government's own bureaucracy—the permanent civil servants in the ministries and in the Bank of England. It is impossible to overrate the influential role of these dimly known individuals in the framing of public policy in Britain. Governments and ministers may come and go, but the civil service remains throughout to provide unity and continuity to policy. Newly appointed ministers—in the British tradition, often nonexperts with little (if any) training or experience in their areas of ministerial responsibility—rely inordinately on their permanent secretaries and other non-political subordinates for information, education, and guidance. This is perhaps the principal reason why underlying preferences in British policymaking circles tend to remain so remarkably stable, and why there have been so few major discontinuities in the last century and half of British foreign economic policy. However much voter sentiment may fluctuate from one election to another, however frequently political power itself may change hands, the same bureaucrats sit in Whitehall and Threadneedle Street giving the same advice to their transient political "masters."

During the 1960s the bureaucracy too underwent a process of reeducation, not only with regard to the relative economic merits of the Commonwealth and European alternatives (as did the country's industrialists and other economic interests), but even more crucially with regard to the differing implications of these two options for Britain's national prestige. For the civil service, Britain's historic conception of itself as a major economic power was more than just a matter of patriotism or the "national interest" (as important as these concerns may have been); in addition, it was a matter of some purely personal self-interest. A global presence for Britain meant leadership roles for many Britons. Prestige for the nation also meant prestige for many individuals. And these individuals gradually became convinced that in these terms too, not just in terms of national economic welfare, a new connection with Europe would be far more rewarding than the old connection with the Commonwealth. Beset by centrifugal forces, the old Commonwealth was fast fading as an influence on the world stage. The new European Community, on the other hand, was clearly a bright and rising star. Many in the British government thus saw the prospect of membership in the Common Market as a unique opportunity. Here was a chance not only to reinvigorate the British economy. Here also was a chance to reestablish Britain's status as a great power—and incidentally to enhance the personal status of Britain's civil servants as well. Indeed, though their French and

German counterparts would likely have a say on certain issues, it was confidently expected within the British civil service that ultimately they themselves—qualified as they were by history, talent, and inherited skills—would become the natural leaders of the emergent Europe. Careers would certainly be made in London and in Brussels. Not surprisingly, therefore, much of the British governmental bureaucracy also eventually fell behind the idea of a European connection.

Of course, there were also constituencies that remained unreconciled to the idea. The labor-union movement, in particular, persistently opposed Common Market membership throughout the 1960s—to some extent because of fears that Britain might lose control over its economic planning, but above all because of worries regarding the distributional implications of the Community's common agricultural policy. Higher prices for food, it was clear, would mean lower real purchasing power for workers; the gains to the British farming establishment would come largely, if not entirely, at the expense of the living standards of the laboring poor. The unions could not accept a foreign economic policy that threatened to gore mainly their own ox. The unions' opposition was reflected politically in the left wing of the Labor Party. Other groups hostile to the idea of a European connection included industrial and financial interests with business ties to the Commonwealth, who also stood to have their ox gored; and sentimental imperial types who were simply reluctant to see the sun finally set over the old British empire. The views of these groups were reflected politically, for the most part, in the right wing of the Conservative Party.

However, over the course of the 1960s the balance of opinion among dominant elites in Britain clearly swung in favor of a European connection.[11] Within the government, important elements of the permanent bureaucracy (particularly in the Foreign Office and the Board of Trade) began changing its advice to the politicians. Outside the government, pressures were applied by such influential lobbies as the Confederation of British Industries, the National Farmers Union (both of which together with the Trades Union Congress, enjoy the right to consultation on a regular and continuing basis with the British government on matters of vital interest to their members), the British National Export Council, and the Committee on Invisible Exports. Inevitably members of both the Labor and Conservative Parties responded: the moderate wings of both parties, following the example of the Liberal Party (which had declared itself in favor of Community membership as early as 1958), gradually moved toward the idea of joining the Common Market on some terms or other. Organized opposition outside Parliament came mainly from the Trades Union Congress, but this proved insufficient to prevent the majority vote approving membership in October 1971.

The education of Britain's elites was hardly an instantaneous process. In 1961, when Harold Macmillan's cabinet made Britain's first application to join the Common Market, attitudes were still relatively uncompromising on such issues as Imperial Preference and the Sterling Area. Most Britons as yet did not really comprehend how much their economic world was changing and were still largely unprepared to abandon their traditional Commonwealth connection. In the negotiations of 1961-1962, the British delegation to Brussels, led by Edward Heath, adopted the hardest possible line, bargaining arrogantly and endlessly over a multitude of safeguards, modifications, and exceptions to the Rome Treaty. The government wanted membership for Britain—but its motivation was largely to avoid the potentially adverse economic consequences of nonmembership, rather than any genuine enthusiasm for participation in the European adventure. Consequently, it insisted on terms that would not interfere with any of the country's existing commercial or financial interests in the Commonwealth. Few concessions were offered. In effect, the government wanted to have its cake and eat it too. With the wisdom of hindsight, it is not difficult to see why Charles de Gaulle saw fit to veto Britain's application in January 1973.

By 1967, when Harold Wilson's cabinet made Britain's second application to the Common Market, attitudes had already begun to change significantly. The very fact that the approach was initiated by a Labor government, despite strong left-wing opposition in the party and in the unions, suggests the extent to which assumptions and perceptions were being modified during this period. Prime Minister Wilson apparently felt that he could cope satisfactorily with the problem of farm prices. He was most attracted by the prospective stimulus to economic growth that access to the European Community could provide. The hallmark of the moderate wing of the British Labor Party has always been a certain willingness to trade off the distribution objectives of policy for the goal of overall economic welfare—that is, to seek improvements for the laboring poor more through economic growth than through the redistribution of income shares. This seems to have been the strategy that the Wilson cabinet adopted in 1967, a strategy embodying preferences not noticeably different from those that the Macmillan cabinet evidently had in mind in 1961-1963. Despite Wilson's greater readiness to compromise, however, de Gaulle vetoed this application too.

Britain's third application in 1969, following de Gaulle's departure from the scene, marked the completion of the education process of the country's elites. No longer did the British try to set their own terms for membership in the Common Market. Throughout the lengthy negotiations in 1970-1971— which were begun by the Wilson cabinet and concluded, after the change of government, by the Heath cabinet—the British delegation's attitude in Brussels was refreshingly open and candid. Britain now wanted to join the Community even if it meant jettisoning the traditional Commonwealth connection. Neither Imperial Preference nor the Sterling Area would be allowed to stand in the way any longer. This was certainly a dramatic transformation in the orientation of British foreign economic policy. In this discussion I have argued that the explanation may be found in the sharply revised assessments of objective circumstances by nearly all the most influential groups in Britain.

Implications of Britain's Choice

What are the implications of this transformed orientation for the substance and direction of the decisionmaking process in British foreign economic policy in the future? Are there likely to be significant changes in either the machinery of government in Britain or in the country's prevailing attitudes toward major international economic organizations such as the GATT and the IMF?

In the short run, at least, changes are likely to be comparatively modest. The machinery of government in Britain is already well adapted to the decisionmaking requirements of membership in the European Community. The British have long belonged to a variety of multilateral intergovernmental organizations, and over the years London has effectively shaped its administrative apparatus to deal with the kinds of problems raised by participation in such organizations. Moreover, from 1961 onward, through their successive attempts to negotiate entry, the British acquired a considerable familiarity with the Community's administrative procedures as well. Consequently, the feeling in Whitehall is that no substantial changes in the established machinery of British government will be required, at least for the time being, particularly since very few governmental functions have as yet been transferred to the Community's institutions in Brussels. Wallace and Wallace say, "There appears to be general satisfaction with the efficient functioning of the machinery during the negotiations, which has bred confidence for the future. . . . The predominant mood is one of confidence in the capacity of existing structures and procedures."[12]

Likewise, for the time being, neither are existing attitudes toward major international economic organizations likely to be altered significantly because of the country's new European connection. Although Britain's high degree of involvement in the world economy has traditionally dictated a preference *in principle* for liberalism and multilateralism in global economic relations—as embodied in the rules and practices of the GATT and the IMF—*in practice* the country's policies were of course long qualified by the requirements of the Commonwealth connection. Imperial Preference constrained Britain's role in successive rounds of multilateral trade negotiations in the GATT; similarly, the Sterling Area moderated Britain's role in monetary reform negotiations in the IMF. British attitudes toward the GATT and the IMF are unlikely to change, in the short run at least, as a result of the shift from one regional orientation to another.

In the longer run, though, more substantial changes may be anticipated, as the European Community moves toward ever closer integration of its members' economies, and as more and more governmental functions are transferred directly to the Community's institutions in Brussels. The machinery of government in Britain will be challenged both by the blurring of distinctions between foreign and domestic economic policy and by the need for closer central coordination of the decisionmaking process in London. Traditionally, four departments monopolized responsibility for the management of British foreign economic policy—the Foreign Office, the Treasury, the Bank of England (nominally part of the Treasury, but in practice quite independent), and the Board of Trade (now the Department of Trade)—with the Foreign Office attempting to assure some semblance of central coordination.[13] However, as integration within the Community proceeds in future years, it will increasingly draw into international discussions questions that until now have been treated as matters solely of domestic concern, and as a result many of the "domestic" ministries will demand a louder voice in the decisionmaking process. This has already occurred in the case of the ministry of Agriculture, owing to the supplanting of national farming policies by the Community's common agricultural policy; other ministries (such as the department of Industry) can be expected in time to follow the same pattern. Accordingly, machinery for more formal coordination among different policy areas will ultimately be required. Because of the growing sensitivity of Community questions for domestic policies, it is unlikely that the Foreign Office can continue to play this coordinating role. More probably, responsibility for the function will pass to the Cabinet Office, which is best suited for the purpose.[14]

In turn, these developments will inevitably influence as well Britain's attitudes toward the GATT and the IMF. Britain's regional orientation toward the Commonwealth was always limited in scope, the degree of integration remaining small. Accordingly, it was natural for Britain to continue to take a prominent (if not an unqualified) role in promoting liberal, global solutions to problems of international commerce or finance. However, as integration in the Common Market proceeds, the British will be called upon to "think European" on a growing range of issues, and increasingly to sacrifice external interests for the sake of the European connection.[15] Britain's foreign economic policy will necessarily become much more regional, in a fundamental sense, than it ever was in the days of Imperial Preference and the Sterling Area, and its prominent role in the GATT and the IMF will necessarily be compromised. British attitudes on international trade and monetary problems can be expected to become progressively less inclined toward multilateral solutions.

However, none of these changes are apt to come about very rapidly. Much will depend on the actual pace achieved in the integration process in Europe, which until now has been anything but rapid. On issues as disparate as exchange rates and energy, so far Britain's European connection has not prevented the pursuit of policies that can be described only as highly nationalistic. Also, the underlying stability of the British decisionmaking process cannot be overstressed. What is most probable is not radical discontinuity but rather a process of gradual adaptation and small marginal adjustments of policy. Many years will pass before the transformed orientation of British foreign economic policy is likely to find expression in terms of significant alterations of governmental machinery or of attitudes toward major international economic organizations.

Notes

1. See for example Benjamin J. Cohen, *American Foreign Economic Policy: Essays and Comments* (New York: Harper & Row, 1968), Part 1.

2. Walter W. Heller, *New Dimensions of Political Economy* (New York: Norton, 1967), p. 5.

3. Cohen, *American Foreign Economic Policy*, pp. 20-29.

4. Cohen, *American Foreign Economic Policy*, pp. 1-10.

5. See, for example, Maxwell Stamp Associates, *The Free Trade Area Option: Opportunity for Britain* (London: Atlantic Trade Study, 1967); Lionel Gelber, *World Politics and Foeign Trade: Britain, USA and the West* (London: Atlantic Trade Study, 1968); Hans Liesner, *Atlantic Harmonization: Making Free Trade Work* (London: Atlantic Trade Study, 1968).

6. See Sir Roy Harrod, *Dollar-Sterling Collaboration: Basis for Initiative* (London: Atlantic Trade Study, 1967).

7. See, for example, U.W. Kitzinger, *The Challenge of the Common Market* (Oxford: Basil Blackwell, 1961); R.W.G. Mackey, *Towards a United States of Europe* (London: Hutchinson, 1961); John Pinder, *Britain and the Common Market* (London: Cresset Press, 1961).

8. See, for example, Robert L. Pfaltzgraff, Jr., *Britain Faces Europe* (Philadelphia: University of Pennsylvania Press, 1969); William Pickles, *Britain and Europe-How Much Has Changed?* (Oxford: Basil Blackwell, 1967); Edgar Pisani et al., *Problems of British Entry into the EEC*, Reports to the Action Committee for the United States of Europe (London: Chatham House and PEP, 1969); Harry G. Johnson et al., *Economics: Britain and the EEC*

(London: Longman, Green, 1969); James E. Meade, *UK, Common-wealth and Common Market: A Reappraisal*, 3rd ed. (London: Institute of Economic Affairs, 1970). (First edition was published in 1962.)

9. See Benjamin J. Cohen, *The Future of Sterling as an International Currency* (London: Macmillan, 1971), pp. 116-127.

10. Cohen, *The Future of Sterling*, pp. 128-141.

11. See, for example, Robert Pfaltzgraff, Jr., *Britain Faces Europe* and Robert Lieber, *British Politics and European Unity: Parties, Elites, and Pressure Groups* (Berkeley: University of California Press, 1970).

12. Helen Wallace and William Wallace, "The Impact of Community Membership on the British Machinery of Government," *Journal of Common Market Studies* (June 1973): 254-261.

13. William Wallace, "The Management of Foreign Economic Policy in Britain," *International Affairs* (London) (April 1974), pp. 251-267.

14. See Wallace and Wallace.

15. William Wallace, "British External Relations and the European Community: The Changing Context of Foreign Policy-Making," *Journal of Common Market Studies* (September 1973), pp. 28-52.

7

Europe's Money, America's Problem*

The United States and its allies are increasingly at odds over the direction of international monetary policies. More than a decade of monetary instability, which in European minds was brought on by America's self-serving leadership and policies, has once again fanned the desires of Europe's leaders to be more independent from the monetary policy of the United States. In spite of previous failures, high risks, and bleak prospects for success, the Europeans are once again going ahead with plans to create a monetary union—this time under the label European Monetary System (EMS). Whether or not they succeed, this latest attempt at monetary unification will create serious problems for the United States.

The last time the members of the European Economic Community (EEC) tried to create a monetary union was in 1971, when they agreed on an experimental narrowing of the margins of exchange-rate fluctuations among their currencies. Their currencies were to continue moving as a group vis-à-vis outside currencies within the range set by the fixed exchange rates established at the Bretton Woods conference in 1944. This was the origin of the "snake in the tunnel" (the snake referring to the narrow band within which Community currencies moved relative to one another, and the tunnel referring to the wider band within which the group moved vis-à-vis outside currencies).

Because of the monetary disturbances in 1971, when the gold convertibility of the dollar was suspended, the system was not put into effect until April 1972, and it ran into trouble almost immediately. Five of the Community's nine members—Britain, France, Denmark, Ireland, and Italy—were forced by economic

*Reprinted with permission from *Foreign Policy* 35 (Summer 1979). Copyright 1979 by the Carnegie Endowment for International Peace.

problems to withdraw from the arrangement (though Denmark later rejoined, while France tried and failed), and the tunnel itself was lost in March 1973, when fixed exchange rates were abandoned. It was clear that the experiment had not worked. All that remained, in effect, was a European monetary zone based on the mark.

Why did the Community's experiment fail? Originally, monetary unification had two motivations: to take another step on the road toward full economic and political union in Europe and to diminish dependence on the dollar while enhancing the EEC's own monetary independence. Lacking a common currency of their own, the European countries were obliged to rely on the dollar to achieve a kind of informal monetary integration. Since this also meant dependence on U.S. monetary policy, it implied a partial loss of sovereignty in this area.

The Europeans believed that formal currency unification was the necessary condition for the elimination of the dollar's hegemony. In addition, they thought a common currency, which would undoubtedly become attractive to others for private transaction and official reserve purposes, might enhance Europe's bargaining strength in international monetary discussions.

The experiment failed because member countries lacked the political will to adopt a common currency. National administrative hierarchies resisted all encroachments on their bureaucratic power and privileges; central bankers, in particular, were unwilling to become submerged in a European federal reserve system. National political leaderships refused to relinquish their traditional decisionmaking autonomy: governments were unwilling to transfer any significant portion of their formal policy sovereignty to Community institutions. The motivations for the experiment were insufficient to overcome these critical political obstacles. As a result, the dream of monetary unification itself lost momentum. As Fred Hirsch wrote in 1972:

> In this sense one can conclude that European monetary integration is not a serious issue. It belongs to that category of commitments that are endorsed by national authorities at the highest level, but are in fact ranked low in their priorities when it comes to the test.[1]

Yet the dream refuses to die. In April 1978, West German chancellor Helmut Schmidt unexpectedly put forth a radical new plan for a "zone of monetary stability" in Europe, and the momentum of monetary unification was suddenly regained. The proposed EMS was formally endorsed three months later at the Community summit meeting in Bremen. For most of the partner countries, the same motivations were at work—the desire both to promote political and economic union in Europe and to enhance European monetary independence in the world—as in 1971. In addition, specific national interests encouraged participation in the new plan. For Schmidt, the EMS offered an opportunity to slow the appreciation of the Deutsche mark, which had been hurting German exports. For others, it offered enlarged credit facilities to support weaker currencies in the exchange market.

After protracted negotiations, the Community agreed on the details of the EMS at a second summit in Brussels in December and launched the experiment in March 1989. Yet because national authorities continue to rank monetary union low in their practical priorities, despite their high-level rhetorical commitments, the fate of this new attempt will probably be no different from that of its predecessor.

A New Supersnake

The EMS essentially consists of three related elements, each building on already existing Community structures: first, an arrangement for linking exchange rates; second, a projected European Monetary Fund (EMF); and third, a system of credit facilities for mutual balance-of-payments support.

The arrangement for linking exchange rates builds on the old snake. In effect, the exchange rates of currencies that dropped out of the previous arrangement will gradually be brought back within the narrow margins of fluctuation ($\pm$ 2.25 percent) set by the joint float of the Deutsche mark and its satellite currencies, creating a new supersnake.

The French government immediately committed itself to reentry. After some hesitation, so too did Ireland; Italy agreed to join, although initially only within a broader band of movements of up to 6 percent in either direction (the so-called boa). Britain has thus far refused to commit itself at all, arguing that its balance-of-payments position is still too precarious to permit it to join. The pound will therefore continue to float independently, as it has since 1972. (As a result, the Irish and British pounds are no longer interchangeable; thus, one short-term effect of the EMS is to emphasize the separation between Ulster and the Irish Republic.)

The new system operates in much the same manner as its predecessor—that is, by linking the exchange rate of each currency directly to that of every other currency in a matrix known as the parity grid. Moreover, each currency is in theory tied indirectly to a European Currency Unit (ECU)—also the name of an ancient French silver coin—that is equal to a weighted basket of all the currencies. In principle, the ECU will be used as a sort of alarm bell (the "rattlesnake") to indicate when any single country's currency begins to diverge too far from the weighted average of currency values. However, because there is no obligation for that country to act, either in the exchange market or by adjusting domestic policies, it is not clear that the rattlesnake will have any real sting at all.

The projected EMF builds on the European Monetary Cooperation Fund (known as FECOM by its French initials), which was first established in April 1973 as part of the Community's earlier experiment with monetary unification. Intended as an embryonic European central bank, FECOM has not until now existed in anything but name. The EMS breathes life into FECOM, renamed the EMF, by pooling under its authority 20 percent of the gold and foreign currency reserves of all Community members. In exchange, members receive deposits in the EMF, denominated in ECUs, to be used in settling all kinds of intra-Community debts.

In effect, the ECU becomes a full-fledged reserve asset similar to the International Monetary Fund's Special Drawing Rights, although initially the ECU will be used only within the EEC. ECUs will be available to all members of the Community, even Britain. This should help strengthen the British pound and thus encourage Britain to participate in the joint float.

Eventually, all Community credit facilities are supposed to be brought under the aegis of the EMF, but for the time being the Fund is intended simply to be a mechanism for swapping existing reserves for ECUs. As in the past, credit will continue to take the form of loans made directly between member countries. The EMS increases the amount of credit available for short-term monetary support from the equivalent of 4.5 billion to 11 billion

ECUs (approximately $14 billion) and for medium-term mone-
tary support from the equivalent of 5.5 billion to 14 billion ECUs
($18 billion). These credit increases amount to a substantial con-
cession by West Germany, potentially the largest creditor in the
Community, to weaker members such as Britain, Ireland, and
Italy.

Weaker members have also been offered additional financial
concessions in the form of subsidized loans from the European
Investment Bank. Such transfers of resources are essential if the
weak countries are to withstand successfully the harsh disciplines of a joint float. Britain, Italy, and Ireland made clear all
along that increased transfers were an absolute condition for
their agreement to re-enter the snake. Italian and Irish hesitations were overcome only when sufficient financial concessions
were arranged. British hesitations were never overcome.

The Enshrined Dollar

International monetary stability presupposes national policy
coordination. If all countries set their policies independently,
policy conflict is the inevitable result (not all countries can
have balance-of-payments surpluses simultaneously), and the
stability of the system itself will be threatened. To preserve
monetary stability, governments must adhere to an organizing
principle that will insure consistency among national policies
and reduce the risk of policy conflict.

In the absence of a world central bank or automatic rules, consistency must stem from either a system organized around a
single country with acknowledged responsibilities and privileges as leader (hegemony) or a system of shared responsibility
and decision making (negotiation). The history of monetary
relations consists of a succession of attempts by the international
community to find such an organizing principle.

In practice, only a system of hegemony—which characterized
the operation of both the classical gold standard in the last decades before World War I and the Bretton Woods system in the
first decades after World War II—has ever succeeded in preserving stability for any length of time. In both cases, the monetary
system was organized around a single hegemonic leader—Great
Britain in the earlier period, the United States in the latter—
and the comparative lack of policy conflict was directly attrib-

utable to the stabilizing influence of the dominant national power.

The classical gold standard was dominated by Great Britain, the supreme economic power of the day. The British ensured international monetary stability by maintaining an open market for the exports of countries in balance-of-payments difficulties, providing contracyclical foreign long-term lending and acting as lender of last resort in times of exchange crisis, three tasks that only they had the resources to take on. These were not roles that Britain deliberately sought or even particularly welcomed. In fact, they were acquired, like the British Empire itself, in a fit of absent-mindedness.

After World War II, the United States, dominant then as Britain had been in the nineteenth century, rapidly assumed the same three managerial roles and took over as money manager of the world. Since international monetary reserves were in short supply, the United States became the principal source of global liquidity through its balance-of-payments deficits. America was accorded the unique privilege of liability-financing its deficits, and the dollar became enshrined not only as the principal currency for international trade and investment but also as the principal reserve asset for central banks. America's deficits became the universal solvent to keep the machinery of Bretton Woods running.

Like Britain in the nineteenth century, the United States did not deliberately seek the responsibility of global monetary stabilization. However, once it had the responsibility, Washington soon came to welcome it, clearly for reasons of self-interest. Being money manager of the world fit comfortably with America's new-found leadership of the Western alliance. The privilege of liability-financing deficits meant that America was freed from all balance-of-payments constraints and could spend as freely as necessary to promote national objectives. The United States could issue the world's principal currency in amounts consistent with its own policy priorities and not necessarily with those of foreign dollar holders. Foreign dollar holders conceded this policy autonomy to the United States because it contributed directly to their own economic rehabilitation. America's pursuit of self-interest also was seen as being in their interest.

In effect, Washington's allies granted the United States

special privileges to act unilaterally to promote American interests. Washington, in turn, condoned its allies' use of the system to promote their own economic prosperity, even if this was occasionally done at the short-term expense of the United States. American policy was demonstrably nationalistic, but it was a nationalism that could credibly be described as benign rather than malign. The United States acknowledged the connection between its own interest and the stability of the overall system and acted accordingly, even when that meant compromising national policy to accommodate the interests of others.

Frustration and Deadlock

Since the breakdown of the Bretton Woods system, the United States has continued to pursue what has always been the key objective of its policy, to reduce any balance-of-payments constraint on the government's decisionmaking capacity in order to increase the country's self-interested freedom of action in domestic and foreign affairs. America's nationalistic approach to monetary policy has not changed and is still largely benign rather than malign.

What has changed is the system itself or, more specifically, the conditions required to organize and maintain a hegemonic monetary system like Bretton Woods. Two conditions are essential. First, hegemonic leadership must in fact be responsible. The economic policy of the world's money manager must be truly stabilizing, transferring neither inflationary nor deflationary impulses to the rest of the world. Second, hegemonic leadership must be regarded as legitimate, generating neither resentment nor policy conflict over the system's benefits and costs. Today, neither of these conditions exists.

In a hegemonic regime, the possibility always exists that sooner or later, accidentally or deliberately, the leader will act irresponsibly and take advantage of its special position to initiate policies that destabilize the world economy. That is precisely what happened in 1965 when Lyndon Johnson made his decision to fight a war in Vietnam and a war on poverty simultaneously. America's economy began to overheat, the virus of inflation began to spread, and ultimately the whole world was infected. This set the stage for the pivotal year 1971, when the

Bretton Woods system was brought down by President Nixon's decision to suspend the gold convertibility of the dollar.

American policymakers did not fully anticipate the disruptive consequences of their own actions and in the years since have needed little encouragement to try to act more responsibly in international monetary affairs. But now the genie is out of the bottle. America's leadership has proved it can be destabilizing, and as a result foreign distrust of American policy has grown to epidemic proportions, particularly since the Carter administration took office.

Today the political and economic conditions that originally made American hegemony acceptable—or, at any rate, tolerable—no longer exist. America's dominant international position has been seriously eroded. Foreign economies are no longer as weak and uncompetitive as they were immediately after the war, and foreign governments are no longer willing to accept a political role subordinate to that of the United States. America's leadership has come under increasing challenge. The United States is still acknowledged as *primus inter pares* in the world economy, but it is by no means still universally accepted as *primus motor*.

The effect of these changed attitudes and perceptions was evident in the heated debate in 1976-1977 between the United States and its major allies over the so-called locomotive approach to recovery from the Great Recession of 1974-1975. America's own expansionary monetary policy was being guided essentially by domestic considerations. But since expansion at home could credibly be argued to aid recovery abroad, the United States urged other locomotive economies, such as Germany and Japan, to follow America's lead and stimulate their own growth rates, too, in hopes that this would help to pull weaker economies out of the stagnation that had persisted since 1975.

At one time, America's leadership might have been heeded. In the changed circumstances of the 1970s, however, it was resisted, and the result was frustration and deadlock. Germany and Japan retorted that stagnation elsewhere was not their problem. Further expansion of their economies, they argued, would be neither desirable (because of the inflationary pressures that might be generated) nor even possible (because of domestic political and institutional constraints on policy). Moreover, they claimed that in any event the stimulative impact on weaker economies would probably be comparatively small. Instead of following the United States, they criticized it for allowing its own balance-of-payments to get out of control and its currency to depreciate sharply in the exchange markets. In some quarters, America was even accused of trying to use dollar depreciation to gain an unfair advantage in trade—malign nationalism at its worst.

These attacks on the United States have recently cooled down because the economic performance of the major industrial economies is converging. But the underlying tensions between the United States and its allies in Europe and Japan remain and are symptomatic of a far deeper malaise in international monetary relations. Conditions are no longer propitious for an American hegemony, yet the Europeans and Japanese have so far resisted American blandishments to share explicitly in the responsibility for global monetary stabilization. Some organizing principle remains necessary to ensure consistency among national policies. The lesson of the locomotive debate is that American hegemony is failing, and the means for establishing a new cooperative regime of shared responsibility have yet to be found.

Europe's Gain, America's Loss

This is where the EMS comes in—more accurately, where it could come in, if successfully implemented. Until now, a fundamental problem for the Europeans in international monetary relations has been their inability to negotiate with the United States on an equal basis, because they are divided by separate currencies and disparate policies. Only Germany enjoys anything near America's international monetary influence. Other countries are individually unable to challenge America's leading role in monetary affairs, a role they may resent but can do little about. A regime of shared responsibility constructed on these terms would only perpetuate the political subordination of the Europeans—and this, in turn, would no doubt only insure more discord than harmony in international decisionmaking.

In creating the ECU, the EMS could reduce Europe's historical dependence on the dollar and the monetary policy of the United States by offering Community members (and perhaps eventually other countries) an attractive alternative asset for reserve, and possibly even transaction, purposes. U.S. policymakers have already begun to relax their traditional resistance to reform proposals intended to reduce the dollar's reserve role.

The problem, however, is that no suitable alternative to the dollar presently exists. The only other national currency that has come to play any significant reserve role is the Deutsche mark, and that has been in spite of the determined opposition of German monetary authorities, who do not wish to find themselves in the same position in the future as the Americans are today. The ECU could fill this void and bring about greater monetary independence for Europe. Successful creation of its own common asset is the *sine qua non* for Europe to be able to address the United States on a basis of parity. And that in return is the *sine qua non* for successful stabilization of global monetary relations.

Europe's enhanced bargaining strength would be gained at the expense of America's traditional freedom of action in monetary affairs. Hence, in this limited sense, Europe's gain would necessarily be America's loss. But America's traditional freedom of action is scarcely what it used to be. Policy autonomy, in reality, has already been seriously eroded in spite of—or even because of—continued international use of the dollar.

To be sure, insofar as foreigners continue to acquire dollars, the United States is able to continue liability-financing its deficits. But because of the magnitude of foreign accumulations over the years, the dollar's international role has now become a two-edged sword. The dollar overhang—the amount of U.S. currency held overseas—numbers in the hundreds of billions of dollars, and when confidence in U.S. policy wanes, as it has in recent years, and dollar holders decide to switch into available foreign currencies, the United States finds it much more difficult than before to pursue its objectives without regard for its balance of payments.

In this sense, the United States has little to lose and much to gain from Europe's enhanced bargaining strength. As the locomotive debate made abundantly clear, U.S. policy leadership today is as likely to be resisted as heeded, and the United States surely loses more from such conflict than it could possibly gain by insisting on the prerogatives of a failing hegemony. Insofar as the EMS encourages the Europeans to share explicitly in the responsibility for global monetary stabilization, America could benefit from the reduced risk of international policy conflict.

The EMS could enable the Europeans to speak with one voice and thus greatly enhance their overall bargaining strength in international monetary discussions. A regime of shared responsibility could then be established that would not perpetuate Europe's political subordination and that would have a better chance of producing concord instead of conflict. In place of an obsolete hegemony, a new organizing principle of cooperative management would finally be within reach.

In fact, however, the chances that the EMS will hold together are slight. Present conditions are not auspicious for linking the Community's currencies together on a sustained basis. Inflation rates in Europe remain highly divergent, from 3 percent in Germany to more than 12 percent in Italy, and consequently the arrangement is bound to come under strain. Schmidt has been obliged to promise a tight rein on credit transfers in order to placate his domestic critics, who have no wish to finance the presumed inflationary excesses of others.

Policy coordination in practice, therefore, is likely to bring the high inflation rates of some countries downward toward Germany's inflation rate, as it has in the existing system, and this in turn is likely to create unemployment problems in those countries. The potential for price discipline built into the joint float is attractive to President Valéry Giscard d'Estaing of France, since it complements and reinforces his present anti-inflation policies. By contrast, the implied discipline threatens the Irish and Italians and explains their insistence on increased transfers of resources through the European Investment Bank. Similar fears prompted Britain's decision to remain outside the exchange-rate arrangement.

Other strains could develop in the joint float. Policy coordination might fail to equalize inflation rates sufficiently, or some of the weaker members might not be able to bear up under the joint price discipline. Either way the arrangement would be put under stress, and speculators would have a field day. Member governments would be faced with the Hobson's choice of either altering their exchange rates frequently to avoid speculative buildups or futilely defending their linked rates with prolonged and costly intervention. Either course would make a mockery of their avowed goal of creating a "zone of monetary stability."

The chances of failing are further aggravated by doubts about the dollar. Investors wishing to switch out of dollars are not attracted to weaker currencies such as the Italian lira or the

French franc. They want strong currencies such as the German mark, the Dutch guilder, the Japanese yen, or the Swiss franc. Renewed dollar sales would create additional pressure to raise the price of the stronger currencies relative to their weaker partners and consequently add even greater strains to the arrangement.

A Bitter Pill

In the face of these problems, the priority that member governments attach to participation in the system becomes telling. In order for it to succeed, the EMS must be a serious issue and not merely the product of preoccupation with outside instabilities. Governments must be willing to sacrifice some of their sovereignty, and this they have yet to do. They have once again endorsed the idea of monetary union at the highest political level, but they have not yet ranked it high among their practical policy objectives. Community spirit has not been conspicuous as member governments have all approached the project in a relentlessly self-interested manner, seizing the occasion to extract maximum national advantage for themselves.

The most probable outcome, therefore, is that the EMS, like its predecessor, will simply fail. Sooner or later, some weaker members will again be forced to abandon the joint float, while the rest struggle to preserve a truncated zone of stability around the mark.

The failure of the new supersnake would not necessarily have any serious destabilizing impact on international monetary relations. After all, the dissection of the previous snake was managed in a harmonious fashion. But given the high hopes attached to this latest experiment, it is difficult to imagine all traces of discord being avoided. More likely, failure would formalize the monetary fragmentation inside the Community, relegate nonparticipants to second class status, and make the goal of European monetary independence even more remote. Moreover, it would probably unsettle the exchange markets further and put additional pressure on the dollar.

On the other hand, the EMS could beat the odds and somehow manage to stay together. Even then, however, it would not necessarily succeed in increasing monetary stability in Europe. If member governments are constantly under pressure to outguess or outgun speculators, the situation could be even more dangerous and unstable than if their currencies were not linked.

An additional complication could arise to destabilize economic conditions further. In principle, the EMS participants maintain the joint float by buying and selling one another's currencies rather than the dollar. This was the rule in the old arrangement, too. But in practice, intervention was often in dollars, and at times of strain it was poorly coordinated if not openly at cross-purposes. Similarly uncoordinated intervention with dollars in the new system would add greatly to the volatility of the exchange markets and could even further complicate America's attempts to stabilize the dollar.

Even if the EMS stays together and succeeds in reducing inflation differentials and effectively coordinating national policies, it is doubtful that the goals of a cooperative monetary regime or international monetary stability will be any closer. Successfully linked exchange rates could boost confidence in most of the Community's currencies and thereby broaden considerably the array of currencies available to investors anxious to switch out of dollars. If and when the ECU, which now is intended solely for use by central banks within the Community, becomes available to nonmember central banks or to private investors, sales of dollars could become a flood, making the dollar's prolonged depreciation in 1977-79 appear modest by comparison. That, too, clearly would not be in the U.S. interest.

Ultimately, the success of the EMS in stabilizing currency values and bringing the world closer to a cooperative monetary regime depends on the Europeans themselves—specifically, on what motivates them to try yet again for monetary union. Greater monetary independence is manifestly one of their primary motivations. But monetary independence for what purpose? Are the Europeans trying to secure their position and take on part of the responsibility for global monetary stabilization? Or are they simply trying to shield themselves from a hegemonic leadership that they no longer regard as responsible? Put differently, are they animated by a sense of confidence in their relations with the United States or by a sense of distrust? This is the real issue of the EMS for the United States.

An EMS motivated by a sense of confidence would pose few difficulties for the United States. The problem, however, is that cooperation with the United States does not seem to be what the Europeans have in mind. Much more crucial to their thinking is endemic distrust of American policy, symbolized by the system's stated purpose of creating a zone of monetary stability in Europe. Because the sharp decline of the dollar in 1977-1979 wreaked havoc in European financial markets, the principal attraction of the EMS for most members is that it would help shield them from similar instabilities.

Thus, isolation from America, not cooperation, seems to be the main purpose of the experiment, and this clearly poses difficulties for the United States. Most likely, the Europeans will choose to distance themselves from perceived malign American nationalism, pursuing instead their own policy priorities within the framework of their Community. This certainly will not reduce the potential for policy conflict in global monetary relations.

The U.S. dilemma is that it has few responses to this latest European attempt at monetary unification. With its dominant international position seriously eroded, the United States can no longer shape its external environment unilaterally to suit its own interests. As the locomotive debate made abundantly clear, Americans must learn to accommodate the interests of other nations—a bitter pill to swallow for those whose memories go back to the halcyon days of hegemony. The United States cannot attempt to block or influence the evolution of the EMS, for the Europeans regard it as a strictly Community affair. Any intervention by Washington would be regarded as meddlesome interference and would only further complicate the situation.

The most America can hope to do, therefore, is to influence events indirectly by acting to restore confidence in the responsibility of American policy. The Europeans must be convinced that there is really no need to isolate themselves from the United States; that whatever may have happened in the past, America is determined not to be a source of instability in the future. At the technical level, this means that Washington must not weaken its commitment, announced in November 1978, to intervene more actively in the exchange markets to counter disorderly conditions. More broadly, it means reinforcing current programs to deal with energy and inflation.

In short, the only possible response by the United States to the EMS is to get its own economic house in order and find a basis for mutual trust with the other major nations of the West—a necessary condition for cooperative management of global monetary affairs. If the United States could do that, it would not have to worry about the EMS.

Notes

1. Fred Hirsch, "The Politics of World Money, *The Economist,* August 5, 1972, p. 57.

8
European Financial Integration and National Banking Interests*

Why is the European Community unable to achieve formal financial integration? At a time of rapid innovation, deregulation, and structural change in global financial markets, the persistent refusal of such key EC members as France and Italy to fully liberalize capital flows on a regional basis seems curious, even anachronistic.[1] Here is a group of countries—ostensibly a "Community"—whose very *raison d'être* is supposed to be creation of a Common Market. In 1985, the ambition of an "area without frontiers" was solemnly reaffirmed when all twelve member-governments adopted a Single European Act, aiming for "completion" of the so-called Internal Market by 1992. And in late 1986 this was followed by a formal agreement to remove controls on a wide variety of capital movements within the Community—the first such EC accord in nearly a quarter century.[2] Yet, in practice, resistance to the collective goal of full financial integration remains strong in individual European states. How can we explain this apparently anomalous behavior?

The short answer, of course, is "politics." Elements of politics as well as economics are obviously entangled here. But what exactly do we mean by "politics" in this context? That is the question to be addressed in this essay, focusing on the main political factors that may help to explain continued resistance to the economic goal of financial integration in Europe. Although particular reference will be made to the three core continental countries of France, Germany and Italy, the scope of the essay is purely conceptual. The aim is to aid in developing a possible research agenda for future empirical study.

---

*From Pier-Carlo Padoan and Paolo Guerrieri (eds.), *The Political Economy of European Integration* (London: Harvester Wheatsheaf, 1989), ch. 6.

Because of the tangle of economics and politics here, the question addressed in this essay is best approached using formal analytical concepts and models drawn from the contemporary scholarly literature on International Political Economy (IPE). Methodologically, I shall argue below, financial integration may be understood as a kind of public good in scarce supply. That scarcity of supply, in turn, may be understood as the consequence of strategic interactions among key actors at two separate but interrelated levels of operation: at the Community level, where the actors are the member governments, each one pursuing its own national policy preferences within the web of regional economic interdependence; and at the national level, where actors include all domestic groups with actual or potential influence over those governmental policy preferences. The challenge for the analyst is to comprehend the dynamics of each of these two levels of operation as well as how they interact and evolve over time. The purpose is to gain insight not only into what it is that constrains the supply of the public good of financial integration in Europe but also how its supply might eventually be increased in the future.

Meanings   of   Financial   Integration

To begin, we must be clear about what we mean by financial integration. In common usage, the word "integration" simply denotes the bringing together of constituent parts into a whole. In economics, however, the meaning of the term is not nearly so clear-cut. Three distinctions, in particular, have to be borne in mind.

First is a distinction between integration as a *process of change* and as a *state of being*. Regarded as a process, integration in economics encompasses measures designed to abolish permanently various forms of discrimination between actors belonging to different national states; viewed as a state of being, it can be represented by the permanent absence of such discrimination between national states. The process of integration takes place over the period of transition during which actors adjust to the abolition of discrimination. When these adjustments are completed, integration as a state of being comes into operation.

Second is a distinction between integration in a *negative* sense and in a *positive* sense. In a negative sense, integration simply means the removal of barriers at the frontier to economic intercourse between actors belonging to different national states; in a positive sense, it involves in addition standardization or harmonization of all relevant *domestic* policies, requirements and regulations. Integration in the negative sense is a necessary condition for the promotion of economic intercourse, but may not be sufficient. Integration in the positive sense may be sufficient but not necessary.

Third is a distinction between variations in the *scope* of integration, depending on the range of transactions involved. The scope of integration may be conceived narrowly or broadly, depending on the number of types or categories of operations encompassed by the abolition of discrimination.

Each of these three distinctions is important in defining the meaning of financial integration for the purposes of this essay:

Process of change versus state of being. This distinction is important because it relates directly to the time profile of the benefits and costs of financial integration. The benefits of financial integration, as we shall see, largely accrue only when integration operates as a state of being; the costs, by contrast, are largely associated with the transition period when adjustments are still required of many of the actors involved. As a result, a trade-off is generated between (fairly certain) costs in the short term and (rather less certain) benefits in the longer term, with the formal or informal comparison of the two affected by each actor's own effective discount rate for comparing present and estimated future values. Since such a calculus is undoubtedly a key factor in helping to explain the persistence of resistance to financial integration in Europe, it is clear that this essay must take explicit account of *both* stages in defining the meaning of financial integration for analytical purposes.

Negative versus positive. This distinction is important because of the heavily regulated nature of the financial-services sector as an industry. In a negative sense, financial integration may be understood simply to be synonomous with free trade in financial assets (capital mobility); that is, with the elimination of all exchange controls on relevant transactions. But given the vast differences in domestic policies applied to financial activity in each country, affecting rights of establishment or operation, integration in this sense alone would be far from sufficient to remove all forms of discrimination between national states. Integration in a positive sense would be required as well, in the form of standardization or harmonization of all domestic requirements and regulations relating to rights of establishment and operation for financial enterprises, to truly achieve an "area without frontiers." This is the meaning that will be employed in this essay. Financial integration will be understood to be synonomous not just with capital mobility but with mobility of institutions and institutional activity; that is, with the freedom to provide financial services anywhere in the Community—one genuine market.

Scope. This distinction is important because of the close functional links that exist between different types or categories of financial transactions. Commercial banking *per se*, stripped to its essence, consists simply of the business of taking deposits and making loans. But banks in practice also engage in a wide variety of other related market activities, from securities underwriting and trading to investment management or leasing, all overlapping in one way or another with other classes of financial intermediary (e.g. investment banks, brokerage houses, thrift institutions). And these activities, in turn, are closely related to and affected by the public policies and operations of a variety of relevant governmental agencies, including most importantly the central bank of each country. Where do we draw the line for analytical purposes?

For the purposes of this brief essay, the line must certainly be drawn to exclude the policies and operations of central banks and other purely governmental (i.e. non-market) agencies. We must not confuse financial integration with other broader concepts such as monetary union or currency union. A monetary union involves the unification and joint management of the monetary policies of participating countries; a currency union (or exchange-rate union) involves the permanent fixing of exchange rates between participating countries. Neither one of these is a necessary prerequisite for the other: historical examples abound both of currency unions between countries with formally independent central banks (e.g., the Scandanavian Currency Union of the nineteenth century) as well as of monetary unions between countries with formally independent exchange rates (e.g., the Belgium-Luxembourg Economic Union of the twentieth century). Nor is either monetary or currency union a necessary prerequisite for full liberalization of nongovernmental capital movements and activities (as, e.g., the old British-led sterling area well demonstrated in the years during and after World War II). The definition of financial integration to be used here will thus assume the continued existence of both formally independent central banks and potentially variable exchange rates. Our focus will be on the integration of market operations alone.

Furthermore, within the broad range of market operations, our focus will be on commercial-banking operations alone, excluding the related activities of other classes of financial intermediary. The excuse here is purely one of convenience: concentrating on banks alone makes the problem a good deal more analytically tractable, albeit at some loss in terms of descriptive richness. Fortunately, the loss would not appear to be great, since, as we shall see, much of what can be said about banks (whether private or state-owned) may easily be extended to other market institutions as well. Once developed in the more narrow context of banking relations, this essay's analytical approach can be readily applied to a much wider range of financial transactions and transactors.

In summary, then, financial integration is defined for the purposes of this essay as a process of change as well as a state of being, encompassing all measures of liberalization or harmonization required to create a single market for commercial banking services anywhere in the European Community. The problem, once again, is to explain why this objective is so difficult to achieve.

Benefits of Financial Integration

Resistance to the objective of financial integration in the Community would be relatively easy to understand if there were little or no potential benefit to be derived from the phenomenon. However, that does not seem to be the case. Quite the contrary, in fact. Conventional economic analysis suggests quite convincingly that, in practice, rather substantial gains could be expected to accrue to such a group of countries from the creation among them of a single market for commercial banking services. Economic welfare would be increased to the extent that opportunities for efficient financial intermediation are effectively enhanced.[3]

Intermediation through banking operations contributes to

economic welfare in at least five separate ways: (a) by providing mechanisms for the disposal of savings or financial
surpluses and the financing of investments or financial deficits;
(b) by helping to bridge the different portfolio preferences of
surplus and deficit actors; (c) by allocating funds to the most
efficient users; (d) by enabling risks to be diversified and transferred from ultimate savers, and (e) by allowing changes to be
made in the structure of portfolios. These five effects have a
positive impact on real-resource efficiency, as compared with a
world of no banking intermediation, by influencing not only the
allocation of investible funds among competing claims but also
the aggregate volume of saving and investment. Such gains
accrue to each country separately from the operation of its own
national banking system. By extension, an integration of
national systems may confidently be assumed to add to such
gains *in toto* by opening up new opportunities for savers or
investors to take advantage of any cross-border differences in
the price or non-price characteristics of available banking
services, leading toward equalization of rates of return on
comparable assets and liabilities and/or closer covariance of
such rates. In effect, the economies of participating countries
would be brought closer to the elusive ideal of Pareto-optimal-
ity in general-equilibrium terms.

Note, however, the two words "general" and "equilibrium."
The key to understanding the persistence of resistance to
financial integration in Europe, despite its evident potential
benefits, lies therein.

Consider first the word "equilibrium," a central concept in
conventional economic analysis, which following standard
practice has been defined by one economist as synonomous with
"a constellation of selected interrelated variables so adjusted to
one another that no tendency to change prevails."[4] This concept clearly implies a state of being rather than a process of
change. That is, it focuses thought on conditions prevailing
after all adjustments have been completed, rather than on the
ease or difficulty of the adjustments themselves. Quite naturally, use of the equilibrium concept tends to distract attention
from any burdens or losses that may be associated with the
requisite period of transition. Or to put the point differently: it
encourages thinking about comparative statics, contrasting before and after, rather than about the dynamics of adjustment,
how we get from here to there. Benefits of final outcomes are

stressed, rather than the costs of the process of change required to achieve them.

All of this is perfectly legitimate, of course, for the purposes of pure economic theory or model-building. But it can be seriously misleading when applied unquestioningly to practical problems of political economy such as the issue of financial integration in Europe. To understand why financial integration is resisted (its "politics"), analysis must stress costs as well as benefits, the difficulties of transition as well as the allure of the final outcome—because that is surely what the key actors themselves are always doing! In any given actor's rational calculation of the attractiveness of a single market for banking services, the burden of adjustment is bound to figure prominently, particularly since costs must be borne "up front" long before most benefits can be expected to accrue. Costs, moreover, being immediate, can be calculated with a higher degree of certainty than more remote potential gains. It would hardly be surprising, therefore, if quite a high discount rate were to be used by many of the most important actors involved when estimating the present value of future gains to be compared with losses in the short term. Resistance may result directly from this difference in the time profile of the benefits and costs of financial integration.

Related to this is the word "general," another central concept in conventional economic analysis, which may be taken to be synonomous with effects for all actors together rather than for any one actor separately. As most commonly applied, this concept is allowed to imply an identity of interest between the particular and the whole. That is, if something is regarded as beneficial *in toto*, then it tends to be assumed to be beneficial *inter se* as well. Quite naturally, such usage serves to distract attention from any divergences that may exist between individual incentives and collective incentives. Or to put the point differently: it encourages thinking of all "public" goods as if they were "private" goods as well. Resistance to anything that can be expected to raise economic welfare in the aggregate, such as financial integration in Europe, may therefore be dismissed simply as myopic or irrational.

In reality, however, not all "public" goods are "private" goods too. Quite the contrary, in fact. Public goods are defined by two key characteristics: (a) non-rivalry (meaning that one individual's consumption or use of the good does not reduce its availability to anyone else); and (b) non-excludability (meaning that once the good is provided, it is available to all).

Private goods, by contrast, exist where one individual's consumption precludes use by others, and where providers can ensure that only those individuals who pay for the good may obtain it. In the case of private goods, obviously, market incentives exist for adequate overall supply by individual producers. In the case of public goods, on the other hand, as is well known, market production in the aggregate is bound to be suboptimal because of the lack of such incentives. A divergence exists between individual interests and the collective interest, and "free riding" is encouraged even where *general* benefit can be demonstrated. Why should potential providers be willing to bear any of the costs of production if supply must be more or less automatically available to all? Why should potential consumers be willing to pay any price if no one can be excluded from use? Resistance in such cases is by no means myopic or irrational.

European financial integration is arguably one such case. True, individual services to savers and investors are essentially private goods that would presumably continue to command a price even after creation of a single banking market in the Community. But there are also undeniable public-good elements in the broader externalities to be expected from the enhancement of opportunities for efficient financial intermediation—the anticipated positive impacts on the allocation of investable funds and the aggregate volume of a savings and investment—that would be freely available for all. Insofar as this is true, financial integration may therefore be understood as a kind of public good in scarce supply. General welfare advantages notwithstanding, integration will be resisted to the extent that divergences exist between collective incentives and individual incentives, with such divergences in turn arising from differences in the gains and losses that can be anticipated by each actor separately. For the question addressed by this essay— Why is European financial integration so difficult to achieve?— the answer most appropriately must be sought in these public-goods aspects of the problem. There, ultimately, is where we find the real meaning of "politics" in this context.

Systemic Analysis of Financial Integration

Analysis of financial integration as a public good necessarily focuses attention on strategic interactions among the key actors involved. And foremost among these actors are of course the Community's several national governments, which as formally sovereign entities still retain ultimate political authority in Europe. A useful starting point for discussion, therefore, is to be found at the Community level, in the incentives that may exist for either cooperation or conflict among EC member states on this sensitive issue of economic policy. As indicated, particular reference will be made here to the core continental countries of France, Germany and Italy.

Models for discussion at the Community level are provided by that branch of contemporary IPE literature that is devoted to so-called *systemic* analysis of the politics of international economic relations.[5] The basic unit of analysis in this type of literature is the "state," ordinarily identified with each country's central governmental decisionmakers. States are assumed to be unitary, rational, and egoistic actors. "Unitary" means that the internal processes by which state policy preferences are determined may, in effect, be disregarded. "Rational" means that policy preferences are consistent and ordered, and that states are capable of calculating the costs and benefits of alternative courses of action in order to maximize their utility in terms of those preferences. And "egoistic" means that their utility functions are independent of one another, in the sense that no state actor gains or loses utility simply because of the gains or losses of others. (They are self-interested, not altruistic.) The methodological value of these assumptions is that they make state preferences constants rather than variables for purpose of analysis: conceptions of self-interest are given and invariant. Discussion is thus able to focus entirely on constraints and incentives for state behavior that derive from the broader system of inter-state relations—hence the rubric "systemic" analysis. Behavior, in Kenneth Waltz's language, is studied from the "outside-in."[6]

Viewed from this perspective, the resistance of individual EC members to the collective goal of financial integration seems less anomalous than may have appeared at first glance. Certainly the broad economic benefits to be expected from creation of a single Community banking market would seem to accord with each government's rational conception of its own self-interest. Incentives clearly do exist for members to cooperate in pursuit of this objective—but only insofar as prospective gains to them individually may safely be assumed to exceed any future losses they might incur; that is, only insofar as the trade-off between the joint goal of financial integration and egoistic national policy preference appears on balance to remain favorable in each state's separate benefit-cost calculation. Otherwise, the public good will be perceived by at least some of them as a private "bad." Member governments may rationally resist increasing the supply of a public good if it threatens to conflict seriously with the achievement of other established objectives of national policy.

In practice, financial integration is indeed likely to threaten (or be thought to threaten) conflict with at least two established policy objectives of at least some EC members. Creation of a single banking market, as noted, would mean free movement of capital leading towards equalization and/or covariance of rates of return on comparable assets and liabilities. At the macroeconomic level, these effects obviously would make it more difficult, if not impossible, for governments individually to preserve autonomy of national monetary policy for domestic stabilization purposes. Likewise, at the microeconomic level, they would make it more difficult, if not impossible, for governments individually to influence the allocation of available financial resources among different industrial sectors or regions of the domestic economy. Independence of monetary policy and discretion in credit allocation are both highly valued "nationalistic" goals in the utility functions of most EC states: the former, especially, in Germany and Italy; the latter, especially, in France. The risk of losses to any of these countries in terms of either of these goals would suffice to make a single banking market seem to them a private bad rather than a public good, creating divergences between collective incentives and individual incentives for promoting the integration objective.

The risk of losses might not in actual fact be very serious. The public good might not really be so bad. At the macroeconomic level, for instance, many economists assert that autonomy of national monetary policy is in practical terms illusory owing to the assumed absence of any long-run trade-off between inflation and unemployment in individual economies. The basic argument in favor of an independent monetary policy is that it can presumably be used to achieve and maintain a welfare-maximizing balance between inflation and unemployment; in technical language, to achieve and maintain some preferred point on the country's Phillips curve, which is assumed to be negatively sloped. In the long run, however, most economists agree, the Phillips curve is likely to be not negatively sloped but rather vertical, at the "natural" rate of unemployment, owing to the inevitable impact of all attempts to alter the inflation-unemployment mix on inflationary expectations. In effect, the (negatively sloped) short-run Phillips curve merely shifts up or down along the (vertical) long-run Phillips curve, with only transitory effects on output or unemployment rates. And indeed, if the private sector's expectations are "rational" in the sense used in economic theory today, not even transitory effects will occur; and independent monetary policy merely permits a government to choose its own inflation rate, but does nothing to achieve domestic stabilization in real terms. In that "ideal" case, loss of monetary policy would threaten no true loss at all.

The world in which we live, however, is not so ideal. Expectations in reality normally are not "rational" in this sense. Stickiness of wages and prices does make for a negatively sloped Phillips curve in the short run, which in turn means that an independent monetary policy is indeed capable of influencing the inflation-unemployment mix at least transitorily. The longer such transitory effects may be expected to persist, the greater will be a government's incentive to do all it can to preserve its own monetary autonomy; and this incentive will be greater still if, in practice, the authorities tend to employ an effectively high discount rate in comparing the benefit of such transitory effects (which would be immediately lost in the event of financial integration) with the present value of financial integration's potential future gains. The nationalistic goal of an independent monetary policy is by no means an illusion.

Likewise, at the microeconomic level, many economists assert that discretion in credit allocation is illusory owing to the fungibility of money in financial markets. If a government tries to use the banking system as an instrument of industrial planning or regional development, encouraging certain kinds or directions of lending at the expense of others, the markets will in this view simply make appropriate adjustments to ensure that available financial resources still go to sectors or regions where rates of return appear highest; and the more "perfect" the markets, the swifter the adjustments. But, of course, in the real world markets are rarely as "perfect" as that—certainly not in countries like France or Italy. In such countries, governments are indeed capable of effectively channelling credit allocation, at least to a degree; and the incentive to preserve that capability will obviously vary directly both with the degree of *de facto* control at present and with the effective discount rate applied to the potential gains of financial integration in the future. The nationalistic goal of discretion in credit allocations is no illusion either.

If neither goal is an illusion, then it is not at all surprising that individual EC members like France or Italy, behaving as rational egoistic actors, would persist in their resistance to the collective goal of financial integration despite the broad economic benefits to be expected. For at least some such countries, the public good does undoubtedly look like a private bad. That is, prospective costs in terms of their own established policy preferences undoubtedly do diminish incentives to cooperate on this Community issue, particularly if each separately can hope to free ride on any joint initiatives by others—in effect, enjoying the efficiency gains of a freer EC banking market without having to pay any of the price. In this respect, the situation is a prime example of the classic problem of collective action analyzed so cogently by Mancur Olson more than two decades ago[7] and recently summarized by Robert Keohane as follows:

> In situations calling for collective action, cooperation is necessary to obtain a good that (insofar as it is produced at all) will be enjoyed by all members of a set of actors, whether they have contributed to its provision or not. When each member's contribution to the cost of the good is small as a proportion of its total cost, self-interested individuals are likely to calculate that they are better off by not contributing, since their contribution is costly to them but has an imperceptible effect on whether the good is produced. Thus . . . the dominant strategy for an egoistic individualist is to defect, by not contributing to the

production of the good. Generalizing this calculation yields the conclusion that the collective good will not be produced, or will be underproduced, despite the fact that its value to the groups is greater than its cost.[8]

The problem of collective action, in turn, may be efficiently analyzed using the intellectual tools of formal game theory. The observable tendency towards underproduction of public (collective) goods is equivalent, in game-theoretic terms, to saying that any potential for joint gain through cooperation may well be destroyed by competition over relative shares. In a variable-sum game, by definition, players have interests that are neither completely irreconcilable nor entirely harmonious. Incentives exist, therefore, not only for cooperation but also for conflict (noncooperation, defection), depending on how potential "payoffs" happen to be structured in any particular instance.

In principle, any number of "payoff structures" may be conceived where cooperation rather than conflict would be encouraged as the dominant strategy for all players. In practice, however, such games appear to be comparatively rare in relations among sovereign states. Much more common is a broad class of games where quite the contrary lends to hold true; that is, where despite the prospective benefits of cooperation, the payoff structure is such that at least some state players can rationally hope to gain more by instead defecting to act on their own. That is where the parallel with public goods comes in. For if some or all states do try to act unilaterally rather than cooperatively, the outcome most likely will turn out to be inferior overall; that is, unrestrained competition over relative shares is likely to become so severe that it will end up reducing the size of the pie for all, eliminating all potential for joint gain. (The public good will be underproduced.) This class of games features such familiar names as Stag Hunt, Chicken, and of course the notorious Prisoner's Dilemma.[9] All are regarded by most IPE scholars as reasonably accurate facsimiles of strategic interactions among national governments, including EC governments, in the real world today.[10]

The common characteristic of such games is that cooperation in the collective interest is desirable but not automatic. Preconditions necessary to inhibit defection are lacking: cooperation must be *promoted* to be successful. The question is: Can the nature of such games be changed in ways that will enhance prospects for cooperation? In other words, can strategic choices be modified? Given established state preferences, are there any elements in the broader inter-state system that may be manipulated to favorably alter environmental constraints and incentives for national behavior? Can the benefit-cost calculations of rational and egoistic state actors be so influenced as to make commitment to collective action appear significantly more attractive for any or all of them separately? This is the central challenge that has been taken up at the level of systemic analysis in the contemporary IPE literature. Applied to the subject of financial integration in Europe, that literature suggests a number of potentially important topics for future empirical study, which for the purposes of a possible research agenda may be grouped under a trio of headings corresponding to the three component variables of any such rational calculus: (a) the *benefits* of cooperation; (b) the *costs*, and (c) the *discount rate* used in comparing them.

Benefits. It is a well-known insight of game theory that, in principle, incentives for cooperation in any given strategic interaction may be considerably enhanced by supplementing the benefit side of a state's benefit-cost calculation with "side-payments" (in plain language, bribes) of one kind or another. Side-payments may be either "issue-specific" (i.e., offered within the specific game itself) or "issue-linked" (i.e., offered in more or less closely related games). In the present context, one intriguing question for future study is whether, in practice, side-payments of either type could conceivably be developed on a scale sufficient to reduce individual state resistance to the collective goal of financial integration in Europe. Could recalcitrant governments, in brief, be bribed to cooperate?

Certainly the means for such bribery are available—if they are wanted. There are two reasons for this. First, financial integration is not a "single-play" game, with payoffs limited to the outcome of a single strategic choice. Rather, it is a continuing interaction, the equivalent of an iterated game where decisions must be repeated and hence where supplementary benefits over time can be offered to discourage defection—where the "shadow of the future" looms large, to use Robert Axelrod's phrase.[11] Second, financial integration is not an isolated game, with payoffs unrelated to other areas of interaction among the players. Rather, it is quite obviously "nested"[12] within a whole set of institutionalized relationships among EC governments, any or all of which could possibly be tapped to provide potentially attractive side-payments in return for desired national commitments. The setting is ripe for rewarding cooperative behavior.

For example, if a country such as Italy resists financial integration because of a perceived threat to its monetary autonomy, the Community's existing short-term and medium-term mutual credit facilities could be made specially available, possibly even at subsidized interest rates, to offset any destabilizing capital movements that might result—an illustration of a possible issue-specific side-payment. In similar fashion, if a country like France is resistant because of a perceived threat to its discretion in credit allocation, supplementary financial resources could be made available to it for planning or regional development purposes, again possibly at subsidized interest rates, through the European Investment Bank or parallel EC institutions. Or, alternatively, issue-linked concessions might be offered in a non-financial area such as agriculture, where the Community's common farm policy could conceivably be redirected to provide additional benefits as an incentive for cooperation in creating a single banking market. Given the dense and continuing network of relationships in existence within the EC, opportunities for bribery along these lines are clearly not in scarce supply.

The key question, then, is not supply but demand: Will the available means be wanted? Since side-payments of either type must be paid for, some actor or actors must be prepared to absorb their costs—which means that we are still caught in the classic collective-action dilemma of how to avoid underproduction of a public good. At least one state individually must be willing to pay disproportionately for the collective goal of financial integration. Is there any such state in the EC today?

The obvious candidate is Germany, which is already the dominant financial power on the European continent. With the possible exception of Great Britain, no other Community member would appear to have more to gain from creation of a single EC banking market. Germany's "universal banks" seem well prepared, in terms of size, experience and expertise, to take full advantage of new rights of establishment and operation in other member countries; Frankfurt might well find itself the continent's leading financial center, ranking perhaps second only to London in the Community as a whole. And not even Britain can rival the Federal Republic of Germany in material resources at hand to invest in suitable side-payments to countries like France or Italy. If bribery is to be the route to financial integration in Europe, Germany would seem the only plausible paymaster.

Indeed, were Germany to play this role, it would be perfectly consistent with the so-called "theory of hegemonic stability" as it has been developed in the IPE literature—the popular argument that provision of public goods like "order" or "openness" in international economic relations requires the presence of a single, strongly dominant actor (a hegemon) prepared to absorb the necessary costs.[13] Large actors, unlike small ones, cannot assume that they have imperceptible effects on whether a public good is produced; furthermore, being large, they presumably stand to lose more from underproduction. Hence, it may be assumed that they have more of an incentive to take the lead in ensuring cooperation by all players, even should that mean bearing a disproportionate share of the cost. In the European context, this clearly means Germany.

But will the hegemon's incentive *suffice* to persuade Germany to play the role of paymaster on behalf of financial integration? As critics of hegemonic stability theory have contended, hegemonic leadership may not in fact be a sufficient condition for the emergence of cooperative relationships, nor even a necessary condition.[14] Cooperative relationships may develop in the absence of a strong, dominant power; they may fail to develop even in the presence of one. Yet not even the theory's critics question that hegemony can in practice help to *facilitate* cooperation in economic relations. This is because the asymmetry of incentives makes achievement of successful collective action more *probable* than it would otherwise be. The issue is whether the hegemon's incentive can somehow be translated into genuine action; that is, whether the leader can indeed be persuaded to lead. The availability of means for bribing other EC governments is not enough. Germany also has to want to use them.

Thus one topic for a future research agenda concerns the potential leadership role of Germany in underwriting possible side-payments through Community institutions to overcome individual state resistance to creation of single EC banking market. Until now, the hegemon's incentive has *not* sufficed to persuade Germany to play such a leadership role on this issue. Many explanations are possible. In the eyes of the German government, the incentive may simply not seem sizable enough to warrant the requisite commitment of resources; alternatively, having already served for so long as the biggest net contributor to the EC budget, Germany may be reluctant in an era of fiscal stringency to take on yet more financial responsibilities. Or it may reflect a broader and possibly growing disaffection with the Community in Germany, as reported in some recent polls of the German population.[15] The need is to sort through these and other possible explanations for the correct answer. Does the Federal Republic in fact have a disproportionate incentive to ensure cooperation on the financial integration issue? And if so, why has it until now not shown more willingness to bear a disproportionate share of the cost? In short, why has Germany not led?

Costs. Another well-known insight of game theory is that "sticks" as well as "carrots" may be useful, in principle, to enhance incentives for cooperation in any given strategic interaction. That is, it is possible not only to reward players via side-payments if they cooperate; it is also possible to punish them, via sanctions of one kind or another, if they refuse—in effect, working on the cost side rather than the benefit side of a state's benefit-cost calculation. Like side-payments, sanctions may be either issue-specific or issue-linked. Another intriguing question for future study, then, is whether, in practice, sanctions rather than side-payments might be developed on a sufficient scale to promote the objective of EC financial integration. In brief, if recalcitrant governments cannot be bribed to cooperate, could they be coerced into doing so?

The logic of sanctions is that they serve in effect to "privatize" a public good, depriving noncooperators of a free ride. As some IPE scholars have been careful to note,[16] the distinction between private goods and public goods—so neat in theory—is in reality more one of degree than of kind, particularly as concerns the characteristic of non-excludability. Even goods that are truly non-rival may nonetheless be excludable, in the sense that free riding could be penalized. Individual players might possibly be excluded directly from the benefits of collective action via issue-specific sanctions; or else they might be made to pay some price for those benefits, via issue-linked sanctions, insofar as they cannot be excluded directly. Either way, where such possibilities do exist, the principle of reciprocity can be invoked, establishing a direct connection between actors' present behavior and anticipated future gains. Defection can be made a costly strategic option.

Financial integration is clearly one such case. As with side-payments, means for coercing recalcitrant governments are certainly available within the dense and continuing network of EC relationships, if they are wanted. The setting is as ripe for punishing defection as it is for rewarding cooperation. Instead of offering linked concessions through such programs as the common farm policy, for example, benefits could conceivably be withheld from those who refuse to commit themselves to collective action on the financial-integration issue, instead of making more resources available through the Community's mutual credit facilities or the European Investment Bank, access to financing for such states could be partially or even wholly curtailed. Or, more directly, sanctions could be imposed within the specific context of financial integration itself, e.g., by denying Community-wide rights of establishment and operation to the banking institutions of noncooperating members or by denying citizens of those members access to various services available in the newly created Community banking market. Opportunities along one or another of these lines are manifold. Sticks, like carrots, are not in scarce supply.

Thus the key question here too is not supply be demand: Will the available means be wanted? Sanctions do not occur spontaneously—certainly not if, as with side-payments, they must be paid for. Where costs are involved, the imposition of sanctions requires a positive decision on the part of cooperating states to effectively privatize the public good. (Even where the imposition of sanctions results automatically from activation of some trigger mechanism, creation of the mechanism itself requires a positive decision.)   Hence we are still caught in the classic collective-action dilemma of how to gain the commitments needed to avoid underproduction. As Joanne Gowa has written, "costly exclusion is itself a public good."[17] One free-riding problem (the risk of noncooperation in the game as a whole) is replaced with another (the risk of noncooperation in the imposition of sanctions within the game). States cooperating in the creation of a single banking market must also be willing to penalize other members for noncooperation; that is, they must be prepared to genuinely commit themselves to a credible policy of reciprocity. Is there any such prospect in the EC today?

In some respects prospects appear good, owing precisely to the nesting of the financial-integration issue in a preexisting Community. IPE scholars identify several possible inhibitions to a credible policy of reciprocity among states, including especially: (a) difficulties in monitoring behavior; (b) difficulties in focusing sanctions on defectors, and (c) difficulties in apportioning responsibility for sanctions.[18] All three of these kinds of inhibitions, however, can be eased by the operation of established EC institutions, which both increase the "transparency" of state actions and facilitate the swift and effective enforcement of rules. A policeman, if needed, is readily available in the European Commission; a judge, in the European Court of Justice. It is not necessary to persuade governments (e.g., Germany) to suffer the possible opprobrium of taking on either of these unpopular roles themselves.

In other respects, however, prospects ironically may be impeded by those very same institutions, insofar as they permit defectors to retaliate more easily against any sanctions imposed upon them. Penalty may be returned for penalty, stick for stick, in a pattern of "echo effects" that could be repeated virtually ad infinitum, threatening mutually harmful policy conflict across a broad range of linked issue-areas. As Robert Axelrod has regretfully remarked, "the trouble with [reciprocity] is that once a feud gets started, it can continue indefinitely."[19] The result may well be to leave all players far worse off than before, unless defenses can be established to prevent an endless cycle of reprisals. And this in turn may lead back to a necessity for side-payments, to bribe defectors in the financial area to forego opportunities for retaliation that might otherwise be available to them through the network of EC relationships. Reciprocity, clearly, is a two-edged sword.

Thus another topic for a future research agenda concerns the potential for a credible policy of reciprocity to overcome individual state resistance to the joint goal of a single EC banking market. Can effective sanctions be designed that would not provoke mutually harmful echo effects? Or must penalties necessarily be packaged together with attractive rewards in order to ensure all players' commitments to collective action? In short, how far can the Community go in using coercion to achieve cooperation?

Discount Rate. Finally, there is the discount rate that states effectively use in their benefit-cost calculations. In principle, this variable too may be modified to enhance prospects for cooperation in any given strategic interaction. In most games, as in the case of EC financial integration, potential gains tend to be both more remote and less certain than prospective losses. On the one hand, this means that most players can be expected to value future benefits at a considerable discount when comparing them with more immediate costs. (In technical terms, they implicitly have a positive rate of time preference or high discount rate.) On the other hand, it means that an opportunity exists for increasing incentives for cooperation—even apart from any possible side-payments or sanctions—insofar as players can be induced to place a higher value on future payoffs. (In technical terms: insofar as their positive rate of time preference, or discount rate, can be reduced.) A third intriguing question for future study, then, in the present context, concerns whether this is an opportunity that could be successfully seized in practice. Could the resistance of individual governments to the EC's collective goal of financial integration conceivably be reduced, to any significant extent, by somehow persuading them to revise their customary rate of time preferences?

That rates of time preference can in principle be revised is without question, since the process of discounting is by definition subjective rather than objective in nature. That is, any value attached to the future is in the eye of the beholder, a matter more of cognition than fact. As Robert Axelrod and Robert Keohane have written: "Perceptions define interests . . . Decisionmaking in ambiguous settings is heavily influenced by the ways in which the actors think about their problem."[20] It follows that if ways of thinking can be altered, incentives for behavior will be changed as well, hence leading to a modification of strategic choices.

This is not to suggest that decisionmaking, being grounded in perception, is therefore irrational in any meaningful sense. Rather, it means simply that rationality may be *bounded* significantly, owing to the ambiguity of the setting in which decisions have to be made. Governments' abilities to make calculations and compare alternatives may be constrained by limits imposed by uncertainty on their information-processing capacities. The concept of bounded rationality was first developed by Herbert Simon.[21] A key implication of the concept is that if uncertainty can be reduced by one means or another, constraints on rational benefit-cost calculations will be reduced as well, raising the value that actors attach to remote future payoffs and thereby making commitment to collective action appear relatively more attractive in the short term. A key question, then, for the analytical purposes of this essay, is whether any such means can be found in the EC today. Can member governments, in effect, be provided with a better understanding of the prospective benefits of a single banking market?

The question necessarily focuses attention on the European Commission, the body best placed to help provide that understanding. At the center of the Community's institutionalized network of relationships the Commission has already established itself as a primary source of sound and reliable information relevant to all members; with its reputation for organizational impartiality and disinterested commitment to the collective good, it can be assumed in general to be trusted by individual governments. Thus a third topic for a future research agenda concerns the potential educative role of the Commission in promoting financial integration. Can the Commission successfully alter states' perceptions of their own interests on this issue? Can an information campaign be mounted that would substantially alter existing rates of time preference? In short, can EC governments be persuaded to change their customary ways of thinking?

Unit Level Analysis of Financial Integration

Until now, our discussion has focused on strategic interactions strictly at the *Community* level, with state behavior studied exclusively from the "outside-in." Useful as such systemic analysis is, however, it is clearly not enough. States in the real world obviously are not purely unitary actors with invariant utility functions: conceptions of national self-interest do not simply materialize out of thin air. As numerous scholars have pointed out, full understanding of state behavior in the international political economy demands analysis from the "inside-out" as well; that is, at the national level too, encompassing strategic interactions among all *domestic* actors with actual or potential influence on state actions abroad.[22] In short, we must also investigate the domestic basis of foreign economic policy. The assumption that we may casually disregard the internal processes by which state policy preferences are determined is unrealistic and potentially misleading—helpful as a first approximation, but certainly not the last word. In methodological terms, the approach is parsimonious but partial. As Keohane has written:

> No systemic analysis can be complete. We have to look beyond the system toward accounts of state behavior that emphasize the effects of domestic institutions and leadership on patterns of state behavior. That is, we will have to introduce some unit-level analysis as well. We have to look from the inside-out as well as from the outside-in.[23]

Models for discussion at the national level are provided by that branch of the IPE literature devoted to so-called *unit-level* analysis of the politics of international economic relations.[24] The basic unit of analysis in this type of literature is the "domestic structure," variously identified with different social or economic forces capable of exercising some degree of influence on the country's central governmental decisionmakers. Just which aspects of the domestic structure may matter most in any particular circumstance will differ, obviously, from country to country and from issue to issue, depending on the general substance of each problem as well as the specifics of each state's own internal organizational arrangements. It is not at all surprising, therefore, that in practice the number of models developed by scholars working at this level of analysis, for application in given instances, tends to be quite large. What distinguishes the many alternative models from one another are the specific elements of internal policy networks that are picked out in each case for special emphasis. What unites them is a common perception of domestic structure as a crucial intervening variable between the international system and individual national behavior.

Precisely because the number of such models is so large, unit-level analysis has often been criticized for going too far in sacrificing parsimony for the sake of realism. Remarks Keohane, a sympathetic critic: "Parsimonious theory, even as a partial 'first cut,' becomes impossible if one starts analysis here, amidst a confusing plethora of seemingly relevant facts."[25] Adds Bruno Frey, a less sympathetic critic: "The most important shortcoming is its non-analytical structure. . . . The approach is descriptive, historical and (sometimes) anecdotal."[26] Even conceding these criticisms, however, unit-level analysis remains essential to highlight the role of internal characteristics of states in explaining external policy preferences. Systemic analysis can identify only the outer parameters (constraints and incentives) for state behavior; it cannot explain what specific "nationalistic" strategies and goals a government will actually choose within the context of any given issue. These choices, in each case, will depend as well on the nature of their purely domestic strategic interactions. As Frey himself admits: "[The approach] is useful in pointing out problems, to give general insights, and helping to grasp the particular forms of institutions and political processes relevant for international political economics."[27]

In general, unit-level models can be grouped into two broad classes: *governmental* models, which focus on strategic interactions within the narrow organization of government itself; and *societal* models, which focus on strategic interactions within the broader economic and political structure of a nation. Most familiar among governmental models is the so-called bureaucratic-politics paradigm, stressing bargaining and negotiation specifically between the state's various central decisionmakers. Government is seen not as homogenous but rather as a conglomerate of institutional actors with differing perceptions of national (and personal) interests; policy preferences are seen as the product of a never-ending process of tugging and hauling among them. Most familiar among societal models is the so-called interest-group approach, stressing bargaining and negotiation on a broader scale, between central decisionmakers on the one hand and other societal actors on the other. A distinction is drawn between the "state," identified with the public sector (the apparatus of political authority), and "society," identified with the private sector (various economic and political groups); and policy preferences are seen as the product of the interrelationships of the two sectors. The IPE literature abounds with studies comparing the explanatory power in individual countries of models drawn from each of these two classes.[28]

Does this mean that one of the two classes is necessarily preferable to the other? Not at all: the two are really complementary rather than competitive. They simply call attention to different sets of relevant actors. In the present context, both may potentially contribute to our understanding of the "politics" of EC financial integration, though clearly it would be impossible within the limits of this brief essay to use them to give more than a hint of all the complex forces and relationships involved. Unit-level analysis, as indicated, is by definition empirical, whereas this essay is purely conceptual. The discussion in the following few paragraphs is therefore intended to be no more illustrative of the various elements of internal policy networks that ought to be included in a future research agenda.

Governmental models, for example, point to the critical role that may be played by key bureaucratic entities whose institutional interests might seem threatened by creation of a single banking market. Incentives for individual actors in the public sector may diverge quite sharply from collective incentives on this issue. I have already mentioned the risk that financial integration poses for the autonomy of national monetary policy, for instance. For central banks, this would inevitably translate into losses of power, prestige, and privileges within the apparatus of political authority, implying an unfavorable benefit-cost trade-off as seen from their own point of view. Whatever net gains there may be for the nation as a whole, therefore, central banks themselves—or at least some officials of those institutions—might well persist in opposing any new Community initiatives in the banking area, hence exerting a crucial particularist influence on the shape of overall government policy. And the more powerful is the central bank's bargaining leverage in state councils, of course, the greater that influence is apt to be. In the EC today, the central banks of Germany and Italy are especially prominent in their respective national policy networks.

Similarly, the risk that financial integration poses for state discretion in credit allocation might well lead to opposition from other important governmental actors as well—in particular, from finance ministries (or at least from those offices or individuals in finance ministries with responsibilities in this area). Here too there are threatened losses of institutional power, prestige, and privileges. Hence here too there may be a crucial particularist influence on the shape of overall government policy. That would appear to be especially likely in the case of France, where there is a long history of state involvement in the channelling of available financial resources.[29]

In parallel fashion, societal models point to the critical role that may be played by key actors outside the public sector, where individual incentives could also diverge sharply from collective incentives. Here it is perhaps most useful to draw a distinction between the handful of leading commercial banks in each country, on the one hand, and the much greater number of small institutions on the other. Every EC member's banking system is characterized by a hierarchy of some sort. In Germany, below the few well known universal banks (including especially the Big Three: Deutsche, Dresdner, and Commerzbank) can be found a myriad of lesser known specialized and/or localized intermediaries, e.g. regional and savings banks and agricultural and commercial credit cooperatives. Likewise, in France a narrow circle of giant money-center institutions (e.g., Banque Nationale de Paris, Credit Lyonnais, Société Generale) operates side-by-side with a much wider outer circle of smaller specialist establishments. And even in Italy, with the most fragmented banking system of the three countries, there are evident differences between the very largest financial intermediaries (e.g., Banca Nazionale del Lavoro, Banca Commerciale Italiana, Credito Italiano) and other participants in Italian credit markets. The importance of these hierarchies, in the present context, stems from the typically far greater involvement of leading banks in international—as opposed to purely domestic—banking business. This comparative difference of international involvement is likely to mean that a rather deep cleavage exists between the attitudes of most big versus small institutions on the subject of a single banking market in Europe.

Europe's biggest banks, by and large, already earn a sizable portion of their profits from cross-border operations of one kind of another. Tested by competition on a global scale, they are apt to view a single regional market more as an opportunity than a threat. Just the opposite reaction, however, can probably be expected from many smaller banking intermediaries, for whom national restrictions on rights of establishment and operation are perceived virtually as a guarantee of continued commercial viability. Small local banks may well calculate that their own interests are not served by financial integration no matter how great net gains may be for the nation as a whole, and hence lobby accordingly—creating yet another particularist influence on the shape of overall government policy.

A similar distinction might be made between the suppliers of more or less closely related financial services, whose markets also tend typically to be characterized by hierarchy with varying degrees of international involvement. Bigger investment banks, brokerage houses and insurance companies, like bigger

banks, are more apt to view financial integration as an opportunity; whereas smaller establishments, like most small banks,
could probably be expected to lobby in opposition. And yet more
elements could be added by looking at the various users of
banking or related financial services and the roles they play in
internal policy networks. Bigger non-financial enterprises with
established credit ratings would potentially be in a position to
exploit new opportunities for borrowing outside their accustomed
domestic markets; whereas smaller borrowers might legitimately worry about a decline of credit availability should
integration cause a drainage of funds away from local intermediaries. In fact, the list of potential particularist influences
that could be studied in each EC member is anything but short.

At this level of analysis, then, the practical challenge is to
identify just which domestic forces are most influential on the
specific issue of financial integration and to investigate just how
their interaction in each EC member affects the determination of
observed policy preferences over time. In addition to the strategic game played between states (international politics) is a
game played within states (domestic politics), between supporters and opponents of a single banking market both inside and
outside of government. And as at the level of international
politics, so at the level of domestic politics, the question is
whether the nature of the game can be changed in ways that
will enhance prospects for inter-state cooperation on the issue.
Can opponents be either bribed or coerced by supporters? Can
resistance be reduced by altering the value integration's opponents attach to the future? Technically, can established conceptions of national self-interest be favorably altered by acting to
modify the rational, egoistic benefit-cost calculations of individual domestic actors? That, in essence, is what "inside-out"
analysis is all about.

Two-Level Interactions

However, not even "inside-out" analysis is the last word.
Necessary as it is as a complement to systemic analysis, it is
still not enough, as such, to complete our understanding of state
behavior on issues like EC financial integration. What unit-
level analysis provides is insight into the domestic basis of
foreign economic policy—the effect of the internal on the

external. What it lacks is the reverse—the effect of the external on the internal. The relationship between the two levels of politics, domestic and international, clearly is two-way, not unidirectional. Domestic structure may have systemic consequences; but it may also be affected by systemic considerations. As a final stage of analysis, therefore, we must also explore how and to what extent the internal processes of states may be constrained or influenced by their external environment. In brief, the domestic and international games must be integrated in full. As Peter Gourevitch has written:

> The international system is not only a consequence of domestic politics and structures but a cause of them. . . . International relations and domestic politics are therefore so interrelated that they should be analyzed simultaneously, as wholes.[30]

Regrettably, the task is easier said than done. While links between the domestic and international games are frequently acknowledged in the IPE literature, [31] useful models for integrated two-level analysis—obviously a complex intellectual challenge—are only beginning to be developed by enterprising scholars.[32] Hence here again, as in the previous section, it is possible to give no more than a hint of all that may actually be involved. By way of illustration, I shall concentrate on just one particular dimension of the two-level game—the opportunity created by external interdependencies to alter internal strategic interactions through formation of implicit or explicit transnational coalitions. Such opportunities ought to be plentiful within the EC's already dense network of institutionalized relationships.

Assuming state preferences to be the outcome of domestic politics, it follows that observed policies may be modified insofar as the balance of internal forces can be tipped by the addition of significant pressures from influential external sectors; that is, insofar as effective transnational coalitions may be formed between key bureaucratic entities or interest groups at home and like-minded counterparts elsewhere. Possibilities along these lines are, in principle, manifold. Two examples from recent writings should suffice to demonstrate the relevance of such coalitions in actual practice.

One example is supplied by my own recent book, *In Whose*

Interest? International Banking and American Foreign Policy.[33] The subject of this book is the complex and often conflicting relationship between the private banking system of the United States and the makers of America's foreign policy in Washington. One finding of the book is that when tensions do develop between these two sets of actors on specific international issues, attempts are frequently made by either side to sway the decisions of the other by forging alignments with influential third parties outside the country (e.g., foreign governments or multilateral institutions). Moreover, the evidence is clear that such *de facto* coalitions can indeed lead to changes of official state policies.

A second example is supplied by Robert Putnam and Nicholas Bayne in their 1984 study of the annual economic summits of the seven major industrial nations, *Hanging Together*.[34] As Putnam and Bayne point out, divisions *within* governments are usually thought to hamper, rather than promote, policy cooperation *between* them. But the authors' careful analysis of the summit experience suggests otherwise: internal divisions in some instances have actually served to facilitate interstate cooperation, insofar as opportunities were created for formation of powerful alliances of like-minded officials in different countries. In effect, external pressures worked to alter internal strategic interactions. In the authors' own words:

> International pressures . . . allowed policies to be "sold" domestically that would not have been feasible otherwise. . . . Summits have frequently eased international tensions by strengthening the hands domestically of those within a government who favored an internationally desired policy.[35]

These examples thus suggest one final topic for a future research agenda on EC financial integration, concerning the potential for forming effective transnational coalitions to help promote a single banking market. Could supporters in practice put together effective alliances across national frontiers? Would such efforts be aided or hindered by the EC's existing network of relationships? And what role might the European Commission play, perhaps as planner or catalyst? Attempts to answer these questions would complete the integration of the domestic and international games on this issue.

Conclusions

In summary, I have argued in this essay that the "politics" of EC financial integration can best be understood as a problem of collective action, a "game," involving two separate but inter-related levels of "play": inter-state and intra-state. Financial integration itself is understood as a kind of public good in scarce supply, demanding direct and explicit cooperation among the Community's members to overcome inherent tendencies toward underproduction. Since divergences exist between collective incentives and individual incentives, cooperation must be promoted to be successful. And since this in turn requires a modification of the strategic choices of at least some of the key governments involved, analysis must necessarily focus on the underlying benefit-cost calculations of both state and non-state actors. At issue are national policy preferences: how these interact internationally (systemic analysis), how they are determined domestically (unit-level analysis), and what the connections are between the two levels of politics. Only by such analysis can we hope to gain the full insight needed to help improve prospects for the creation of a single banking market in Europe.

Notes

1. The emphasis here is on the word "fully." Much financial liberation, it must be acknowledged, has indeed occurred in recent years in the Community, even in France and Italy. On France, see e.g., *The Economist*, November 29, 1986, pp. 75-76; on Italy, see e.g., the *International Herald Tribune*, May 23, 1987, p. 1. But it is also true that many barriers still remain in the EC to segment national banking markets, and much opposition obviously still remains to their removal.

2. See e.g., *The Economist*, November 22, 1986, p. 84. The agreement effectively implemented a plan that had been proposed by the European Commission just six months earlier. See Commission of European Communities, *Program for the Liberalization of Capital Movements in the Community* (Brussels, May 23, 1986).

3. See e.g., David T. Llewellyn, *International Financial Integration* (New York: Wiley and Sons, 1980).

4. Fritz Machlup, *International Payments, Debts, and Gold* (New York: Scriber's, 1964).

5. For some particularly noteworthy examples of recent contributions to this literature, see e.g., Robert O. Keohane, *After Hegemony* (Princeton, NJ: Princeton University Press, 1984); and Kenneth A. Oye (ed.), *Cooperation Under Anarchy* (Princeton, NJ: Princeton University Press, 1986).

6. Kenneth Waltz, *Theory of World Politics* (Reading, MA: Addison-Wesley, 1979), p. 63. "Outside-in" or "systematic" analysis corresponds to what in an earlier formulation Waltz had described as his "third image" of international relations, locating the source of state behavior in attributes of the inter-state system. This was in contrast to his "second" and "first" images, which located the sources of state behavior in, respectively, the structure of individual states and the nature of individual men. See Waltz, *Man, the State and War* (New York: Columbia University Press, 1959).

7. Mancur Olson, *The Logic of Collective Action: Public Goods and the Theory of Groups* (Cambridge, MA: Harvard University Press, 1965).

8. Keohane, *After Hegemony*, p. 69.

9. These as well as other games are each distinguished by a unique payoff structure, understood to stand for the preference ordering of players among available alternative combinations of strategies. In an elementary two-player game, four such combinations are available from the point of view of each player separately: mutual cooperation (CC), mutual defection (DD), unilateral defection (DC), and unrequited cooperation (CD). In Stag Hunt, both players' preference ordering is: CC>DC>DD>CD. In Chicken: DC>CC>CD>DD. And in Prisoners' Dilemma: DC>CC>DD>CD. These are all *symmetrical* games. Games may also be *asymmetrical*, where the preference orderings of individual players differ. Two especially prominent examples of the latter are Bully and Called Bluff.

10. See especially the essays collected in Oye, *Cooperation Under Anarchy*. But cf., Duncan Snidal, "Coordination versus Prisoners' Dilemma: Implications for International Cooperation and Regimes," *American Political Science Review*, vol. 79, no. 4, (December, 1985), pp. 923-942.

11. Robert Axelrod, *The Evolution of Cooperation* (New York: Basic Books, 1984).

12. The concept of "nesting" is attributed to Vinod Aggarwal,

Liberal Protectionism: The International Politics of Organized Textile Trade (Berkeley, CA: University of California Press, 1985). This book is based on a doctoral dissertation completed in 1981.

13. See e.g., Charles Kindleberger, *The World in Depression, 1929-1939* (Berkeley, CA: University of California Press, 1973); Stephen Krasner, "State Power and the Structure of International Trade," *World Politics*, vol. 28, no. 3 (April 1976), pp. 317-347; and Robert Gilpin, *War and Change in World Politics* (New York: Cambridge University Press, 1981).

14. See e.g., Keohane, *After Hegemony*, Ch. 3, and Duncan Snidal, "The Limits of Hegemonic Stability Theory," *International Organization*, vol. 39, no. 4 (Autumn 1985), pp. 579-614.

15. *The Economist*, April 11, 1987, p. 46.

16. John Conybeare, "Public Goods, Prisoners' Dilemmas and the International Political Economy," *International Studies Quarterly*, vol. 28, no. 1 (March 1984), pp. 5-22.

17. Joanne Gowa, "Ships that Pass in the Night? Neoclassical Trade Theory in a Balance-of-Power World," paper prepared for a conference on "Political and Economic Analysis of International Trade Policies," 1986, mimeo.

18. Robert Axelrod and Robert O. Keohane, "Achieving Cooperation Under Anarchy: Strategies and Institutions," in Oye, *Cooperation Under Anarchy*, pp. 234-238 and 244-247; and Keohane, "Reciprocity in International Relations," *International Organization*, vol. 40, no. 1 (Winter 1986), pp. 1-27.

19. Axelrod, *Evolution of Cooperation*, p. 138.

20. Axelrod and Keohane, "Achieving Cooperation," pp. 229, 247.

21. See e.g., Herbert Simon, *Models of Bounded Rationality* (Cambridge, MA: MIT Press, 1982).

22. See e.g., Joanne Gowa, "Anarchy, Egoism, and Third Images, The Evolution of Cooperation and International Relations," *International Organization*, vol. 40, no. 1 (Winter 1986), pp. 167-186.

23. Keohane, *After Hegemony*, p. 26.

24. For some particularly noteworthy contributions to this literature, see e.g., Peter Katzenstein (ed.), *Between Power and Plenty: Foreign Economic Policies of Advanced Industrial Countries* (Madison, WI: University of Wisconsin Press, 1978; and Stephen Krasner, *Defending the National Interest* (Princeton, NJ: Princeton University Press, 1978).

25. Keohane, *After Hegemony*, p. 25.

26. Bruno, Frey, *International Political Economics* (Oxford: Basil Blackwell, 1984), p. 9.

27. Ibid.

28. See e.g. the following studies of United States foreign trade and monetary policies; Robert Pastor, *Congress and the Politics of U.S. Foreign Economic Policy* (Berkeley, CA: University of California, 1980); John Odell, *U.S. International Monetary Policy* (Princeton, NJ: Princeton University Press, 1982); and Robert Baldwin, *The Political Economy of U.S. Import Policy* (Cambridge, MA: MIT Press, 1985).

29. Although much liberation has occurred in French credit markets in recent years, use of the banking system by the government to guide lending in desired directions is by no means a thing of the past. According to one estimate, as much as 30-40 percent of loans now outstanding in France are the result of such public intervention. See *The Economist*, November 29, 1986, p. 75. As one recent survey concluded: "The most likely future for French banking . . . will be a continuation of the trend towards greater competition and flexibility, but with the state retaining ultimate control." See D. Marsh, "French Banking and Finance: Winds of Change," *The Banker*, April 1985, p. 95.

30. Peter Gourevitch, "The Second Image Reversed: The International Sources of Domestic Politics," *International Organization*, vol. 32, no. 4 (Autumn, 1978), p. 911.

31. Axelrod and Keohane, "Achieving Cooperation," pp. 241-242.

32. Robert Putnam, "Domestic Politics, International Economics, and Western Summitry, 1975-1986" or "International Cooperation and the Logic of 'Two-Level Games'," paper prepared for the 1986 meeting of the American Political Science Association.

33. Benjamin J. Cohen, *In Whose Interest? International Banking and American Foreign Policy* (New Haven, CT: Yale University Press for the Council on Foreign Relations, 1986).

34. Robert Putnam and Nicholas Bayne, *Hanging Together: The Seven-Power Summits* (Cambridge, MA: Harvard University Press, 1984).

35. Ibid., p. 209.

PART TWO

Issues of Systemic Organization and Management

9

The Political Economy of Monetary Reform Today*

In recent years the world monetary order has been in a state of rapid flux. The rules and conventions that went by the name of the "Bretton Woods system" are honored now more in the breach than in the observance. Repeated efforts to reform the structural framework of international monetary relations so far have ended in near total failure. The few superficial changes in global monetary arrangements that have recently been introduced have been almost purely cosmetic. Why has monetary reform proved so difficult to achieve? What must be done in order to restore stability to international monetary relations? The objective of this essay is to examine the principal issues of monetary reform today. The major stress of the essay will be on the political economy of the problem. I shall argue that underlying and conditioning all of the purely economic aspects of monetary reform is the fundamental political dilemma of how to ensure a minimum degree of consistency among the political objectives of separate national governments. That is the real issue of world monetary reform.

The Failure of Reform

Monetary reform has not failed for want of trying. Intensive discussions of the needs, prospects, and possibilities for reform began more than a decade and a half ago.[1] In the intervening

*From *Journal of International Affairs*, vol. 30, no. 1 (Spring/Summer 1976), pp. 37-50. Published by permission of the *Journal of International Affairs* and the Trustees of Columbia University in the City of New York.

years, few subjects in international economic relations have attracted so much attention. During the 1960s, the debate on reform tended to focus mainly on the triad of broad, interrelated problems known as adjustment, liquidity, and confidence.[2] By "adjustment" was meant the problem of assuring an efficient mechanism for the maintenance and restoration of equilibrium in international payments. "Liquidity" referred to the problem of assuring an adequate supply and rate of growth of official monetary reserves. "Confidence" stood for the problem arising from the coexistence of different kinds of reserve assets and the danger of disturbing shifts among them.

At the level of governmental and intergovernmental agencies, most discussions stressed the latter two problems. To cope with the confidence problem, a variety of partial reforms were introduced into the monetary order. Among them were the General Arrangements to Borrow (GAB) in the International Monetary Fund (IMF); a network of reciprocal swap facilities among central banks; a gold pool; and a two-tier gold price system. All were intended to help governments handle destabilizing shifts among various international monetary assets. To cope with the liquidity problem, deliberations in the so-called Group of Ten culminated in 1968 in the creation of an entirely new international reserve asset, inelegantly labelled the Special Drawing Right (SDR).[3] Most observers at the time hoped that these reforms would be enough to keep the monetary order operating smoothly at least into the medium-term future. Events, however, were to prove them wrong. On August 15, 1971, international monetary arrangements suffered a severe jolt resulting from former President Nixon's declaration of the New Economic Policy of the United States.[4] Within a year and a half, despite the "greatest monetary agreement in the history of the world" at the Smithsonian Institute in December 1971, the world monetary order collapsed completely.

That is not to say that the world monetary system itself collapsed. Analytically, a clear distinction must be drawn between the international monetary system and the international monetary order.[5] A system is "an aggregation of diverse entities united by regular interaction according to some form of control."[6] In the context of international monetary relations, this describes the aggregation of individuals, commercial and financial enterprises, and governmental agencies that are involved, either directly or indirectly, in the transfer of purchasing power between countries. The international monetary system exists because, like the levying of taxes and the raising of armies, the creation of money has always been considered one of the fundamental attributes of political sovereignty. Within national frontiers only the local currency is accepted to serve the three traditional functions of money: medium of exchange, unit of account, and store of value. Consequently, across national frontiers some integrative mechanism must exist to facilitate interchanges between local money systems. That mechanism is the international monetary system.

The international monetary order, by contrast, is the legal and conventional framework within which this mechanism of interchange operates. Control is exerted through policies implemented at the national level and interacting at the international level. By specifying which instruments of national policy may be used and which targets of policy may be regarded as legitimate, the monetary order establishes both the setting for the monetary system and the understanding of the environment by all of the participants in it. As Robert Mundell says: "A monetary order is to a monetary system somewhat like a constitution is to a political or electoral system. We can think of the monetary system as the modus operandi of the monetary order."[7]

What collapsed after 1971 was the monetary order. The monetary system continued to function. Indeed, world trade and payments continued growing at record rates. Now, however, the system was no longer subject to any stabilizing form of control This was the real change in global monetary relations. In 1972, the so-called Committee of 20 (formally, the Committee on Reform of the International Monetary System and Related Issues) was organized under the auspices of the IMF in hopes that agreement on a new framework of rules and conventions could be reached before the end of 1973. Unfortunately, such agreement proved elusive, and, in June 1974, the Committee wound up its affairs without final accord on a comprehensive plan for reform.[8] Instead, the Committee declared that henceforth the process of putting a reformed monetary order into practice would have to be treated as evolutionary, rather than as a task to be concluded in the short one-to-two year period originally envisioned. In the words of the chairman of the deputies of the Committee of 20, "some aspects of reform should be pushed forward and implemented early, while other aspects could be developed over time."[9] In effect, a British-style approach to constitution writing would have to be substituted for an American-style approach. No estimate was given of how long the evolutionary process of reform might actually take.

These aspects of reform, pushed forward by the Committee of 20, were all relatively superficial—mainly, a new system of valuation of and high interest rate on the SDR, and the establishment of an Interim Committee of the Fund's Board of Governors to continue the former committee's work. The same description of superficiality applies as well to the subsequent decisions of the Interim Committee at its meeting in January 1986 in Jamaica, which apart from acknowledging the reality of floating exchange rates, principally concerned enlargement of national quotas in the IMF and disposition of the Fund's own gold holdings.[10] On the specific technical issues which, over the years, have truly agitated governments—issues such as the rules for exchange intervention by central banks, the convertibility of the dollar, and the consolidation of the dollar "overhang"—no significant progress has been made. Reform, to date, has been almost purely cosmetic.

There are several reasons for this. For one thing, deliberations in the Committee of 20, and subsequently the Interim Committee, have been stymied by inertia. The basic issues of reform have been under discussion for so long that most governmental positions have become inflexible. A second cause has been the emergence of unanticipated and unprecedented international economic developments, including rampant global inflation and the enormous increases of oil prices since late 1973. International negotiators were taken unawares by these developments. As is so often true of generals, they were caught preparing for the last war instead of for the next.

The principal cause, however, is simply that negotiators have been caught looking in the wrong direction. Negotiators have kept their eyes on the same triad of problems that dominated the debate through the 1960s. Adjustment, liquidity, and confidence, however, are not really the main threat to the monetary system, even if they remain technical issues in urgent need of resolution. The genuine danger goes much deeper—to the absence of some agreed mechanism to ensure compatibility among the external policy objectives of separate national governments. This is the problem of "consistency." Essentially political in nature, it underlies and conditions all of the traditional economic issues of reform. No economic problem can be solved until the political consistency problem is satisfactorily dealt with. Yet negotiators in the Committee of 20 and Interim Committee have never explicitly confronted this problem. Little wonder, then, that monetary reform has remained an elusive goal.

The Options for Reform

Basically, there are only five possible ways to respond to the consistency problem. Each represents an alternative organizing principle for the international monetary order. These are: (1) anarchy, what Richard Cooper calls a "free-for-all" regime;[11] (2) automaticity, a self-disciplining regime of rules and conventions binding for all nations; (3) supranationality, a regime founded on collective adherence to the decisions of some autonomous international organization; (4) hegemony, a regime organized around a single country with acknowledged responsibilities and privileges as leader; and (5) negotiation, a regime of shared responsibility. An international monetary order must be based on one of these five abstract principles, or on some combination of them. The five together effectively exhaust all possible options for monetary reform.

Which option should governments be aiming for in the evolutionary process of reform that has now begun? In my opinion, the choice clearly lies between hegemony and negotiation. Automaticity and supranationality both have their attractions, but they are politically naive. Sovereign governments will not voluntarily surrender their decisionmaking powers either to automatic rules or to a supranational agency. A free-for-all regime is even less appealing to governments, even though it might conceivably achieve a fairly high degree of technical efficiency through exclusive reliance on private market decisions. Anarchy does not cope with the political consistency problem—it cops out. As Cooper says:

> A free-for-all regime does not commend itself. It would allow large nations to exploit their power at the expense of smaller nations. It would give rise to attempts by individual nations to pursue objectives that were not consistent with one another (e.g., inconsistent aims with regard to a single exchange rate between two currencies),

with resulting disorganization of markets. Even if things finally settled down, the pattern would very likely be far from optimal from the viewpoint of all the participants.[12]

Is hegemony possible? There is no question that the Bretton Woods system was hegemonic. The charter drafted at Bretton Woods in 1944 clearly reflected the dominant position and vital interests of the United States at the time. As David Calleo has written: "Circumstances dictated dollar hegemony."[13] The postwar world needed an elastic supply of new international reserves; the United States desired freedom from any balance-of-payments constraints in order to pursue whatever policies it considered appropriate and to spend as freely as it thought necessary to promote objectives believed to be in the national interest. The result, unplanned but effective, was a gold-exchange standard based on the dollar as the principal reserve asset, with the flow of new monetary reserves being determined mainly by the magnitude of America's annual payments deficit. America's deficits were the universal solvent that kept the machinery of Bretton Woods running. Other countries set independent balance-of-payments targets; the external financial policy of the United States was essentially one of "benign neglect." In effect, America surrendered any payments target of its own in favor of taking responsibility for the operation of the monetary order itself. Consistency was assured by America's willingness to play a passive role in the adjustment process: "Other countries from time to time changed the par value of their currencies against the dollar and gold, but the value of the dollar itself remained fixed in relation to gold and therefore to other currencies collectively."[14]

Naturally, this responsibility was advantageous to the United States—it preserved America's privilege to act abroad unilaterally in promoting its perceived national interest. So too was it advantageous to other countries, which were thereby given assurance of a more stable international monetary environment. America's hegemony was not exploitative. Quite the contrary, it reflected a positive-sum game in which all of the principal players would benefit. At the heart of this order was an implicit bargain, struck early in the postwar period between the United States and the countries of Western Europe, the only countries at the time conceivably capable of challenging America's hegemony. As I have written elsewhere:

Implicitly, a bargain was struck. The Europeans acquiesced in a system which accorded the United States special privileges to act abroad unilaterally to promote U.S. interests. The United States, in turn, condoned Europe's use of the system to promote its own regional economic prosperity, even if this happened to come largely at the expense of the United States.[15]

Ultimately, however, the fabric of the bargain frayed as discontent over its terms grew on both sides of the Atlantic. European governments (especially the French) became increasingly resentful of what Charles de Gaulle called "the exorbitant privilege" given the United States by the dollar's preeminence, to pursue policies many considered abhorrent, such as the U.S. involvement in Vietnam. In the meantime, the U.S. government was becoming increasingly uncomfortable about the economic costs of European regionalism, and, by extension, the economic costs of its benign-neglect policies toward third regions such as Japan. America's trade balance was deteriorating badly. By 1970, protectionist forces were running rampant in the U.S. Congress. Furthermore, in 1971, the United States faced a serious threat of a run on its remaining gold stockpile in Fort Knox. The New Economic Policy of August 1971 was a direct response to these and related developments. The postwar bargain was scuttled because the Nixon administration decided that the United States could no longer afford to play a passive role in the payments adjustment process. Consequently, the Bretton Woods system lost its assurance of consistency.

Today, it is difficult to imagine being able to reconstruct anything like America's postwar hegemony in international monetary arrangements. Circumstances have changed too much. Western Europe and Japan both have long since emerged from under the American shadow, and, more recently, the energy crisis has promoted the countries of OPEC to a new position of prominence as well. No longer are these nations content to play the world money game strictly by American rules. In the Committee of 20 and the Interim Committee, for instance, negotiators were preoccupied with ensuring a greater degree of "symmetry" in the international monetary order. For European governments at least, this was simply a semantic disguise to cloak the more fundamental ambition of ending dollar hegemony.

At the same time, however, none of these nations has grown strong enough to write its own rules for the monetary order. The European Community still has not made significant progress toward making the political concessions necessary for monetary unification. Without a common currency the Community can hardly hope to reduce or eliminate the asymmetries in the global economy that derive directly or indirectly from the dollar's leading role as international "vehicle" currency. The governments of Europe still have not demonstrated that they are prepared to make the fundamental political concessions that a common currency would require. As Fred Hirsch has argued:

> In this sense one can conclude that European monetary integration is not a serious issue. It belongs to the category of commitments that are endorsed by national authorities at the highest level, but are in fact ranked low in their priorities when it comes to the test.[16]

Likewise, Japan, for all its industrial might, can hardly hope to replace the United States as the dominant power. At the same time, the oil states, lacking any financial markets of their own, have actually reinforced America's position by favoring New York and the dollar for the investment of their surplus earnings. The United States may no longer be as clearly dominant as it was in 1944. But it is still the world's leading national economy.

The United States, therefore must continue to bear the responsibility of leadership, even if it can no longer enjoy all its privileges. "Leadership without hegemony," Marina Whitman calls it: "the replacement of leadership based on hegemony with leadership based on persuasion and compromise."[17] Like Samson, we may still be strong enough to bring the temple crashing down around us if we wish; our power of veto remains. If our role is to be constructive rather than destructive, however, we must, as I have argued elsewhere:

> Acknowledge that the United States is no longer the dominant economic power in the world. Deeds must speak as loud as words: the United States must demonstrate that it is in fact prepared to adjust to the new reality in reorganizing economic space—not assertively or in excessively self-interested terms, but on the basis of a genuine reciprocity of interests and purposes.[18]

We must be prepared to give up our "exorbitant privilege" and to accord a greater voice in monetary councils to Western Europe, Japan, and OPEC. The new international monetary order that is evolving must be negotiated rather than imposed, pluralistic rather than hegemonic. The only alternative is inconsistency and the consequent danger of splintering into congeries of competing monetary blocs: a free-for-all regime.

Such self-sacrificing leadership is not easy to achieve. Calleo notes: "It is a hard lesson for an imperial power to learn that it cannot be omnipotent."[19]

Can the United States be happy with such an arrangement? Harry Johnson stresses, "This is a problem in political economy, not in technical economic analysis."[20] Technical economic analysis can illustrate what monetary reforms might be desirable; it can also demonstrate America's shared interest in an order that promotes stability for all. In the end, however, it will not be economics that matters, but politics.

The Adjustment Problem

To give some substance to this general argument, consider again the three technical problems of adjustment, liquidity, and confidence. All are issues still in urgent need of a solution. I have said that in the 1960s the stress of most discussions was on liquidity and confidence. In the 1970s, emphasis must be changed somewhat in the light of recent developments. The collapse of the Bretton Woods system was in essence a breakdown of the rules for central bank intervention in the foreign-exchange market. This means, on the one hand, that attention must now be focused much more on the adjustment problem. On the other hand, the rise of OPEC means that the liquidity and confidence problems have been significantly transformed. At a time when all oil consumers are scrambling to pay for their higher-priced oil imports, much less importance need be attached to such traditional concerns as dollar convertibility and consolidation of the dollar overhang. The key aspect of the liquidity-confidence problem today is the issue labelled "petro-dollars." I shall discuss these problems of adjustment and petro-dollars in turn.

With regard to the adjustment problem, there used to be a great prejudice, at the level of governmental and intergovernmental agencies, against any form of exchange-rate mechanism that would allow currency values to float freely. The Bretton Woods system was a par-value (or "pegged-rate") regime: each government was expected to declare a par value for its currency and to defend its parity within narrow limits by intervening in the exchange market as buyer or seller of last resort. Par values (pegs) were supposed to be shifted only infrequently in response to something called "fundamental disequilibrium." The comparative rigidity of the postwar regime reflected the chaotic experience of the interwar period which, the negotiators at Bretton Woods were convinced, had amply demonstrated the disadvantages of floating rates. With the collapse of the Bretton Woods system, and the subsequent move to generalized floating in 1973, many feared the advent of a new era of wildly fluctuating currency values and competitive exchange depreciations. As events have turned out, however, such fears were excessive. In fact, floating rates have worked remarkably well, considering the unprecedented economic developments of recent years, and governments have been educated about their advantages. With exchange-market pressures now being absorbed mainly by changing currency values—rather than, as in the past, by reserve movements, controls, or adjustments of the level of domestic activity—countries find themselves enjoying an extra degree of freedom in the pursuit of national economic and social objectives. Official opinion is now amenable to greater exchange-rate flexibility than had previously been considered either possible or desirable.

In the Committee of 20, this opinion was expressed by the acceptance (in principle) of a formula of "stable but adjustable par values," indicating the possible willingness of governments but only provided they have the right to make frequent small adjustments of their parities when and if the need arises. The formula itself was ambiguous. What was clear, though, was that any difference between a "stable but adjustable" regime and a regime of "managed" floating under multilateral surveillance would likely be more apparent than real. A reasonable conclusion, therefore, was that reform ought to do away entirely with the fiction of par values, and concentrate instead on establishing rules and procedures to guide a regime of continuously floating exchange rates. The reality of floating exchange rates was formally acknowledged by the Interim Committee, at its

January 1986 meeting in Jamaica, in the form of a new amendment of the IMF charter legalizing abolition of par values.[21]

The principal advantage of floating rates is that they provide a mechanism for continuing adjustment in the face of all the myriad influences that impinge daily on a country's balance of payments. The principle disadvantage of floating rates is that they are prone to destabilizing activity by private speculators or government officials. Private speculators may increase the frequency and amplitude of fluctuations of exchange rates around their long-term trend; government officials may be tempted to intervene to influence in mutually inconsistent ways the long-term trends themselves ("dirty floating"). Both types of activity create uncertainties and exchange risks that could discourage a certain amount of legitimate foreign trade and investment. Economic theory teaches that normally private speculation tends to be stabilizing except when the economic environment is clouded by unpredictable governmental policies. This suggests that the first need of a floating-rate regime is agreement on guidelines for official intervention in the foreign-exchange market. Intervention must be encouraged to reduce the frequency and amplitude of fluctuations of rates around trend, but not to influence the trends themselves ("clean floating"). A tentative set of such guidelines was recommended by the Committee of 20 when it wound up its affairs in 1974, but these were too general to be of much practical use to governments.[22] Unfortunately, the new amendment adopted by the Interim Committee at Jamaica did nothing to make the guidelines more specific. Further refinement of intervention rules and procedures is still necessary.

The second need of a floating-rate regime is agreement on the respective adjustment obligations of countries in balance-of-payments of surplus or deficit. This is a subject discussed at considerable length in the Committee of 20 and the Interim Committee. During the 1960s, a serious political conflict developed between the United States, which was demanding currency revaluations by Western Europe and Japan, and the countries of continental Europe, led by France, which were insisting upon devaluation by the United States. This was the origin of the "symmetry" issue. It reflected the weakening of the postwar bargain between the United States and Europe. The Europeans felt that they were being discriminated against by America's exorbitant privilege to finance deficits by issuing what amounted to IOUs. America felt discriminated against because it had no effective control over its own rate of exchange. Since other governments used the dollar not only as their main reserve asset but also as their principal intervention medium to support par values, the U.S. could not change its exchange rates unilaterally unless all other countries agreed to intervene appropriately in the exchange market. This was an asymmetry in the monetary order that favored the Europeans rather than the U.S. which could not easily devalue to be rid of its deficit.[23]

In the negotiations in the Committee of 20 and the Interim Committee, both the United States and Europe have agreed that a more symmetrical adjustment process is needed. Since they are talking about different kinds of symmetry, however, they find it difficult to agree on an approach to the problem. Each side is prisoner of its own perception of the past. As Peter Kenen wrote in 1973:

> As usual, the parties are arguing from history as each reads it. Americans believe that the U.S. deficits of the 1950s and 1960s were prolonged and led finally to the collapse of the par value system because surplus countries—the Europeans and Japan—could not be compelled to alter their policies, and the United States could not easily initiate a change in exchange rates. Europeans read this same postwar history to argue that the blame and obligation to change policies rested with the United States, yet it was not compelled to act because it was not losing reserves.[24]

What criteria might be used for refining intervention procedures and the respective adjustment obligations of countries in payments surplus or deficit? Clearly, this is one of those areas where politics must take precedence over economics. No monetary order can remain stable for long if some governments feel seriously discriminated against. As Anthony Lanyi has pointed out:

> If the cost of cooperation is too great for a country at a particular time, it will prefer to take measures which, if often only in a minor or partial way, "break down" or diverge from the purposes and methods of the agreed-upon system. . . . Therefore, the more equally the costs of

cooperation are distributed, the better is the chance that
the system will be maintained unimpaired.[25]

In short, procedures and obligations must be shared more or
less equally. This does not mean that governments must submit to
automatic rules enjoining specific policies in the event of particular types of disturbances; nor does it mean that they must
always follow the dictates of some autonomous international
organization. I have already argued that sovereign states will
not voluntarily surrender their decisionmaking powers either to
automatic rules or to a supranational agency. Governments demand a certain leeway in their effective range of policy options.
What it does mean is that all governments must be expected to
take an active role in the management of the exchange-rate
regime—countries in payments surplus as well as those in
deficit, reserve centers as well as those who do not enjoy an
exorbitant privilege. All must share in the collective costs of
cooperation. That indeed is the essence of a negotiated order.

Special responsibility falls on the largest countries which,
because of their power to disrupt, have no choice but to take a
constructive attitude toward the problem of adjustment. This
includes the United States, of course; it also includes, in
particular, Germany and Japan, the next two largest economies
of the noncommunist world, which share with America an
interest in a stable exchange-rate regime. Among currencies
today, the currencies of these three countries are clearly
dominant—the Deutsche Mark in Europe (as linchpin of the
European "snake," which is as close to monetary unification as
Europeans have yet been able to come), the yen in the Far East,
and the dollar in Latin America and elsewhere. Successful
stabilization of relations among these three currencies is a
prerequisite for stabilization of the exchange-rate mechanism
as a whole. In 1936, the monetary chaos of the interwar period
was finally brought to a close by a Tripartite Agreement among
the three most influential currencies of that day—the dollar,
the pound, and the French franc. In the 1970s, a similar sort of
tripartite agreement is needed among the dollar, the mark, and
the yen in order to end present uncertainties about exchange-
intervention procedures and payments-adjustment obligations.

Such a stabilization agreement could be more or less
formal.[26] Preferably, it should be carried out under the
auspices of the IMF, in order to confer a certain "legitimacy" on

the rules and procedures agreed to by the major financial powers. The Fund is an ideal forum for this because it can provide an institutional mechanism for the management of the exchange-rate regime without imposing on governments any special elements of supranationality. Fund recommendations tend to reflect a consensus of views of all the principal members. Consequently, governments can accede more easily to its recommendations than to the decisions of one or a few large countries acting unilaterally. Still, any agreement at all is better than none. There is a need for some form of managed floating under multilateral surveillance. If negotiation within the Fund proves too slow or cumbersome, a tripartite agreement among the major powers would be far preferable to the only conceivable alternative, an unpalatable free-for-all regime.

The Petro-Dollar Problem

With regard to the petro-dollar problem, the key question is what to do about the huge surplus earnings of OPEC. The oil-price increases since 1973 have resulted in enormous current-account surpluses for oil producers as a group—$60 billion in 1974, $92 billion in 1975, and additional large surpluses in 1976 and thereafter.[27] The world has never before been confronted with such an immense transfer of wealth. As Winston Churchill said in another context, never before have so many owed so much to so few. Projections of future OPEC surplus accumulations vary considerably, depending on the source.[28] According to even the most sanguine projections, petrodollar surpluses are expected to reach a minimum of $180-190 billion (in current dollars) by 1980. Even that is a substantial sum, and the situation has profound implications for global economic and political relations. Two issues in particular stand out as far as the international monetary order is concerned: how governments can ensure that petro-dollars will be effectively "recycled" to the oil consumers that are most in need of them, and how they can ensure that OPEC surplus accumulations will not become a new source of instability in world monetary arrangements.

The recycling issue highlights the fact that oil-price increases affect different oil-consuming countries differently. Some consumers are more dependent on oil imports than others; some are less able to offset the higher cost of oil imports either by increasing exports of goods and services to OPEC members or by attracting loans and investments from them. Consequently, some consumers have found themselves in serious payments difficulty since the energy crisis, while others have been enjoying relatively healthier external accounts. In the long run, consumer countries must evolve toward a structure of trade relations compatible with the emerging pattern of OPEC capital flows to consumers as a group. In the short run, however, the key need is to channel oil revenues from consumers presently receiving the benefit of OPEC capital flows to those who are most in need of them. Private international financial markets cannot be relied upon to perform this financial intermediation function entirely on their own. There is no assurance that an allocation of loans based on traditional banking considerations (creditworthiness, relative interest rates, etc.) will coincide with the requirements of global balance-of-payments equilibrium. In the words of IMF managing director Johannes Witteveen: "[T]he Euro-currency markets alone cannot cope with the new situation because they cannot channel funds on reasonable terms to countries whose economic position is precarious. The need of these countries is perhaps the most urgent, but precisely for this reason their ability to attract private funds is weakest."[29] For this reason, the private markets must be supplemented by bilateral and multilateral credit facilities among governments, such as the IMF "oil facility" and the OECD's proposed Financial Support Fund.

Until now, such governmental recycling facilities have not been used frequently. This has led some observers to suggest that the private markets indeed can be relied upon to handle the problem by themselves. This is, however, an overly sanguine conclusion based on an unrepresentative sample of experiences. In 1974, the first year of the energy crisis, there was still much scope in international financial markets for absorbing the higher cost of oil imports. The most seriously affected industrial countries, such as Britain and Italy, as well as many less developed countries, were able to borrow extensively to cover their oil deficits. Now, however, many of these same countries seem to be reaching the limit of their foreign borrowing capacity. Fully 80 percent of the combined current-account deficits of oil consumers in 1974 was borne by primary-producing countries, including primary producers in the periphery of Europe and Australia. The deficits of Third World primary producers alone totaled $28 billion in 1974 and $35 billion in 1975.[30] These poor countries have already attracted about as much private money as they are capable of doing; for most of them, monetary reserves are simply too low to take up much of the remaining burden of financing. Without access to governmental recycling facilities, they will be forced to endure cutbacks in imports and development programs, and perhaps even starvation. LDCs would not be participants in the OECD Financial Support Fund, and the amounts of funds that were committed to the IMF oil facility before it was allowed to lapse were derisively small. For these poorest countries, an expansion of intergovernmental recycling facilities is still a fundamental imperative.

All this imposes a special responsibility on the United States. Because of our favorable endowments of oil and alternative energy resources, our balance of payments has been less adversely affected by higher oil prices than have the external accounts of most other consumer nations. At the same time, a disproportionate share of OPEC surpluses have been placed either in the United States or in Euro-dollars. (Either way, the American balance of payments benefits, since the dollars paid to oil producers are returned to the United States—in the former instance directly, in the latter, indirectly—rather than converted into foreign currencies.) New York is an especially attractive investment center as it is probably the only financial market in the world large enough to absorb without serious strain sustained capital movements of the magnitudes involved. The dollar is an especially attractive investment medium because it continues to be the world's leading vehicle currency for private transactions. The United States, therefore, must take the lead in facilitating the recycling of OPEC funds. In the interest of promoting prosperity at home as well as abroad, the U.S. must see that other governments are not forced into mutually harmful payments policies by oil-induced deficits.

The second issue is the disposition of OPEC surplus accumulations. OPEC countries have begun to diversify a portion of their investments. Yet for a long time to come, a large proportion will undoubtedly continue to be concentrated in short-maturity assets (bank deposits, etc.). By the end of 1975, the official monetary reserves of Saudi Arabia had soared to over $24 billion, second only to Germany's; reserves of the oil producers as a group had risen to $55 billion, one-quarter of the world total. In the next few years, OPEC countries could accumulate reserves in excess of $100 billion, most of which will be concentrated in the hands of five Persian Gulf nations and Libya. A monetary order cannot remain stable when such a large proportion of international liquidity is unilaterally controlled by such a small number of countries—particularly countries with such a poor record of economic and political volatility. In the interest of assuring monetary stability, multilateral controls should be instituted to ensure that these funds are not shifted about frequently in a chaotic or irresponsible fashion. The objective should be to induce OPEC nations to treat their surpluses as long-term savings rather than as short-term investments.

This would require new investment facilities to absorb OPEC's surplus funds. There has been no lack of proposals along these lines.[31] The problem is to ensure that such facilities are sufficiently attractive to induce OPEC participation. OPEC nations might have to be offered concessions to protect the purchasing power of their investments against losses from exchange-rate depreciation or price inflation. They might have to be offered a role in the administration of such facilities as well as some degree of control over the terms by which their funds are relent to final borrowers. Without such concessions, the oil producers might not consider cooperation worthwhile.

The three largest economies of the noncommunist world have a clear common interest in the problem of adjustment. With regard to the petrodollar problem, however, the interests of the United States, Germany, and Japan are more divergent. Because the latter two countries are more dependent on OPEC oil than the United States, they are less reluctant to offer concessions to OPEC in order to attract a reflow of their surplus earnings. The U.S., in contrast, is in a position to make fewer concessions to oil producers because of its more favorable energy endowment. Nowhere has this divergence of interests been more apparent than in the debate, in 1974, over the relative merits of the IMF oil facility versus the OECD Financial Support Fund. The Germans and Japanese favored a considerable expansion of the IMF oil facility, which would have offered OPEC countries not only a relatively riskless haven for funds but also a substantial voice in administration. For these reasons, however, Secretary of State Kissinger preferred to bypass the IMF with his alternative proposal for a "safety net" to be established solely within the OECD. Ultimately, the American position prevailed. Therefore, the petro-dollar threat to the stability of the monetary order remains acute.

Successful solution of the petro-dollar problem also requires agreement among the largest national economies; the divergent interests of the United States, Germany, and Japan must be reconciled. Again, it would be preferable to implement such agreement through the IMF, in order to confer a certain degree of legitimacy on decisions, and as with the adjustment problem, any agreement at all would be better than none. The key need is to avoid a situation in which inconsistency of national policies, a failure to compromise, leads to great instability. The United States is no longer in a position to dictate from a position of hegemony. Others are not yet ready to pick up the mantle of leadership. Consistency can be assured today only in the context of a negotiated system—more a matter of politics than economics. One can only hope that the politicians are up to the job.

Notes

1. Credit for intiating the modern debate on world monetary reform must go to Robert Tiffin. See his landmark *Gold and the Dollar Crisis* (New Haven: Yale University Press, 1960).

2. This trichotomy goes back to the deliberations of a celebrated international study group of 32 economists in 1964. See Fritz Machlup and Burton G. Malkeil, eds., *International Monetary Arrangements: The Problem of Choice* (Princeton: International Finance Section, 1964).

3. For more on the reforms of the 1960s, see Fritz Machlup, *Remaking the International Monetary System* (Baltimore: Johns Hopkins Press, 1968).

4. See Benjamin J. Cohen, "The Revolution in Atlantic Economic Relations: A Bargain Comes Unstuck," in Wolfram Hanrieder, ed., *The United States and Western Europe: Political, Economic and Strategic Perspectives* (Cambridge, Mass.: Winthrop Publishers, 1974), pp. 106-133.

5. See Robert A. Mundell, "The Future of the International Financial System," in A. L. K. Acheson, J. F. Chant, and M. F. J. Prachowny, eds., *Bretton Woods Revisited* (Toronto: University of Toronto Press, 1972), p. 92; and Richard N. Cooper, "Prolegomena to the Choice of an International Monetary System," *International Organization*, vol. 29, no. 1 (Winter 1975), p. 64.

The terminology of "order" and "system" employed in the test is Mundell's.   Cooper prefers the term "regime" to "order."

6. Mundell, "International Financial System," p. 92.

7. Ibid.

8. The results of the Committee's deliberations were published in the form of an Outline of Reform, detailing areas of both agreement and disagreement among the negotiators.   See *International Monetary Reform: Documents of the Committee of Twenty* (Washington: International Monetary Fund, 1974).

9. Jeremy Morse, as quoted in *IMF Survey*, 8 April 1974, p. 97.

10. See *IMF Survery*, 19 January 1976.

11. Cooper, "Prolegomena," p. 64.

12. Ibid., p. 65.

13. David P. Calleo, "American Foreign Policy and American European Studies: An Imperial Bias?," in Hanrieder, *The United States and Western Europe*, p. 62.

14. Marina v.N. Whitman, "The Current and Future Role of the Dollar: How Much Symmetry?", *Brookings Papers on Economic Activity*, no. 3 (1974), p. 542.

15. Cohen, "Atlantic Economic Relations," p. 118.

16. Fred Hirsch, "The Politics of World Money," *The Economist*, 5 August 1972, p. 57.

17. Marina v.N. Whitman, "Leadership Without Hegemony," *Foreign Policy*, no. 20 (Fall 1975), p. 160.

18. Cohen, "Atlantic Economic Relations," p. 133.

19. Calleo, "American Foreign Policy," p. 70.

20. Harry G. Johnson, "Political Economy Aspects of International Monetary Reform," *Journal of International Economics*, vol. 2, no. 4 (September 1972), p. 405.

21. *IMF Survey*, 19 January, 1976.

22. See *International Monetary Reform: Documents of the Committee of Twenty*, Annex 4.

23. A second asymmetry unfavorable to the United States, also deriving from the dollar's exclusive intervention role, was the fact that market exchange-rates involving the dollar could move by only half as much as the exchange-rate between any other pair of currencies.   This is an asymmetry that persists even today, and will continue to persist as long as governments intervene in the exchange markets principally in dollars.

24. Peter B. Kenen, "After Nairobi—Beware of the Rhinopotamus," *Euromoney*, November 1973, p. 19.

25. Anthony Lanyi, *The Case for Floating Exchange Rates Re-*

considered, Princeton Essays in International Finance no. 72 (Princeton: International Finance Section, 1969), pp. 23-24.

26. For a formal proposal along these lines, see Ronald I. McKinnon, *A New Tripartite Monetary Agreement or a Limping Dollar Standard?* Princeton Essays in International Finance, no. 106 (Princeton: International Finance Section, 1974). For a similar proposal involving just the dollar and the mark, see C. Fred Bergsten, "The United States and Germany: The Imperative of Economic Bigemony," in C. Fred Bergsten, *Toward a New International Economic Order: Selected Papers of C. Fred Bergsten, 1972-1974* (Lexington, MA: D. C. Heath, 1975), ch. 23.

27. International Monetary Fund, *Annual Report 1975,* pp. 12-16.

28. See, e.g., Morgan Guaranty Trust Company, *World Financial Markets,* 21 January 1975; First National City Bank, *Monthly Economic Letter,* June 1975; Thomas D. Willett, "The Oil Transfer Problem," *Department of the Treasury News,* 30 January 1975; Hollis B. Chenery, "Restructuring the World Economy," *Foreign Affairs,* vol. 53, no. 2 (January 1975), pp. 242-263; and W. J. Levy Consultants, *Future OPEC Accumulation of Oil Money: A New Look at a Critical Problem* (New York: June 1975).

29. Quoted in *IMF Survey,* 6 May 1974.

30. International Monetary Fund, *Annual Report 1975, loc. cit.* The deficits of the primary producers reflect the severe deterioration of their terms of trade in 1974 and 1975—partly caused by the high rate of inflation in the industrial world, as well as the oil price increases, which raised the prices of their imports, but mainly attributable to the severity of the recession in the industrial world, which sharply reduced the prices of their exports.

31. See, e.g., Khodada Farmanfarmanian, Armin Gutowski, Saburo Okita, Robert V. Roosa, and Carroll L. Wilson, "How Can the World Afford OPEC Oil?" *Foreign Affairs,* vol. 53, no. 2 (January 1975), pp. 201-222.

10

Balance-of-Payments Financing: Evolution of a Regime*

In few areas of international economic relations has there been as much change in recent years as in the area of monetary relations. At the start of the 1970s, the international monetary system was still essentially that established at Bretton Woods, New Hampshire, a quarter of a century earlier. Exchange rates were still "pegged" within relatively narrow limits around declared par values. Currency reserves were still convertible, directly or indirectly, into gold at the central-bank level. And the main source of external financing for balance-of-payments deficits was still the International Monetary Fund (IMF).

A decade later, all that has changed. Exchange rates of major currencies are no longer pegged; they float. Currency reserves are no longer convertible into gold; they are inconvertible. And the main source of balance-of-payments financing is no longer the IMF but private banking institutions. The role of the private banks in international monetary relations has been greatly enhanced as a result of repeated increases in oil prices since 1973, which have generated enormous financing problems for many oil-importing countries (the petrodollar recycling problem). The recycling of the surplus earnings of OPEC countries, via bank credits and bond issues, to nations in balance-of-payments deficit has, in lieu of commensurate increases in financing from official sources, fallen primarily to private credit markets. As a result, the markets have come to play a role once reserved (in principle) exclusively for official institutions such as the Fund. As one former central banker has put it, "the private banking system took over the functions proper to an official institution possessed of the power to

*From *International Organization*, vol. 36, no. 2 (Spring 1982), pp. 457-478.

finance balance-of-payments disequilibria through credit-granting and to create international liquidity. . . . The function of creating international liquidity has been transferred from official institutions to private ones."[1]

Not that the practice of private lending for balance-of-payments purposes is entirely new. Even in the late 1960s, as much as one-third of all payments financing was intermediated by banking institutions between surplus countries (in those days, mainly countries of the Group of Ten) and deficit countries. But up to 1973, the private markets' role tended to be relatively modest. It was only with the emergence of the petrodollar recycling problem that the markets came into their own as an alternative source of payments financing. A special report to the OECD in 1977 (the McCracken Group Report) perhaps best described the development in historical perspective:

> The shift to increased reliance on private lenders for official financing purposes marked the culmination of a secular transformation of the process of liquidity creation. This transformation had already been going on for some time. Its roots lay in the development of the international financial markets—in particular, the growth of the Euro-dollar market—which gradually made it easier for governments to rely on private international financial intermediation rather than on the deficits of reserve centres to obtain new monetary reserves. The international markets act as worldwide financial intermediaries between the lenders and borrowers of loanable funds (including official as well as private lenders and borrowers). Private capital and the accumulated reserves of surplus countries flow into the market and then ultimately are lent on to countries in balance-of-payments difficulties. Increases of demand for credit in borrowing countries are financed by the markets, within the usual institutional and legal constraints, by borrowing or attracting deposits from the banking systems of surplus countries with available loanable funds. The events of 1974-1976 simply confirmed and accelerated a trend in the process of liquidity creation that had been evident well before the oil price increases of 1973.[2]

This may be only a change of degree—but it is a change of degree so profound that it appears to border on a transformation of kind. This seeming transformation of the regime governing access to balance-of-payments financing is the subject of this essay.

I shall first summarize the role of balance-of-payments financing in international monetary relations, and then describe the key elements of the financing regime that was established at Bretton Woods. Next, the evolution of the regime will be analyzed, and I shall argue that no matter how profound the regime's recent change may appear, it does not in fact add up to a transformation of kind. Rather, to borrow John Ruggie's phrase, it represents an example of "norm-governed change." At the level of principles and norms, the regime remains very much as it was. In the final two sections of the essay, I shall briefly consider what inferences may be drawn from the analysis regarding, first, the relationship between the financing regime and behavior; and second, the jurisdictional boundaries between this and other international economic regimes.

The Role of Financing

The regime for payments financing encompasses the set of implicit or explicit principles, norms, rules, and decisionmaking procedures governing access to external credit for balance-of-payments purposes. This is clearly a very disaggregated notion of a substantive issue-area. In fact, payments financing as an issue is firmly embedded in the broader question of balance-of-payments adjustment (which in turn is embedded in the still broader question of the structure and management of international monetary relations in general). My choice of issue-area for analysis is based on convenience for a relatively narrow case study; it implies no claim regarding what may or may not be the most appropriate level of aggregation for the study of regimes in other international issue-areas.

Payments financing arises as an issue essentially because of the insistence of national governments on their sovereign right to create money. The existence of separate national moneys requires some integrative mechanism to facilitate economic transactions between states. In practical terms, this function is performed by the foreign-exchange market, which is the medium through which different national moneys are bought and sold. The basic role of the foreign-exchange market is to transfer purchasing power between countries—that is, to expedite exchanges between a local currency and foreign currencies ("foreign exchange"). This role will be performed effectively so long as the demand for foreign exchange in any country (representing the sum of the demands of domestic importers, investors, and the like, all of whom must normally acquire foreign currencies in order to consummate their intended transactions abroad) and the supply of foreign exchange (representing the sum of demands by foreigners for domestic goods, services, and assets, which must be paid for with local currency) remain roughly in balance at the prevailing price of foreign exchange— that is, so long as the exchange market is in *equilibrium*. Difficulties arise when demand and supply do not tend toward balance at the prevailing price—that is, when the market is in *disequilibrium*. Then, either the price of foreign exchange (the exchange rate) must be brought to a new equilibrium level or other actions must be taken or tolerated in order to remove or suppress the disequilibrium. This is the problem of balance-of-payments adjustment.

When confronted by a payments disequilibrium, national governments have two basic policy options. Either they may *finance* the disequilibrium, or they may *adjust* to it. Adjustment implies that the authorities are prepared to accept an immediate reallocation of productive resources (and hence of exchanges of real goods, services, and investments) through changes of relative prices, incomes, exchange rates, or some combination thereof. In effect, they are prepared to accept a reduction of domestic spending on goods, services, and investments (in technical terms, real domestic absorption) relative to national output (real national income). Financing, by contrast, implies that the authorities prefer to avoid an immediate reallocation of resources or a reduction of the ratio of real absorption to production by running down their international monetary reserves or borrowing from external credit sources or both. Politics aside, decisions by individual governments regarding the preferred mix of these two options tend to reflect the comparative economic costs of each.

The economic costs of adjustment have both macroeconomic and microeconomic dimensions. At the macroeconomic level, there may be a decline in the overall level of employment of resources, an increase in the rate of price inflation, or both. At the microeconomic level, there may be a decline in the overall productivity of resources because of distortions introduced into the pattern of resource allocation, as well as frictional costs of the sort that occur whenever resources are reallocated. The magnitude of the costs of adjustment will depend not only on the macroeconomic and microeconomic conditions of the economy but also on the particular strategy of payments adjustment that is chosen—whether that strategy relies most heavily on income changes via variations of monetary policy and fiscal policy (expenditure-reducing policies), or on relative price changes via a modification of the exchange rate, or on direct restrictions on trade or capital movements (expenditure-switching policies). The distinguishing characteristic of adjustment costs is that they must be borne currently, whatever happens to the balance of payments in the future (even if subsequently the causes of the deficit should prove to have been transitory).

The costs of financing, by contrast, are borne not in the present but in the future, when monetary reserves must be replenished and foreign debts repaid. The country will then have to generate a greater net volume of exports to gain the requisite increment of foreign exchange. But until that time, no reduction of current absorption relative to production is required.

The choice between adjustment and financing thus reduces to a choice between reducing the absorption-production ratio today or reducing it tomorrow. Put differently, it reduces to a (necessarily subjective) evaluation of the present values of two different kinds of cost, one (the cost of adjustment) to be borne in the present and one (the cost of financing) in the future—a classic discounting problem.

For political and other reasons, governments often prefer to attach a rather high discount rate to future costs as compared with present costs; that is, they prefer to postpone nasty decisions for as long as possible. Consequently, the greater the level of their reserves or access to external credit or both, the greater is the risk that they may be tempted to alter their policy mix away from adjustment and toward financing—even in situations where an immediate reallocation of resources might be the more appropriate response. Thus it has long been felt that, on principle, governments ought not to enjoy unlimited access to balance-of-payments financing. That principle was formally incorporated into the design of the international monetary system established by a conference of forty-four allied nations at Bretton Woods in 1944.

The Bretton Woods System

The Bretton Woods conference represented the culmination of more than two years of planning, particularly in the treasuries of Great Britain and the United States, for reconstruction of the monetary system after World War II. In agreeing on a charter for an entirely new international economic organization, the International Monetary Fund, the conferees in effect wrote a constitution for the postwar monetary regime—what later became known as the Bretton Woods system.[3]

Provision of supplementary financing. One of the cardinal principles established at Bretton Woods was that nations should be assured of an adequate supply of international liquidity. Since it was widely believed at the time that the interwar period had demonstrated (to use the words of one authoritative source) "the proved disadvantages of freely fluctuating exchanges,"[4] the conferees decided that countries should be obligated to declare a par value (a "peg") for their currencies and to intervene in the exchange market to limit fluctuations within relatively narrow margins. But since, at the same time, it was also widely recognized that exchange-market intervention "presupposes a large volume of . . . reserves for each single country as well as in the aggregate," the conferees agreed that there should be some "procedure under which international liquidity would be supplied in the form of prearranged borrowing facilities."[5] It was in order to ensure the availability of such supplementary financing that the IMF was created.

Access to the IMF's resources, however, was not to be unlimited. On the contrary, access was to be strictly governed by a neatly balanced system of subscriptions and quotas. In essence, the Fund was created as a pool of national currencies and gold subscribed by each member country. Members would be assigned quotas, according to a rather complicated formula intended roughly to reflect each country's relative importance in the world economy, and would be obligated to pay into the Fund a subscription of equal amount. The subscription was to be paid 25 percent in gold or currency convertible into gold (effectively the U.S. dollar, which was the only currency still convertible directly into gold) and 75 percent in the member's own currency. In return, each member would be entitled, when short of reserves, to "purchase" (i.e., borrow) amounts of foreign exchange from the Fund in return for equivalent amounts of its own currency.

Maximum purchases were set equal to the member's 25 percent gold subscription (its "gold tranche") plus four additional amounts each equal to 25 percent of its quota (its "credit tranches"), up to the point where the Fund's holdings of the member's currency would equal 200 percent of its quota.[6] (If any of the Fund's holdings of the member's initial 75% subscription in its own currency were to be borrowed by other countries, the member's borrowing capacity would be correspondingly increased: this was its "super-gold tranche.") The member's "net reserve position" in the Fund would equal its gold tranche (plus super-gold tranche, if any) less any borrowings by the country from the Fund. Net reserve positions were to provide the supplementary financing that the Bretton Woods conferees agreed was essential.[7]

Formally, within these quota limits, governments were little constrained in their access to Fund resources. The IMF charter simply provided that "the member desiring to purchase the currency [of another member] represents that it is presently needed for making in that currency payments which are consistent with the provisions of the Agreement"[8]—for example, that it "avoid competitive exchange depreciation" and that it "correct maladjustments in [its] balance of payments without resorting to measures destructive to national or international prosperity."[9] In short, the member would play by the agreed rules of the game. It was only with the passage of time that access to financing from the Fund came to be governed explicitly by what has become known as policy "conditionality."[10]

As such, the word "conditionality" does not appear anywhere in the IMF Articles of Agreement. Indeed, in the Fund's early years, there was some question whether the organization even had a legal authority to make borrowing subject to conditions; and for a time debate raged over the issue. Very soon, however, as a result of accumulating experience and precedent, a recognized interpretation of the Fund's prerogatives did in fact emerge to govern members' access to credit. Two landmark decisions of the Fund's governing board of executive directors[11] stand out in this connection. In the first, in 1948, the board agreed that the IMF could challenge a member's request for finance on the grounds that *inter alia* it would not be "consistent with the provisions of the Agreement," and indeed that the Fund could "postpone or reject the request, or accept it subject to *conditions.*"[12] In the second, in 1952, "conditions" were defined to encompass "policies the member will pursue . . . to overcome the [balance-of-payments] problem"[13]—in other words, policies that promise a genuine process of adjustment to external deficit. Since 1952, this has been the accepted meaning of the term "conditionality."

The 1952 decision was also important for establishing a practical distinction between a member's gold tranche and its four credit tranches, by ruling that borrowing in the gold trance (plus the super-gold tranche, if any) would receive "the overwhelming benefit of any doubt."[14] Subsequent practice also created a distinction between a member's first credit tranche and its remaining ("upper") credit tranches, as summarized in the Fund's 1959 *Annual Report*:

> The Fund's attitude to requests for transactions within the first credit tranche . . . is a liberal one, provided that the member itself is also making reasonable efforts to solve its problems. Requests for transactions beyond these limits require substantial justification.[15]

Integral to the evolution of these distinctions were two further developments in IMF practice—stabilization programs and standby arrangements.

Over the course of the 1950s, the Fund evolved a practical expression of policy conditionality in the form of stabilization programs, which members were obliged to submit when applying for financing in their credit tranches. Such a program may be quite comprehensive, covering monetary, fiscal, credit and exchange-rate policies as well as trade and payments practices. In the case of a request in the first credit tranche, members may express their policy intentions at a relatively high level of generality. But for upper credit tranches, programs have to be correspondingly more precise and rigorous in design. Common to most stabilization agreements are, first, a "letter of intent" from the member-government to the Fund spelling out its program to correct its external deficit; and, second, the use of "performance criteria" to express, in quantitative terms, the policy objectives of its program.

Also over the course of the 1950s, the Fund evolved what has become one of the primary instruments used in applying policy conditionality—the standby arrangement. Under a standby, a member is assured of access to a specified amount of Fund resources for a fixed period of time under agreed conditions, without further consideration of the member's position beyond that provided for in the initial agreement. A key characteristic of most standbys is "phasing," which provides that specified amounts of finance will be made available at specified intervals during the standby period. At each interval the member's access to finance is made dependent on compliance with the performance criteria spelled out in its stabilization program. These criteria usually operate automatically to suspend (in Fund terminology, "interrupt") the member's access to finance if the policy objectives of its program are not being observed.[16]

Standbys normally originate from negotiations between a mission composed of officials of the Fund secretariat, operating under the instructions of the Fund's managing director, and representatives of the member-government. From these negotiations, which may be quite protracted, a letter of intent emerges, usually signed by the member's finance minister or central-bank governor (or both). The Fund secretariat then, through a decision process involving both "area" departments (responsible for individual countries and regions) and "functional" departments (responsible for individual policy issues such as exchange and trade restrictions, fiscal or monetary policy, etc.), formulates the standby arrangement by reference to the letter of intent. That arrangement in turn is submitted by the managing director to the executive board for final approval. The board then makes its decision, usually without benefit of a formal vote. If a formal vote is required, executive directors vote on behalf of all the members, with the vote of each member weighted in proportion to its individual quota.[17]

The financing regime summarized. The regime for payments financing embedded in the postwar Bretton Woods system can be readily summarized in terms of the four elements of the standard definition of an international regime.

Principles. The basic principle underlying the regime was that nations should be assured of an adequate but not unlimited supply of supplementary financing for balance-of-payments purposes. The principle was formally articulated in the IMF Articles of Agreement and backed by explicit organizational arrangements in the Fund.

Norms. Standards of behavior were defined in terms of formally articulated treaty rights and obligations accepted by each nation pursuant to its membership in the Fund. Rights consisted of access to IMF resources within quota limits. Obligations consisted of the general pledge to avoid policies inconsistent with the provisions of the IMF charter (i.e., to play by the agreed rules of the game).

Rules. Specific prescriptions or proscriptions for action derived from the Fund's prerogative of policy conditionality. Members' access to financing, particularly in the upper credit tranches, was subject to explicit conditions embodied in Fund stabilization programs and standby arrangements.

Decisionmaking procedures. Arrangements for determining the amount of financing to be made available and the policy conditions, if any, to be imposed in individual instances combined bargaining (in negotiations between the deficit country and the Fund), administrative decisionmaking (within the Fund secretariat) and, if necessary, voting (in the executive board).

Evolution of the Regime

The regime remained relatively intact until barely more than a decade ago. What accounted for its creation and subsequent maintenance for more than a quarter of a century? And what then explains its dissipation and subsequent changes in the 1970s?

Creation. To a certain extent, creation of the postwar financing regime may be attributed to enlightened self-interest on the part of the forty-four nations represented at Bretton Woods. All understood the need for adequate liquidity in any exchange-rate regime other than a pure float. All remembered the so-called "gold shortage" of the 1920s—a by-product of extreme price inflation in almost all countries during and immediately after World War I, which had sharply reduced the purchasing power of monetary gold stocks (then still valued at their prewar parities). And all remembered the financial chaos of the 1930s that had ensued when Britain was forced to depart from the gold standard in 1931. None wanted to risk repeating any of that dismal history.

But all understood as well the need to set some upper limit on the availability of supplementary financing for balance-of-payments purposes. The question was, what form should that limit take?

Planning for the postwar monetary system was dominated by the two great reserve centers of the day, Great Britain and the United States. Prior to Bretton Woods the British government, in the person of John Maynard Keynes, had pushed hard for the establishment of an international clearing union endowed with some characteristics of a central bank and in particular, with authority to create a new international currency ("bancor") for lending to countries in deficit. Access to financing, within very broad and flexible limits, would have been automatic and repayment would have followed only after the external imbalance had been reversed. But the Keynes plan was opposed by the American government—in particular, by the chief American negotiator, Harry Dexter White—as being excessively biased in favor of financing rather than adjustment. A much firmer limit on borrowing was needed, White felt: financing should be conditional rather than automatic, and repayment should be at a set time rather than indefinite.

The respective positions of the two governments reflected, in good measure, their national concerns. Britain, facing an enormous task of reconstruction, did not want to be hampered by an inability to finance prospective payments deficits. The United States, by contrast, potentially the largest creditor in the system, did not want in effect to write a blank check. For America, the problem was to avoid financing a massive "give-away" of U.S. exports. For the U.K., the problem was to avoid constraints on the process of postwar recovery.

In the end, the American position prevailed—reflecting, of course, the predominant position of the United States among the allied nations during World War II. What was agreed at Bretton Woods was a compromise between the Keynes and White plans. But as one author has put it, "the compromise contained less of the Keynes and more of the White plans."[18] A contractarian route was used, in effect, to legitimate America's view of what constituted rectitude in monetary affairs. Supplementary financing would be made available to deficit countries, but only subject to strict quantitative limits and contingent upon appropriate policy behavior. Hence the Fund's neatly balanced system of subscriptions and quotas.

Only in one respect did the American position on borrowing not prevail at Bretton Woods, and that was on the issue of repayment. In a compromise with the British, the United States initially agreed to an "automatic" provision requiring members to repay credits only when their reserves were rising (with repayments normally to equal one-half the net increase of reserves in each year).[19] But not long thereafter (in 1952), under U.S. pressure, the Fund's Executive Board agreed to a more precise and rigorous temporal limit, requiring repayment within three to five years at the outside.[20] Thus here, too, America's view ultimately won out.

Maintenance. Two factors were principally responsible for the maintenance of the postwar financing regime in the 1950s and 1960s. On the demand side, the need for supplementary financing generally did not exceed what the IMF could provide. On the supply side, there were few alternative sources of financing to compete with the Fund or compromise its authority to exercise policy conditionality.

The demand side. Implicit in the original charter of the IMF was a remarkable optimism regarding prospects for monetary stability in the postwar era. Underlying the choice of a pegged-rate exchange regime seemed to be a clear expectation that beyond the postwar transition period (itself expected to be brief) payments imbalances would not be excessive. The pegged-rate regime was manifestly biased against frequent changes of exchange rates, reflecting the bitter memory of the 1930s, yet nations were left with few instruments under the charter other than capital controls to deal with external disturbances. Few of the conferees at Bretton Woods appeared to doubt that the new Fund's resources would be sufficient to cope with most financing problems.

As matters turned out, this optimism was not entirely justified, at least not in the near term. In fact, in the immediate postwar period monetary relations were anything but stable, and the Fund's resources were anything but sufficient. Most nations were too devastated by war—their export capacities damaged, their import needs enormous, their monetary reserves exhausted—to pay their own way; and their financing needs far exceeded what the IMF could offer. Consequently, the initial burden fell instead to the United States, which in the years 1946 to 1949 disbursed $26 billion through the Marshall Plan and other related aid programs for deficit countries. Fund lending, meanwhile, after a short burst of activity during its first two years, mainly to the benefit of European nations, shrank to an extremely low level. In 1950, the Fund made no new loans at all.[21]

By the mid-1950s, however, the situation had altered substantially. Economies had recovered from wartime destruc-tion and reserve levels were increased by the U.S. balance-of-payments deficit (which averaged approximately $1.5 billion annually between 1950 and 1956). Thereafter, until the emergence of the petrodollar recycling problem in the 1970s, payments imbalances of most countries tended to be more manageable than formerly, and financing needs tended not to strain Fund resources unduly—particularly after 1962, when the Fund's potential lending authority was substantially augmented by negotiation of an arrangement with ten of its main industrial members (the "General Arrangements to Borrow") to borrow additional amounts of their currencies when necessary.[22] During these years, monetary relations corresponded much more closely than previously to the expectations of the conferees at Bretton Woods. And this in turn reinforced the regime that had been designed there.

The supply side. The regime was also reinforced by the absence of important alternative sources of balance-of-payments financing. Some alternative sources did exist, but none seriously threatened to undermine the central role of the Fund.

For example, from 1950 to 1958 the countries of Western Europe enjoyed access to a limited amount of payments financing through the European Payments Union.[23] Similarly, in the 1960s the larger industrial countries could avail themselves of short-term credit through the network of central-bank swap lines initiated by the American Federal Reserve System as well as through other special arrangements at the Bank for International Settlements (BIS) at Basle (e.g., the special standbys arranged for Great Britain between 1964 and 1968).[24]   And of course a number of countries also had the standing to obtain a certain amount of financing in private credit markets via bank credits or bond issues. But none of these sources was ever posed as a competitor to conditional lending by the Fund. Indeed, most were designed to complement rather than to substitute for IMF credit.

The existence of these alternatives did, of course, bias the system somewhat in favor of the relatively small group of rich industrial countries able to take advantage of them. In effect, only the poorer countries of Europe and Third World nations were fully subject to the ostensible rules of the game. The richer countries had room for a certain amount of "cheating," by borrowing either from one another or (to a limited extent) from the private markets. But it should also be noted that the room for such cheating was not unlimited; witness the fact that Britain required $3.6 billion of IMF loans during the 1964-68 period, despite its access to other lines of credit through the Federal Reserve and the BIS. In any event, the most important of these alternative sources of financing were still official rather than private, thus tending to ensure, in practice, no great inconsistency with Fund conditionality.

In fact, there was only one country at the time that truly had the capacity to avoid Fund conditionality through access to an alternative source of financing. That, ironically, enough, was the principal author of the postwar regime, the United States, through the central role of the dollar in international monetary affairs. Because other countries, eager to build up their currency reserves, were largely prepared to accumulate America's surplus dollars (in effect, America's IOUs), the United States was for the most part freed from any balance-of-payments constraint to spend as freely as it thought necessary to promote objectives believed to be in its national interest. In brief, the United States could simply "liability-finance" its deficits. Not that this meant that America's "exorbitant privilege" (as Charles de Gaulle called it) necessarily exploited or disadvantaged others. In fact, as I have argued elsewhere, the element of mutual self-interest in this arrangement was very strong.[25] But it did mean that the regime was potentially vulnerable to abuse by the reserve center, and eventually, as we know, America's deficits did indeed become too great for the postwar system to bear.

Dissipation. With the emergence of the petrodollar recycling problem in the 1970s, changes occurred on both the demand side and the supply side to alter substantially the appearance of the postwar regime. On the demand side the need for supplementary financing expanded enormously, overwhelming what the IMF alone could provide, while on the supply side the private credit markets emerged as an increasingly important rival to the Fund as a source of such financing.

The demand side. Once oil prices began to rise in late 1973, it was clear that oil-importing countries as a group would for some time face extremely large current-account deficits in their relations with oil producers. Some of the largest members of OPEC simply could not increase their imports of goods and services as quickly as their revenues: their "absorptive capacity," at least in the short term, was too low. Accordingly, the balance of their earnings—their "investable surplus"— perforce would have to be invested in foreign assets or otherwise lent back to oil-importing nations as a group.[26] But since reflows of funds from OPEC could not be counted upon to match up precisely with the distribution of deficits among oil importers, some of the latter (industrialized as well as developing countries) were bound to find themselves in serious payments difficulties. The aggregate need of such countries for supplementary financing far exceeded what the IMF alone could provide.

The IMF tried, of course. What was needed, plainly, was not just an increase of quotas (which in fact occurred twice during the 1970s), but, even more importantly, an increase of members' access to Fund resources beyond the strict limit set by their quotas. Precedent for this already existed in two special facilities that had been created during the 1960s to help members cope with particular types of payments problems. The Compensatory Financing Facility was established in 1963 to assist countries, particularly producers and exporters of primary products, experiencing temporary shortfalls of export revenues for reasons largely beyond their own control. The Buffer Stock Financing Facility was established in 1969 to assist countries participating in international buffer-stock arrangements designed to stabilize the price of a specific primary product. Each of these two facilities initially permitted a member to borrow an amount equal to 50 percent of its quota over and above its regular credit tranches.[27]

Building on these precedents, the Fund in the 1970s erected several more special facilities in an effort to cope with its members' increased need for financing. These included a temporary one-year Oil Facility (1974), to help countries meet the initial balance-of-payments impact of higher oil prices; a second one-year Oil Facility (1975); an Extended Fund Facility (1974), to provide financing for longer periods (up to ten years) and in larger amounts (up to 140% of quota) for members experiencing "structural" balance-of-payments problems; a Trust Fund (1976), to provide special assistance to the Fund's poorest members (for up to ten years) out of the proceeds of sales of a portion of the Fund's gold holdings; and a Supplementary Financing Facility (1979), also known as the Witteveen facility, to provide extra credit to members experiencing very large deficits in relation to their quotas. By 1979, as a result of these initiatives, a country could in principle borrow as much as 467.5 percent of its quota, as compared with the 125 percent authorized under the original Articles of Agreement.[28]

But even this was not enough. Although the Fund found itself lending more money to more countries than ever before, the magnitude of deficits after 1973 was simply too great,[29] and much of what the Fund did was really a case of too little and too late. Deficit countries had to look elsewhere. What they found were the private credit markets.

The supply side. The increased role of the private markets as an alternative source of payments financing was a natural consequence of OPEC's comparatively low absorptive capacity. Insofar as the imports of the largest oil exporters failed to keep pace with their revenues, their investable surplus had to be placed somewhere; and the most attractive options were to be found in Western financial markets. Coincident with the weakening of domestic investment demand in industrialized countries, this in turn spurred Western banking institutions to search for new outlets for their greatly enhanced liquidity. Seemingly among the most attractive of such outlets were countries in need of supplementary financing for balance-of-payments purposes.

After 1973, accordingly, private lending to deficit countries increased enormously, primarily by way of bank credits or bonds issued in national or international (offshore) markets. Private banking institutions came to represent, in quantitative terms, the single most important source of payments financing in the world.[30] Not all countries were able to avail themselves of such financing, of course. Poorer less developed countries, lacking any standing at all in the markets, still had to rely on official bilateral or multilateral sources for most of their foreign borrowing. But for developing countries that were regarded by private lenders as sufficiently "creditworthy," as well as for most industrial countries, the bulk of external assistance now came from private sources. Much as in the manner of the United States after World War II, the markets took over from the IMF the main burden of providing supplementary financing for payments purposes.

The result appeared fundamentally to challenge the IMF's presumed role as final arbiter of access to such financing. Private banking institutions had neither the legal authority nor (usually) the inclination to make loans to sovereign governments subject to policy conditions. As a consequence, countries that were regarded by the markets as creditworthy were formally unconstrained in their access to financing, so long as they were willing and able to pay the going rate of interest. This created a danger that some countries might be tempted by the availability of such relatively "easy" (i.e., unconditional) financing to postpone painful—even if necessary—adjustment measures. Put differently, it suggested that the cardinal principle underlying the postwar financing regime—that governments ought not to enjoy unlimited access to balance-of-payments financing—might have been fatally compromised.

Transformation? The danger was widely acknowledged. Said Wilfried Guth, a prominent German banker, in 1977: "The banks as today's main international creditors are unable to bring about by themselves a better balance between external adjustment and financing."[31] His sentiment was echoed by Arthur Burns, then chairman of the Federal Reserve Board of Governors, who admitted that "Countries thus find it more attractive to borrow than to adjust their monetary and fiscal policies."[32] The problem was best summarized by the IMF:

> Access to private sources of balance-of-payments finance may . . . in some cases permit countries to postpone the adoption of adequate domestic stabilization measures. This can exacerbate the problem of correcting payments imbalances, and can lead to adjustments that are politically and socially disruptive when the introduction of stabilization measures becomes unavoidable.[33]

Nor was the danger merely hypothetical. In fact, the IMF was describing what actually came to pass in a number of individual instances. In Peru, for example, in 1976, at a time when the country's balance-of-payments was under severe pressure owing to plummeting prices for copper (a major Peruvian export) as well as to a mysterious disappearance of anchovy stocks from offshore waters (essential for fishmeal, another major Peruvian export), the government used a new $385 million syndicated bank credit to avoid painful adjustment measures, such as credit restraints or cutbacks of fiscal expenditures. The government even announced, less than a month after the credit was negotiated, plans to purchase $250 million worth of fighter-bombers from the Soviet Union. The result was further deterioration of Peru's external balance, domestic social and political unrest, and eventually stringent austerity measures when the government was finally obliged to adopt an effective stabilization program in 1978.[34]

Similar cases could be cited elsewhere, for example in both Turkey and Zaire after 1975. In these countries, access to market financing apparently encouraged the authorities to postpone needed adjustment measures, with consequences ultimately very much like those in Peru.

But not all countries yielded to the temptation to postpone needed adjustment measures. In fact, for any example such as Peru, one could cite a variety of counterexamples of countries that at one time or another used their access to market financing to underwrite immediate and effective actions to restore balance-of-payments equilibrium. Particularly impressive was the case of South Korea following the rise of oil prices in 1973 and the onset of recession in its principal export markets in the United States and Japan in 1974. While relying on borrowing in international credit markets to bridge a widening balance-of-payments gap, the Korean authorities instituted an intensive program of export promotion supplemented by a modest relaxation of monetary and fiscal policy to cushion the domestic impact of recession in foreign markets. In effect, market financing was used to give the economy a breathing space to reallocate resources to the export sector in a context of continuing real growth. Similar cases could be cited, such as Argentina in 1976 and Spain in 1977.

Still, little comfort could be drawn from such "success stories." As the Peruvian case demonstrated, the danger inherent in the availability of relatively "easy" financing from the markets was real—and no one was more aware of it than private banking institutions themselves. Certainly the banks recognized that it was not in their interest to make loans to any country that would do little to ensure its future capacity to service such debt. They had no wish to throw good money after bad, but the problem from their point of view was one of leverage. What, in practice, could they do to ensure that sovereign borrowers would indeed undertake policies that promised a genuine process of adjustment to external deficit?

Variations of terms on offer in the marketplace (e.g., a rise of interest rates or a shortening of maturities) seemed to have little influence on the policies of borrowing governments. As one central banker conceded, it was difficult to "regard this as more than a very marginal contribution to adjustment."[35] Potentially more effective might have been variations of *access* to the market (whatever the terms on offer)—that is, shifts in market sentiment regarding a sovereign borrower's credit-worthiness. But the difficulty with that approach was that it might cut off a country's access to financing just when it was most needed. It was certainly not in the banks' interest to force a nation into outright default on its foreign debt.

An alternative approach might have been to exert discipline directly on a borrower through imposition of comprehensive policy conditions. In fact, this was attempted only once—in the syndicated credit to Peru in 1976, which was split into two installments, the first to be drawn immediately and the second in early 1977. Peru's creditors thought that they could ensure adherence to an effective stabilization program by establishing a system for continuous monitoring of the Peruvian economy and by making the second installment of their loan formally contingent upon satisfactory performance. The effort was unique. It was also a failure. In the end, when the loan's second installment came due, no delay was ever seriously mooted despite Peru's evident failure to meet its policy commitments. The banks, as private institutions, simply did not have the legal or political leverage to dictate policy directly to a sovereign government. Since that episode, they have not even tried.

Instead, private lenders have turned increasingly to the IMF, the one lender that, as a multilateral institution backed by formal treaty commitments, *does* have such legal and political leverage. In a growing number of instances, where doubts have developed regarding a country's prospective policy stance, borrowers have been told to go to the IMF first: formally or informally, new financing from the markets has been made contingent upon negotiation of a satisfactory stabilization program with the Fund. As a result, the Fund has come to play a role as a de facto certifier of creditworthiness in the markets— the official issuer of an unofficial "Good Housekeeping Seal of Approval."[36] As one banker has said: "Conditional credit from the Fund is increasingly viewed as an 'international certificate of approval' which enhances the ability of a country to borrow in the private market place."[37] The procedure is favored by lenders because of the Fund's high professional standards, access to confidential information, and—above all—recognized right to exercise policy conditionality. The procedure is acceptable to the Fund because, in effect, it "gears up" the IMF's own lending while ensuring that new financing in such cases will indeed be used to support a well conceived process of adjustment.

To this extent, therefore, the Fund's role as arbiter of access to financing has been preserved: for countries whose creditworthiness comes into doubt, it is still the Fund that formally imposes specific prescriptions or proscriptions for action. This suggests that the change in the regime is really less than it first appears.

That profound change has occurred is clear. At the level of decisionmaking procedures, the amounts or conditions of lending are in most instances no longer a matter for negotiation solely between the authorities of a country and the IMF. Now a third set of actors is often prominently involved—private banking institutions. And in the many instances where a borrower's policy stance has not come into doubt, the IMF may not be involved at all. To that extent the Fund's monitoring role has indeed been eroded.[38] Nonetheless, I would argue that this falls short of a transformation of kind.

In the first place, just as the practice of private lending for balance-of-payments purposes is itself not entirely new, neither is the role of the Fund as informal certifier of creditworthiness in the markets. Even as far back as the 1950s, cases could be cited where an IMF stabilization program proved the key to unlocking supplementary financing from private sources.[39] Admittedly, use of that procedure prior to 1973 was relatively infrequent. Still, the very fact that it existed at all suggests that there has been more of an element of continuity in the financing regime than might have been thought.

Even more importantly, there has been a strong element of continuity in the basic principles and norms underlying the regime. The idea that deficit countries ought not to enjoy unlimited access to balance-of-payments financing has not been fatally compromised; nor have commonly agreed standards of behavior been significantly altered. Rather, what has happened is that all the key players—governments, banking institutions, the IMF—have made operational adaptations to the changed circumstances on both the demand and the supply sides of the system. True, as a result norms and rules have tended to become somewhat less formally articulated than before; decisionmaking procedures have become more ambiguous; and the room for cheating (for countries with unquestioned creditworthiness) now is greater than it used to be. But these are changes of degree only—"norm-governed changes," once again to borrow Ruggie's phrase. The important point is that all players, even while making their operational adaptations, still acknowledge the fundamental need to play by the rules of the game. In its maintenance of a balance of recognized rights and obligations for deficit countries, the financing regime remains very much the same as before. In its deeper tenets, it has not in fact changed.

The Relationship Between Regime and Behavior

What conclusions may we draw, from this stylized sketch of the evolution of the postwar financing regime, regarding the relationship between the regime and behavior?

At the time of its creation, it is clear, the regime was the product not of actual behavior but rather of other, endogenous factors—in particular, the experiences of the interwar period and World War II. The interwar experience had generated a broad consensus in favor of establishing some kind of mechanism to provide limited amounts of supplementary payments financing. World War II had confirmed the economic and political predominance of the United States. The fact that a regime emerged from Bretton Woods at all reflected the allies' collective perception of self-interest in monetary affairs. The specific shape of that regime reflected largely the individual concerns and influence of the United States.

Moreover, over the next quarter of a century, it was mostly the regime that influenced behavior rather than the reverse. Deficit countries, with the important exception of the United States, did in fact generally respect IMF policy conditionality when availing themselves of supplementary payments financing—although, to be sure, this reflected conditions on both the demand and the supply sides of the system as much as it did the influence of the regime as such. Governments played by the formal rules agreed at Bretton Woods not only because they were legally committed to do so by an international agreement but also because their need for supplementary financing did not in general exceed what the IMF could provide and because there were few alternative sources of financing to compete with the Fund. Maintenance of the regime in the 1950s and 1960s was attributable as much to the general absence of either need or means to circumvent the regime as it was to the enlightened self-interest of nations.

Conversely, when conditions changed dramatically in the 1970s, so did behavior. The vast increase in the need for financing led countries to search for new sources of external credit; the vast increase of liquidity in financial markets led banking institutions to search for new customers. The result was a profound change in the appearance of the regime as the markets emerged as a major alternative source of financing for deficit countries. No longer did the IMF stand alone as arbiter of access to payments support.

But this cannot be regarded as a transformation of kind. Owing to the informal working relationship that has gradually developed between the IMF and the markets whereby private lenders, in cases of serious payments difficulties, treat negotiation of a Fund standby (with attendant policy conditionality) as a prerequisite for lending, the basic principle underlying the regime as well as commonly agreed standards of behavior for deficit nations have, for the most part, been preserved. While rules and decisionmaking procedures admittedly have become somewhat vaguer than they were, and for some countries the room for cheating has been increased, these changes have been for the most part "norm-governed" in character. In its essential purpose, the financing regime continues to have a real effect on behavior.

Jurisdictional Boundaries of the Regime

Finally, it is of interest to consider the impact of recent events on the jurisdictional boundaries of the financing regime.

Originally, a very clear division of labor was intended to distinguish the work of the IMF from that of its sister organization created at Bretton Woods, the World Bank (formally, the International Bank for Reconstruction and Development). The mandate of the Fund was to lend for relatively short periods of time to help maintain international payments equilibrium. The mandate of the Bank was to lend for much longer periods to help support postwar economic recovery and, subsequently, economic development in poorer countries. The regime to govern access to IMF financing was firmly embedded in the broader question of balance-of-payments adjustment. The regime to govern access to Bank financing was firmly embedded in the broader question of development assistance.

More recently, however, as a result of repeated increases in world oil prices since 1973, the line dividing the Fund's mandate from the Bank's has grown rather more ambiguous. In fact, the Fund has come under a great deal of pressure to extend increased amounts of credit to deficit countries—particularly in the Third World—for longer periods and with more flexible policy conditions.[40]   In an era of persistent OPEC surpluses, it is argued, deficits in non-oil developing countries cannot be treated simply as a short-term phenomenon caused by faulty domestic policies and amenable to traditional policy prescriptions (e.g., devaluation or monetary and fiscal restraint). Oil-induced deficits perforce must be expected to continue for much longer periods, until such time as the nations involved can make the necessary "structural" adjustments to the altered relative cost of energy. In the meantime, the Fund should make a greater effort to supplement private lending by reforms of its own lending policies, such as making more money available for longer-term, structural measures to narrow net dependence on oil imports and to broaden the foreign-exchange earning capacity of deficit countries.

To some extent, the Fund has tried to respond to these pressures. In 1979, the executive board issued a new set of guidelines on policy conditionality explicitly acknowledging that adjustment in many cases might require a longer period of time than traditionally assumed in Fund stabilization programs, and pledging to "pay due regard to . . . the circumstances of members, including the causes of their balance-of-payments problems."[41] And in 1980 and 1981 a new policy of "enlarged access" to the Fund's resources was brought formally into effect, along with a 50 percent increase of all members' quotas. Under the new policy, the maximum amount that a country may in principle cumulatively borrow from the Fund has been raised from 467.5 percent of its quota to 600 percent.[42]   In addition, an increasing proportion of Fund lending is now being directed through the Extended Fund Facility, thus making available more financing for longer periods of time than had generally been available in the past.

However, as these changes have been carried out, the Fund has found itself moving closer to the traditional province of the World Bank—just as, simultaneously, the Bank has been moving the other way. Also under pressure to do more for countries hit hard by the increased relative cost of energy, the Bank in 1979 began to shift from its usual emphasis on long-term project lending to more, relatively short-term, program lending for "structural adjustment" purposes. The object of such lending, in the words of a senior Bank official, is "to provide support for member countries already in serious BOP [balance-of-payments] difficulties, or faced in the years ahead with the prospect of unmanageable deficits arising from external factors which are not likely to be easily or quickly reversed."[43] This sounds remarkably similar to the IMF's explanations of its own lending policies.

In fact, we are witnessing a partial convergence of the roles of the Fund and the Bank—that is, a partial overlapping of the regimes governing access to payments financing and development assistance. Here, in the blurring of the jurisdictional boundary between these two regimes, is perhaps the most significant impact of the events of the 1970s. In the 1980s it will be increasingly difficult to maintain a clear distinction between these two forms of lending.

Notes

1. Guido Carli, *Why Banks Are Unpopular*, The 1976 Per Jacobson Lecture (Washington: IMF, 1976), pp. 6, 8.

2. *Towards Full Employment and Price Stability*, A Report to the OECD by a Group of Independent Experts, chaired by Paul McCracken (Paris: OECD, 1977), para. 159. In a still longer historical perspective, Charles Kindleberger has pointed out that—on an intermittent basis—private bankers at least since the Medici have made a practice of last-resort lending to governments at times of financial crisis; see his *Manias, Panics, and Crashes: A History of Financial Crises* (New York: Basic Books, 1978), chap. 10. Only with the growth of the Eurocurrency market, however, has balance-of-payments lending from private sources tended to become a *regular* practice.

3. Comprehensive histories of the wartime discussions and Bretton Woods conference can be found in J. Keith Horsefield, ed., *The International Monetary Fund, 1945-1965*, vol. 1: *Chronicle* (Washington: IMF, 1969), Part I; and Richard N. Gardner, *Sterling-Dollar Diplomacy* (Oxford: Clarendon Press, 1956), chaps. 5,7.

4. League of Nations, *International Currency Experience* (1944), p. 211.

5. Ibid., pp. 214-218.

6. Although the original Fund charter contained a provision prohibiting members in most circumstances from borrowing more than 25% of quota in any twelve-month period, in practice, as IMF operations evolved, this provision was frequently waived and was finally eliminated entirely in a Second Amendment of the Articles of Agreement of the IMF in 1976.

7. As a result of the Second Amendment in 1976, gold was eliminated from the Fund system of subscriptions and quotas. In lieu of gold, members now have a reserve tranche.

8. *Articles of Agreement of the International Monetary Fund,* Art V., Section 3 (a)(i). The original Articles are reprinted in Horsefield, *The IMF,* vol. 3; *Documents,* pp. 185-214.

9. *Articles of Agreement,* Art. I (iii) and (v).

10. For the evolution of the concept of policy conditionality, see Horsefield, *The IMF,* vol. 2; *Analysis,* chaps. 18, 20, 21, 23; Joseph Gold, *Conditionality,* IMF Pamphlet Series, no. 31 (Washington: IMF, 1979); Manuel Guitian, "Fund Conditionality and the International Adjustment Process: The Early Period, 1950-70," *Finance and Development vol. 17,* no. 4 (December 1980), pp. 23-27; and Frank A. Southard Jr., *The Evolution of the International Monetary Fund,* Essays in International Finance, no. 135 (Princeton: Princeton University, International Finance Section, 1979), pp. 15-21.

11. Formally, the Fund is governed by its Board of Governors, consisting of one Governor (usually the Finance Minister or central-bank Governor) from each member-country. However, since the Board of Governors only meets once a year, in practice most of its powers have been delegated to the Executive Board, which functions in continuous session. Executive Directors now (1981) number twenty-two, seven representing the five largest members of the Fund together with Saudi Arabia (one of the Fund's two largest creditors) and China, and fifteen representing various constituencies comprising collectively the remaining membership.

12. Decision no. 284-4, 10 March 1948, reprinted in Horsefield, *The IMF,* 3:227. Italics supplied.

13. Decision no. 102-(52/11), 13 February 1952, reprinted in Horsefield, *The IMF,* 3:228.

14. Ibid., p. 230.

15. IMF, *Annual Report,* 1959, p. 22.

16. For a model standby arrangement, see Joseph Gold,

Financial Assistance by the International Monetary Fund: Law and Practice, IMF Pamphlet Series, no. 27 (Washington: IMF, 1979), Appendix B.

17. For more on the Fund's decisionmaking procedures, see Horsefield, *The IMF*, 2, chap. 1; and Southard, *Evolution of IMF*, pp. 2-15.

18. Sidney E. Rolfe, *Gold and World Power* (New York: Harper & Row, 1966), p. 78.

19. *Articles of Agreement*, Art. V, Section 7.

20. See, e.g., Southard, *Evolution of IMF*, pp. 16-17.

21. Inadequacy of resources was not the only reason for the Fund's meager contribution during these years. In addition, there was the running debate over conditionality, which was not finally resolved until the Executive Board's landmark 1952 decision. See Southard, *Evolution of IMF*, p. 17.

22. The text of the arrangement is reprinted in Horsefield, *The IMF*, 3:246-56.

23. For more detail on EPU, see Robert Triffin, *Europe and the Money Muddle* (New Haven: Yale University Press, 1957), chaps. 5-6.

24. For more detail on the various support operations arranged for Britain during this period, see Benjamin J. Cohen, *The Future of Sterling as an International Currency* (London: Macmillan, 1971), pp. 97-98.

25. Benjamin J. Cohen, *Organizing the World's Money* (New York: Basic Books, 1977), pp. 95-97.

26. In fact, OPEC's absorptive capacity after the first round of oil price increases in 1973-74 surpassed expectations, and by 1978 its investable surplus (which averaged some $45 billion annually, 1974-76) had fallen to below $10 billion. But with the second round of price increases starting in late 1978, the surplus soared to $68 billion in 1980. Most observers expect this OPEC surplus to persist for much longer. See, e.g., Morgan Guaranty Trust Company, *World Financial Markets*, September 1980, pp. 1-13, and May 1981, pp. 3-5; *Citibank Monthly Economic Letter*, April 1981, pp. 5-6; IMF, *World Economic Outlook* (Washington, D.C., June 1981).

27. More recently, the Compensatory Financing Facility has been liberalized to permit borrowings up to 100% of quota.

28. For more detail on the Fund's various special facilities, see Gold, *Financial Assistance*; and *IMF Survey*, May 1981. "Supplement on the Fund," pp. 6-10. It should be noted that of

these facilities, only three—the Compensatory Financing Facility, the Buffer Stock Financing Facility, and the Extended Fund Facility—represent *permanent* additions to the IMF's lending authority.

29. For more detail, see Benjamin J. Cohen, *Banks and the Balance of Payments*, in collaboration with Fabio Basagni (Montclair, NJ: Allenheld, Osmun, 1981), chap. 1.

30. Ibid.

31. Wilfried Guth, in Guth and Sir Arthur Lewis, *The International Monetary System in Operation*, The 1977 Per Jacobson Lecture (Washington: IMF, 1977), p. 25.

32. Arthur F. Burns, "The Need for Order in International Finance," in *International Banking Operations*, Hearings before the Subcommittee on Financial Institutions Supervision, Regulations, and Insurance of U.S., Congress, House Committee on Banking, Finance and Urban Affairs, (Washington, D.C., March-April 1977), p. 860.

33. IMF, *Annual Report*, 1977, p. 41.

34. For more detail on the Peruvian and other examples cited in this section, see Cohen, *Banks and the Balance of Payments*, chap. 4 and Appendix.

35. J. A. Kirbyshire, "Should Developments in the Euro-Markets be a Source of Concern to Regulatory Authorities?," *Bank of England Quarterly Bulletin vol. 17, no. 1* (March 1977), p. 44.

36. See, e.g., Giovanni Magnifico, "The Real Role of the IMF," *Euromoney*, October 1977, pp. 141-44; Charles Lipson, "The IMF, Commercial Banks, and Third World Debts," in Jonathan David Aronson, ed., *Debt and the Less Developed Countries* (Boulder, CO: Westview Press, 1979); and Carl R. Neu, "The International Monetary Fund and LDC Debt," in Lawrence G. Franko and Marilyn J. Seiber, eds., *Developing Country Debt* (New York: Pergamon Press, 1979).

37. Richard D. Hill, in *International Debt*. Hearings before the Subcommittee on International Finance of U.S., Congress, House Committee on Banking, Housing and Urban Affairs (Washington, D.C., 1977), p. 127.

38. There seems little to be done to reverse this erosion, at least by way of formal reforms, without losing the acknowledged benefits of private lending for balance-of-payments purposes. See Cohen, *Banks and the Balance of Payments*, pp. 171-76.

39. See e.g., Peter B. Kenen, *Giant Among Nations* (New York: Harcourt, Brace, 1960), pp. 93-94.

40. See, e.g., Group of 24, *Outline for a Program of Action on International Monetary Reform*, reprinted in *IMF Survey*, 15 October 1979, pp. 319-23; *North-South: A Programme for Survival*. Report of the Independent Commission on International Development Issues, chaired by Willy Brandt (Cambridge: MIT Press, 1980), chap. 13; and Sidney Dell and Roger Lawrence, *The Balance of Payments Adjustment Process in Developing Countries* (New York: Pergamon Press, 1980). I have associated myself with this point of view in Benjamin J. Cohen, "Balancing the System in the 1980's: Private Banks and the IMF," in Gary Clyde Hufbauer, ed., *The International Framework for Money and Banking in the 1980s* (Washington: International Law Institute, 1981).

41. See *IMF Survey*, 19 March 1979, pp. 82-83; and Gold, *Conditionality*, pp. 14-37.

42. In practice the limit is even higher, since the 600% figure does not take into account loans from either the Compensatory Financing Facility or the Buffer Stock Financing Facility. See *IMF Survey*, May 1981, "Supplement on the Fund," p. 10. The first country to borrow up to this new maximum was Turkey, in June 1980. See *IMF Survey*, 25 June 1980, p. 177. The IMF had never previously lent more than 400% of a member's quota.

43. E. Peter Wright, "World Bank Lending for Structural Adjustment," *Finance and Development*, September 1980, p. 21.

11
A Global Chapter 11*

On the crowded agenda of international economic issues facing the Bush administration, few challenges appear more daunting or less tractable than the festering problem of Third World debt. Seven years after Mexico's dramatic financial collapse in summer 1982, fatigue clearly has set in on all sides as the economies of developing-country debtors continue to stagnate under onerous service obligations to their creditors. Equally clearly, vital American interests are at stake in the search for a durable solution that will not only protect the soundness of the largest U.S. banks but also restore markets for U.S. exports and reduce the threat of political instability in countries ranging from Argentina to the Philippines. The main accomplishment of the Reagan administration was to skillfully steer incipient—and recurrent—debt crises away from the brink through what amounted to a strategy of containment. The Bush administration seems aware that it must aim higher.

Even before he took office in January 1989, George Bush promised a "whole new look" at the issue. In March, Treasury secretary Nicholas Brady duly unveiled a broad new set of proposals that called on banks to help reduce the outstanding obligations of countries prepared to commit themselves to genuine economic policy reforms. Treasury sources indicated that the Brady plan envisaged a reduction of as much as 20 percent for all debtors over the next 3 years. The approach, which Brady said was needed to "reinvigorate a process that has become debt-weary," reflected a growing consensus in the financial community that the prevailing strategy was in serious need of reform. The principle of debt reduction already had become fashionable among bankers and public officials in recent years, with most emphasis placed on the so-called menu

*Reprinted with permission from *Foreign Policy* 75 (Fall 1989), pp. 109-127. Copyright by the Carnegie Endowment for International Peace.

approach of various schemes for debt conversions and buy-backs. What Brady added was the U.S. government's imprimatur for further development and elaboration of the menu approach, backed by the prospect of possible new financing from Japan and perhaps even some guarantees of debt obligations by the International Monetary Fund (IMF) and the World Bank.

The good news in the Brady plan is the administration's willingness to acknowledge the failure of the old strategy and to conclude that direct relief of troubled debtors is necessary. Such a recognition of reality is welcome, even if the magnitude of the relief currently envisaged may be too modest to fully ease the cash-flow strains on debtors. The bad news is the administration's unwillingness to move beyond the past reliance on essentially voluntary approaches initiated by the banking community. In this sense, the administration's program represents no more than a refinement of the prevailing strategy rather than a fundamental reform. Until now, efforts to organize significant concessions by banks have foundered on the notorious free-rider problem—the obvious incentive for individual lenders to avoid participating in costly debt-reduction plans while hoping to reap the benefit of any ensuing gains in the value of their claims. The key question of how to overcome this obstacle to effective collective action remains.

The answer, ideally, would lie in a more concerted approach—imaginative institutional innovation designed to facilitate a negotiated resolution of less-developed-country (LDC) debt-service difficulties on a case-by-case basis that would be consistent with the interests of all concerned parties. Experience suggests, however, that this would require major changes in the political equation underlying creditor-debtor relations, since many on the lender side remain highly resistant to any alternative strategy of concerted debt relief. Progress ultimately depends on the distribution of leverage among the players around the negotiating table. No real solution will be possible without a significant new initiative from Washington to replace—not merely refine—the discredited containment strategy of the past.

One of the most striking features of the containment strategy has been the heavy burden borne by debtors through lost growth and net outward transfers of resources. Equally striking has been the willingness of debtors to acquiesce in this painful result.

With rare exceptions, Third World governments have deliberately chosen not to repudiate their debts or otherwise refuse to acknowledge their full contractual obligations. Most have been careful to preserve their lines of communication with other major actors and to abide as much as possible by the results of creditor-debtor negotiations, however unfavorable they seem. The reason clearly has had most to do with underlying configurations of power in the political arena, both within individual debtor countries and in the broader strategic interaction with creditors. These two factors have typically intersected to make acquiescence appear by far the least-cost choice for LDC policymakers. Domestic politics have encouraged most debtor governments to eschew the option of default, while realistic fears of the consequences of any rash action have been greatly reinforced by the tactics of foreign creditors.

Within individual countries the burden of adjustment typically has fallen most heavily on those groups that are the least well positioned to affect the course of government policy—that is, unorganized labor, peasant farmers, small business, civil servants, and the urban and rural poor. That outcome is no accident. It is, in fact, a direct consequence of their lack of access to options much more readily available to powerful domestic interests. Private industrialists, large landowners, managers of parastatal enterprises, and the military can often use their influence to extract special treatment from policymakers or to win exemption from taxation or repressive economic policies. Many are also able, in extreme circumstances, to take their movable assets elsewhere—otherwise known as capital flight. The more successful local elites have been in exercising these options, the less pressure they have exerted on debtor governments to seek a change in the ongoing debt strategy.

Exercise of influence has also been evident in the interaction with creditors. Commercial bankers, often backed by their home governments and the multilateral institutions, have not hesitated to exploit their abundant potential for side-payments or sanctions to shape outcomes to their advantage. LDC acquiescence has been encouraged by holding out the prospect of more generous rescheduling terms, such as longer grace periods, lower interest margins, and relaxed policy conditions, and perhaps even some "spontaneous" new financing somewhere down the road. Recalcitrance has been discouraged by implicit or explicit threats of retaliatory penalties, which might include not just a cessation of medium-term lending or an interruption of short-term trade credits but also the seizure of exports or even attachment of a debtor's foreign assets, such as commercial airliners, ships, and bank accounts. The more successful creditors have been at such carrot-and-stick tactics, the more pressure they have put on debtor governments not to seek a change in the prevailing strategy. Is it any wonder, then, that LDCs have been willing to do most of the adjusting?

Changing Power Relationships

Configurations of power can change, of course. Indeed, they seem to be changing now, in part precisely because of a growing awareness of the prevailing strategy's bankruptcy. The problem is that underlying relationships do not seem to be changing fast enough to overcome anytime soon the powerful creditor resistance to an alternative strategy of concerted debt relief.

Within many debtor countries power relationships are shifting because of the growing sensitivity of influential economic and social groups to the heavy costs of maintaining full debt service abroad. As the February 1989 rioting in Venezuela demonstrated, the constraints imposed by the debt problem act like a pressure cooker to heat up conflicts of interest among societal forces, eroding the political basis for continuing the acquiescence to creditors. With persistent economic stagnation the domestic political pot could reach the boiling point, raising the specter of disorder or worse. Debtor governments, whether they liked it or not, could then be compelled to look for more radical solutions to their difficulties—up to and including a unilateral moratorium on all outstanding contractual obligations.

The domestic volatility in debtor countries is increasingly being reinforced at the international level by a parallel erosion of the effectiveness of the creditors' carrot-and-stick tactics. The issue here is credibility. Strenuous LDC attempts to improve trade balances have still not earned any renewal of voluntary lending by the international financial markets; even Colombia, the one Latin American country that since 1982 has never requested a rescheduling, has experienced great difficulty in arranging any fresh financing from Western banks. Meanwhile, recent defiant acts by several LDC governments have failed to provoke any damaging penalties from creditors. Even Peru, which under its socialist president, Alan Garcia, has probably been the most confrontational Third World debtor, has not seen any of its exports seized or foreign assets attached. Reportedly the Peruvians are still able to raise an adequate amount of trade financing simply by paying slightly more than standard market rates. Many debtors are becoming increasingly skeptical that they have all that much to fear from creditors.

Such skepticism appears well founded, for two reasons. One is juridical uncertainty: the limited, not to say dubious, basis in law for the usual list of legal sanctions threatened by creditors against recalcitrant debtors. Few court precedents exist to establish the right of international lenders to seize exports or attach the assets of a sovereign borrower. Despite much discussion, lawyers themselves are still unable to agree on just what forms of legal redress, if any, may in principle be applicable under the circumstances, or even whether any court judgments could, in practical terms, be enforced. The second reason relates to the sheer number of debtors that have to be induced or pressured into acceptance to preserve creditor credibility. Neither side-payments nor sanctions are costless. As the ranks of potential defaulters have grown, so, too, have the hesitations of creditors to make actual use of their putative leverage.

Creditors are not unaware of the decline of their own credibility and, to the extent possible, have acted decisively to maintain their bargaining position with respect to debtors by bolstering primary capital and loan-loss reserves, and in some cases by selling off or swapping selected portions of their LDC portfolios. But it is not at all clear that these defensive measures will ever fully restore the creditor side's early capacity to shape outcomes to its advantage. A critical question, therefore, is whether debtors might now seize the opportunity for themselves. Do LDCs on their own now have the power to overcome creditor resistance to debt relief?

Most potent would be some form of collective action by LDC governments to extract concessions from creditors—some variant, in other words, of the long-dreaded debtors' cartel. However, the chances that a cartel would be formed even now must be counted as rather remote. Recent experience, particularly in Latin America, demonstrates that, rhetoric to the contrary notwithstanding, serious obstacles exist to effective coordination among debtors. One fundamental reason is the extraordinary diversity of economic conditions and prospects on the debtor side, which tends to overshadow any underlying common interest in debt relief. Another is national sovereignty, which maximizes each government's incentive to seek out the best deal for itself. Additional obstacles include differences in the timing of financial crises, in foreign strategic relationships, in domestic political systems, and even in the personalities and values of key decisionmakers.

Perhaps the most crucial obstacle of all, however, is that from the debtors' point of view, formal coordination may not be necessary and could well be counterproductive, insofar as it might serve merely to provoke governmental and public opinion in creditor countries. Far less provocative, but not necessarily much less potent, would be the cumulative effect of a series of individual initiatives by troubled debtors—just as has been occurring lately, as a result of changing power relationships at home or abroad, in both Latin America and sub-Saharan Africa. At one time or another in recent years, more than a dozen governments, including most recently Venezuela, have unilaterally ceased debt service or fallen into serious arrears, saving valuable foreign exchange.[1]   Once in arrears, debtors only rarely seem to find both the will and the means to catch up with their interest payments. Yet precisely because of the growing number of countries involved, creditors have become increasingly hesitant to engage in any costly reprisals. So who needs a debtors' cartel when much the same impact can be achieved without the difficulties and risks of formal coordination?

By far the most likely scenario, therefore, at least for the near term, is a continuation of the trend discernible in these sporadic de facto defaults by debtor governments—collective inaction (nonpayment) rather than collective action. The more persistent the trend, the greater the eventual erosion of the bargaining leverage of creditors will be. To that extent, momentum would appear to be flowing to the debtors. The political equation does seem to be changing.

But is it changing enough? That remains in considerable doubt. An ebbing of creditor leverage is one thing; a flow of momentum sufficient on its own to force a fundamental reform of the traditional strategy is something else again. In good part the outcome ultimately will depend on which LDCs may choose to join the ranks of nonpayers. Sustained de facto defaults by three of four of the largest debtor countries plainly would do more to concentrate minds on the creditor side than several times that many unilateral initiatives by smaller players. But since it is impossible to foresee who might actually be tempted or driven to default, it is also impossible to know whether this trend alone would alter decisively creditor attitudes on debt relief. The odds in favor of debtors may be shortening somewhat but hardly enough, it seems, to be able to declare categorically that the game is over.

The American Tune

If any further reform of the prevailing strategy occurs in the near future, it will more likely come from changes on the creditor side than on the debtor side. The creditor side is not a monolith, after all. Underlying alignments among commercial lenders, and between them and public institutions, are becoming more fluid as the debt problem drags on. Here, too, however, the problem is that the resulting shifts of power relationships thus far do not seem to be enough to alter fundamentally creditors' collective behavior toward debtors.

Until now, despite potential coordination problems, creditors have been remarkably successful at maintaining sufficient solidarity in debt negotiations to shape outcomes largely to their advantage. This reflects above all the inordinate influence of the largest commercial lenders—the two or three dozen giants at the peak of the global banking industry. The giants, with their high levels of exposure, have stood to lose the most from any concessions to debtors; so their interests have been served most directly by the containment strategy of the last half-decade. In effect, therefore, it is they who have called the tune—even where other creditors, with other mixes of interest, might well have preferred a different drummer. Creditor solidarity has been maintained by a decisionmaking process dominated, implicitly if not explicitly, by the needs and preferences of the biggest commercial lenders.

In practice, the giants have remained dominant, however imperfectly, by exploiting two basic features of their institutional environment. One is the distinctly oligopolistic and hierarchical structure of the international banking community, which gives larger intermediaries disproportionate influence over the behavior of smaller rivals. As a general rule, the biggest banks first negotiate terms with each other and with debtors, and then seek ratification by smaller institutions, using the usual tactics of side-payments and sanctions. For example, local and regional banks can be induced by offers of privileged access to interbank credit lines or possible participation in lucrative new lending syndicates. They can also be coerced by threats of exclusion from traditional industry networks and correspondent relationships—"peer pressure," as it is politely known in the trade.

The other relevant feature is the distinctly fragmented structure of policy assignments within national governments, which in the capital-market countries as a whole tends to give banks disproportionate influence over official attitudes on the debt problem. In all the capital-market countries, primary responsibility for LDC debt issues has been entrusted to finance ministries or central banks rather than to foreign ministries or industry—or trade-oriented agencies. The result, not surprisingly, has been to accord highest priority to the purely financial aspects of the problem, rather than to the political, security, or commercial implications.

Comparatively little weight has been attached to possible threats of political disruption or lost export opportunities in the Third World. Public policy has been conditioned most directly by concerns for the safety and soundness of financial institutions. And because the largest institutions have the most at risk, their interests have generally received the most attention. The interests of others on the creditor side, such as smaller lenders and exporters, to say nothing of debtors, may not have been wholly ignored as a result, but they certainly have been discounted. It is hardly necessary to invoke some kind of conspiracy theory to account for the tacit alliances that have coalesced on this issue between the big international lenders and their home governments.

Within this configuration of creditor power, no actors have been more influential than those of the United States: the major money-center banks of New York, Chicago, and California together with the Federal Reserve Board and, most important, the department of the Treasury. Other players on the creditor side, including the governments of other capital-market countries, have tended to defer to U.S. leadership in dealing with the problems of Third World commercial borrowers. This reflects the key role of the dollar as the currency of denomination for most LDC bank loans, making the Federal Reserve in effect lender of last resort in the event of a debt-induced financial crisis. Even more to the point, it reflects the dominant market share of U.S. intermediaries in the most prominent troubled debtor countries in Latin America and the Philippines.

The bank advisory committees that negotiate with debtor governments traditionally comprise at most a dozen or so of a country's largest creditors. This has given America's big money-center intermediaries, backed by the Federal Reserve and the Treasury, by far the greatest influence in formulating and managing the containment strategy. It is no accident that the strategy adopted to deal with the debt crisis was first developed at the Federal Reserve and the Treasury department back in 1982. Nor is it an accident that all major adjustments of the strategy since then have also emanated from Washington—the celebrated Baker plan of 1985 (named for its author, then Treasury secretary and now secretary of state James Baker II), the menu approach first formally articulated in 1987, and now the Brady plan of 1989. The tune that has been called over the decade has had a distinctly American ring to it.

Alignments on the creditor side have recently become noticeably more fluid as a result of growing distributional struggles among banks and between them and other interested parties in the capital-market countries. Smaller banks, for instance, increasingly seem prepared to break ranks with the giants of the industry despite peer pressure. Many, especially those with only limited Third World exposure and few other commercial ties to LDCs, are simply getting out of existing syndicates by selling off their paper in the secondary market or by refusing to participate in new reschedulings, thus forcing larger banks to take over their shares. Others, more dramatically, are writing off substantial portions of their portfolios or working out separate deals with debtor governments.

Likewise, even among the major creditors, divergences of interests and priorities now appear to be widening significantly. Certainly this is evident in the mounting dissatisfaction of the continental European banks, which have long chafed under the status quo strategy of rescheduling plus concerted lending favored by the big U.S. banking institutions, the Federal Reserve, and the Treasury. Dissension is also evident within the ranks of the American banks, which have been split on a number of recent occasions, particularly following Citicorp's dramatic unilateral 1987 decision to add to its loan-loss reserves. That initiative was unexpected; and while it is true that it was soon emulated by other U.S. lenders, it was also resented by those money-center banks less profitable or more exposed to Third World debt than Citicorp and therefore less well positioned to meet what then became a new standard for American lenders: a minimum provision of 25 percent against overall LDC claims.

Tensions over the issue were exacerbated near the end of 1987 by a second round of reserve increases, to an even higher standard of 50 percent or more of exposure, started by the Bank of Boston and some other large regional institutions. By early 1988, a distinct leverage had developed between the big New York institutions, together with the San Francisco-based Bank of America, on the one hand, and the remaining money-center banks of California and Chicago, as well as most regional institutions, on the other. The first grouping refused to add yet again to their LDC provisions; the latter opted for the new, higher standard. Increasingly, relations among America's major banks appear to be dominated less by thoughts of preserving industry solidarity than by sentiments of salvaging what they can.

Finally, other parties outside the financial community with their own interests in debtor countries are beginning to voice serious opposition to the prevailing strategy. This is especially true of constituencies in the export sector, in the United States and elsewhere, as awareness grows of the extent to which debt-induced stagnation has shrunk traditional markets in developing countries. Exporters clearly have had their consciousness raised in recent years. Anger has been directed in particular at the Federal Reserve and the Treasury for their evident bias in favor of financial interests. More and more, calls have been made to accord higher priority to commercial and security considerations. Pressures have visibly grown to loosen the close, albeit tacit, bank-government alliances that have dominated decisionmaking on LDC debt.

Yet despite all these strains on the creditor side, no fundamental reform of the ongoing strategy can be expected unless existing coalitions are supplanted by new and even strong alignments of forces, implicit if not explicit, in the capital-market countries. Increased fluidity among the players is not enough. Resentments and frustrations must be translated into effective collective action if the political equation is in fact to be significantly altered. The big banks, backed by finance ministries and central banks, are unlikely to abandon their resistance to debt relief without a struggle. Absent sufficient leverage from the debtor side, resistance can be diminished or overcome only by a superior use of influence from within the creditor side—new tactics of side payments or sanctions to replace those previously exercised by the industry giants. This can be accomplished only through some degree of political organization among other players inside the financial community or outside it.

Unfortunately, there is little evidence to indicate that such organization will occur spontaneously. Inside the financial community, barriers to alternative alignments will remain high so long as the industry remains so oligopolistic and hierarchical. Outside, other interested parties will continue to have difficulty influencing official attitudes as long as finance ministries and central banks retain primary policy responsibility on debt. And any coalescence of links between selected elements of the financial community, like the smaller banks, and other actors, like exporters, will continue to be hampered by the lack of a tradition and an institutional base for collective action. Thus more realistically it must be admitted that here, too, as on the debtor side, the odds are unlikely to shorten enough to allow a categorical declaration that the game is over.

The Need for Leadership

The implication of all this is clear. If collective action to further reform the prevailing strategy is unlikely to occur spontaneously, it follows that a genuinely new approach will have to be promoted. Leadership will be required to bring all the concerned parties to agreement. And that leadership, despite America's own current debtor status, can come only from the United States—still unique in its capacity to exercise effective leverage over lenders and borrowers alike. The increased fluidity of alignments on the creditor side affords the Bush administration a real opportunity for imaginative institutional innovation. The challenge is to organize actively a political coalition that can supplant the past tacit alliance between the big money-center banks and the Treasury and Federal Reserve. Until now, the only serious efforts in Washington along these lines have been launched from the congressional end of Pennsylvania Avenue. But so far such efforts have all run aground because of determined opposition from the executive branch.

An early case in point was the so-called Bradley plan—the well-publicized debt-relief scheme proposed by Senator Bill Bradley (D-New Jersey) in 1986. It would have tied eligibility for concessions on commercial debt directly to a debtor's commitment to trade liberalization designed to promote imports from the United States and other industrialized countries. By linking trade and debt so explicitly, Bradley hoped to attract export interests into the policymaking process as a counterweight to the dominant influence of the money-center banks. Despite some initially favorable reactions, however, his plan soon faded into oblivion owing to the persistent opposition of the Treasury and Federal Reserve. Much the same fate also awaited similar proposals advanced later by other "debt hawks" in Congress, such as Representatives John LaFalce (D-New York) and Donald Pease (D-Ohio). Likewise, Reagan administration lobbying succeeded in watering down far-reaching debt-relief provisions introduced at an early stage into the 1988 omnibus trade bill.

Even so, advocates of a new approach are unlikely to be discouraged, and more efforts of the same kind can be expected. The more the idea of concerted debt relief is floated in the public domain, the more likely it is that many of the diverse parties involved—such as large European banks, smaller U.S. lenders, and exporters—will come to appreciate the extent to which their interests are shared, and hence that a new and stronger coalition of political forces should be forged to promote genuine reform of the prevailing strategy. It was presumably with that thought in mind that the Bush administration moved to preempt critics of past policies with its new proposals for voluntary debt reductions. But the Brady plan is hardly likely to be the end of the story. With the fluidity always associated with the arrival of a new administration in Washington, the alternative of a more concerted approach to relief could yet turn out to be an idea whose time has finally come.

Naturally, much will depend on the design of any alternative reform strategy proposed to large lenders. To be realistic, any new concerted approach must be genuinely responsive to the legitimate concerns of commercial creditors. This might best be

accomplished through the creation of an international mechanism for relief of troubled debtors structured on the model of
Chapter 11 of the U.S. Bankruptcy Code or analogous regulations
elsewhere.

Creditor concerns about debt relief encompass a wide range of
valid issues. First and foremost, lenders worry about possible
"contagion effects" in the financial markets—potentially dis-
astrous ripples and feedbacks that could flow throughout the
system from a widespread markdown of Third World obligations.
They also worry about the serious damage that might be done to
debtors' long-term credit standing and access to future financing.
Another concern is the possible deleterious effects on the policy
behavior of developing countries; debt relief might critically
dilute present incentives to adopt tough domestic adjustment
measures and reforms or even might induce some LDCs to
deliberately worsen their economic performance in order to
qualify for major concessions. And creditors are anxious about
any new intrusion of politics into an already highly charged
negotiating framework, which they prefer to keep as formally
voluntary and market-oriented as possible.

Analysis suggests, however, that these concerns could be
largely allayed by a reform plan incorporating five crucial
safeguards. These are:

Selectivity: a differentiated, case-by-case approach that
limits any forgiveness of contractual obligations to just those
LDCs that, by objective analysis, appear to face something
approximating real insolvency rather than mere illiquidity. A
case-by-case approach has been an integral part of the prevailing strategy. An equivalent approach, if applied in the context
of debt relief, would substantially diminish any risk of contagion effects in financial markets.

Flexibility: changes or reinterpretations of existing account-
ing regulations with the intention of permitting commercial
creditors to stretch out the capital losses or other costs when
LDC obligations are reduced. This, too, would lower the risk of
contagion in financial markets.

Conditionality: a direct link between relief and appropriate
policy commitments by debtors, another practice that is already
well established. Making concessions contingent upon implementation of needed adjustment measures would surely minimize any
risk of deleterious effects on LDC credit standing and policy
behavior.

Mutuality: explicit recognition of rights and obligations on both sides, a norm vital to the success of any strategy.

Autonomy: preservation of an essentially voluntary and market-oriented negotiating framework to avoid further politicization of the debt issue.

These five safeguards provide the working principles for a new and truly reformed debt strategy. The challenge is to translate them into a specific design that is likely to be practicable and effective.

A useful model is Chapter 11 and similar mechanisms elsewhere already established to deal with insolvency at the national level. Under Chapter 11, debtors unable to meet their contractual obligations can appeal for protection from creditors while they reorganize their affairs under the supervision of a bankruptcy court and work out mutually satisfactory terms for resolving their difficulties. The procedure embodies all five of the working principles just enumerated. Mutuality and autonomy are preserved by an essentially voluntary and market-oriented negotiating framework based on explicit recognition of respective rights and obligations. Selectivity is maintained in the debtor's right to make the initial decision to seek protection. Flexibility is inherent in the virtually unlimited scope provided for final terms of settlement. And conditionality is reflected in the court's assignment to a supervisory role over the debtor's ongoing operations. Debtors benefit from the opportunity to restore order to their economic affairs without being driven to the wall. But creditors, too, are protected insofar as conditions are attached to the assistance thus provided.

Emulating this model at the international level would first require the establishment of an institution authorized to play a role in LDC debt negotiations comparable to that of the bankruptcy court in the Chapter 11 procedure, though to be acceptable to sovereign debtors it would presumably not have the court's formal powers of adjudication and arbitration. If creditors and debtors were to be persuaded to accept the risks of an alternative debt-relief strategy, some impartial intermediary would have to exist that could assure both sides that their rights and needs would be respected. Players would be entitled to a degree of confidence that the new strategy would be interpreted and implemented objectively and equitably, ensuring creditors, on the one hand, that irresponsible economic management in developing countries would not be encouraged, and ensuring debtors, on the other, that the price of relief would not be too steep. In short, they would need a mediator.

Such a mediating institution could be called the International Debt Restructuring Agency (IDRA) and would have to be established by multilateral convention. Ideally it would be organized as a wholly new and independent entity to underscore its impartiality and objectivity. In practice it might be more feasible—and certainly would be quicker—to start IDRA as a joint subsidiary of the two multilateral agencies most involved in the problem, the IMF and the World Bank. It could thereby rely on the expertise and experience of existing staff members who would be detailed for this project. IDRA's general mandate would be to facilitate fair negotiations between creditors and debtors. More specifically, its role would be to promote agreement between creditors and debtors—for example, by enfranchising representative committees for each class of claimant, setting timetables for discussions, acting as a conduit of communication, and perhaps even proposing formulas for settlements—while exercising general surveillance over the relevant policy decisions of debtors.

Once the institutional framework was established, LDC debtors would have the right to apply to IDRA if they believed their circumstances warranted some relief. However, in doing so they would commit themselves irrevocably to a process of conciliated negotiation with their creditors, as well as to some IDRA surveillance of their policies. Relief would be provided only where all the parties concerned concurred that it was justified. The terms of relief would be anything to which the debtor and a qualified majority of creditors agreed. Following agreement, adherence to the terms would be supervised by IDRA until the country was back on its feet and its external creditworthiness was restored. Creditors would be permitted to withdraw all concessions on such matters as interest rates if IDRA determined that a debtor was out of compliance with its policy commitments.

Would such a design be politically feasible? Commercial banks as well as developing countries ought to find it attractive since, like the Chapter 11 procedure, it embodies all five of the principles that seem necessary to make an alternative strategy acceptable. The banks' home governments should also find it appealing since it puts a minimal demand on scarce public revenues. In this respect the design stands in stark contrast to most other plans for institutional innovation that have been proposed since 1982 in that they usually call for the creation or designation of some international facility to aid in the consolidation of LDC debt. The distinguishing characteristic of all such proposals is that a sizable financial liability, outright or contingent, would have to be assumed by a public institution as part of a multilaterally negotiated program of debt relief. All, therefore, would require some level of funding or financial risk for the governments of the capital-market countries. IDRA, by contrast, calls for mediation, not intermediation. Hence it would entail no explicit financial commitment beyond the comparatively trivial amounts needed for its own operating expenses. This would surely count as a plus in practical political terms.

Implicitly, to be sure, there would be some cost to taxpayers, insofar as they would be obligated to compensate for any tax deductions or credits legitimately taken by banks when LDC obligations were marked down. This could give rise to charges that public money was being used to bail out private lenders. In reality that would be true only to the extent that the loss of taxable bank earnings implied by any settlement negotiated under IDRA could otherwise be averted—a dubious proposition at best if current discounts in the secondary debt market and other signs of doubt in the financial community are to be believed. In any event, the pain for taxpayers would be eased no less than that for banks by any regulatory changes stretching out the costs of debt relief. Any remaining discomfort should not be politically intolerable; it would be a small price to pay, really, for a genuinely effective solution.

But it might be argued that the proposed IDRA mechanism would not actually add all that much. After all, creditors and debtors already negotiate directly, case by case, on a formally voluntary and market-oriented basis; and even now many bankers seem ready to agree with the Bush administration's new emphasis on selective concessions to help ease the plight of certain troubled debtors. Then why interpose some new player in a game where all the old players already know the rules? The answer should be evident: It is the failure of the current containment strategy, which inevitably generates frustration, confrontation, and conflict. The disadvantage of present procedures is that they encourage actors to concentrate mainly on their differences—the free-rider problem—rather than on areas of common interest. The great advantage of the IDRA approach, by contrast, is that it would structure incentives in a far more positive way for all the parties concerned.

In the end, of course, an IDRA mechanism would be only as effective as creditors and debtors wanted it to be. However, in a situation where both sides could potentially benefit, as compared with the prevailing strategy, good will ought not to be in short supply. The presence of IDRA arguably would help to reduce greatly or eliminate existing obstacles to further debt reform. With the stakes as high as they are, that would certainly be no mean accomplishment.

Notes

1. They include: Argentina, Bolivia, Brazil, Costa Rica, the Dominican Republic, Ecuador, Honduras, the Ivory Coast, Morocco, Nigeria, Peru, Venezuela, Zaire, and Zambia.

12

Toward a General Theory of Imperialism*

There are two issues of particular importance to any study of the subject of imperialism: (1) the *form* of dominance-dependence relationships, and (2) the *force(s)* giving rise to and maintaining them. These are the very meat of analysis. This essay will focus on the question of underlying motivating forces. Is there a common "taproot" (borrowing John Hobson's word)[1] to all of the various forms of imperialism?

What the Taproot Is Not

Marxists and radicals have no doubt that there is indeed a common taproot to the various forms of imperialism, and it is to be found in the presumed material needs of international capitalism. However, there is remarkably little evidence to support this point of view. The strictly economic interpretation of imperialism is substantiated neither by logic nor by the facts.

At the level of logic, there is little validity to any of the economic theories that have been developed by marxist or radical writers. Intellectual weaknesses are evident in the original underconsumption hypothesis as well as in Marx's alternative concept of the rising organic composition of capital. Parallel weaknesses are evident in the several contemporary lines of argument derived from these early approaches. None of the theories of marxists or radicals can prove that economic imperialism is necessary or inevitable as part of mature capitalist development, or that poor countries are necessarily retarded or exploited. The theories are all much too highly deterministic.

Neither is there much validity to any of these theories at the level of empirical observation. The nations of the periphery have rarely assumed the importance ascribed to them as markets or investment outlets, or even as sources of raw materials. This was true during the era of the so-called "new imperialism" of the late nineteenth century; it is equally true during the modern era of decolonization and the multinational corporation. In fact, for many LDCs economic relations with the metropolitan center have actually proved to be enormously beneficial in economic terms. The gains of the international capitalist economy do not all necessarily go to the rich.

All through history there have been innumerable examples of imperialism having nothing to do with the international capitalist economy or the presumed needs of its most advanced constituents. Some of the most aggressive imperial powers of the late nineteenth century could in no way be described as mature capitalist societies. (Nor could some of the most mature capitalist societies in any way be described as aggressive imperial powers.) In fact, the political form of imperialism both antedates and postdates the development of modern capitalism. Empires were known long before the industrial revolution began; empires still persist even where capitalism has been swept away. The behavior of the Soviet Union today in eastern Europe and elsewhere certainly qualifies for description as imperialistic.

In short, marxist and radical theories of economic imperialism do not stand up to close analytical scrutiny. All that needs to be said about them has by now been said. As intellectual constructs, they are like elaborate sand castles—a few waves of the incoming tide, and much of their substance gradually dissolves and washes away.

What the Taproot Is

Does this mean that there is no common taproot of imperialism—that it is impossible to account for all of its various forms within a single analytical framework? On the contrary, evidence is strong that a single theme does effectively explain each major variation. That theme, to recall Richard Hammond's phrasing, is "the good old game of power politics."[2]

Power politics. Power politics figure prominently as a guide to explaining imperial behavior in the nineteenth century, before as well as after the revival of formal empire-building around 1870. It also appears to be a principal motive for more contemporary forms of political imperialism, and is the basic force behind modern economic imperialism. In all these variations, major emphasis may be laid on considerations of politics, power, and national prestige. I suggest that the condition of international inequality has been actively affirmed by dominant nations because of the strategic needs of the state, not the commercial or financial needs of private business.

Not that the theme of power politics is particularly original in this connection. The political interpretation of imperialism has often been stressed by non-marxist or non-radical writers. As the British economic historian, W. H. B. Court, stated: "It is reasonable to believe that man is a political as well as an economic animal."[3] However, with only a few exceptions, most political interpretations of imperialism have unfortunately tended to be more superficial than profound. Most scholars writing in this vein have relied more on the hasty generalization or the pithy aphorism than on thorough and reasoned analysis. A prime example is Hans Morgenthau, who has written: "What the precapitalist imperialist, the capitalist imperialist, and the 'imperialist' capitalist want is power, not economic gain."[4] Taken in context, the idea is simply stated rather than explained: this is an obiter dictum, not an argument. The same is true of Raymond Aran, who has referred to a nation's "will to power,"[5] and of Court, who speaks of the "temptations to domination."[6] Consider also American economic historian David Landes, who speaks of the "logic of dominion":

> It seems to me that one has to look at imperialism as a multifarious response to a common opportunity that consists simply in a disparity of power.[7]

I agree that this is the way to look at imperialism, but it is hardly *all* one has to look at. Remarks such as these share the common virtue of being pointed in the right direction, but they also share the common vice of not going far enough. To gain a truly complete comprehension of this complex and "multifarious" phenomenon, one must ask what lies behind this logic of dominion, this will to power. It is not enough to assert simply, as political scientist Robert Tucker does, that "dominion is its own reward."[8]   That by itself is no more enlightening than to assert the contrary, as marxists and radicals in effect do, that dependence is its own punishment. Neither is it enough to assert simply, as Landes does, that "whenever and wherever such disparity [of power] has existed, people and groups have been ready to take advantage of it."[9] That by itself is no more convincing than the "dependencia" model, which also confuses opportunity and necessity. The real question is *why* people and groups have been ready to take advantage of a disparity of power. Why do nations exercise a will to power? Why do they yield to the temptations to domination? Here is where we approach the real nub of the matter.

In essence, this is the same question that has intrigued students of international relations at least since the days of Aristotle and Plato. It is the central problem of all international political theory, the problem of the cause of war and conflict among nations. Many different answers have been offered, perhaps more than could be fully comprehended by any single scholar in a lifetime. In his classic *Man, the State and War*, Kenneth Waltz comprehended as many as any scholar might, and suggested that all causes could usefully be ordered under three broad headings: (1) within man; (2) within the structure of the separate nation-states; or (3) within the structure of the system of nation-states.[10]   The first of these three images of international relations stresses defects in the nature and behavior of man; the second, defects in the internal organization of states; and the third, defects in the external organization of states (the state system). Together they exhaust all possible explanations (unless, of course, one cares to entertain metaphysical or extraterrestrial hypotheses).

Marxist and radical theories of imperialism clearly fall under the second of Waltz's headings. They are all variations on the same image of international relations; indeed, as Waltz himself notes, they "represent the fullest development of the second image."[11]   Nations exercise a will to power because they are organized internally along capitalist lines. Domination and conflict among nations are the direct result of the defects in social and economic structures within nations. The alternative theme that I suggest, by contrast, falls under the third of Waltz's headings. The "good old game of power politics" focuses deliberately on the state system itself, rather than on systems within states. The logic of dominion, I wish to argue, derives directly from the defects in the external organization of states.[12]

National security. As we know it, the state system consists of a relatively small number of separate national constituents—150 or so social collectivities, each organized within a particular constitutional order prevailing over some specific geographic terrain. The principal characteristic of the system is that each constituent claims the right to exercise complete sovereignty over its own internal affairs. As Waltz summarizes it: "The circumstances are simply the existence of a number of independent states that wish to remain independent."[13] The principal consequence of the system is that no constituent can claim the right to exercise even partial sovereignty over the external affairs of nations. No body of law, no rules, can be enforced in the realm of international relations. There is no automatic harmony, no automatic adjustment of interests. Each state is the final judge of its own ambitions and grievances. The system as whole, though interdependent, is formally in a condition of anarchy.

What is significant about this condition, from our point of view, is that in anarchy there can be no such thing as absolute security. No state can afford, without risk, to take its own national survival for granted. Uncertainty prevails. With every state left to its own devices, all are free to use force at any time to achieve their individual objectives. Therefore, all must be constantly prepared to counter force with force, or pay the price of weakness. All must be able to defend themselves against outside attack and to protect themselves against outside control, to be concerned, in other words, with self-preservation. It is in the sense that one scholar has written that "the basic objective of the foreign policy of all states is preservation of territorial integrity and political independence."[14] Preoccupation with national security is the logical corollary of the state system as we know it.

At a more immediate level, the practical problem facing each state is to translate the basic objective of national security into an operational strategy of foreign policy. This is no easy matter, for two reasons. First, the state itself is not a unitary policy-maker. Much of international political theory, unfortunately, has traditionally regarded the state more or less in this way.

Foreign policy has been treated as if it were the reasoned product of farsighted and creative leadership—concerted, purposive action arising out of a rational perception of the fundamental interests of the state. In fact, nothing could be further from reality; the political processes out of which policies normally spring are just not that simple. The state is not the proverbial "black box" but a social collectivity, a society of groups of all kinds, many with extensive foreign as well as domestic interests, and each with its provisional conception of the overall national interest related ideologically to its own special interest. To the extent that interest is institutionalized, particular interest expresses itself with political power, and out of governmental processes of tension and conflict the foreign policy of the state emerges—a consensus of purposes and actions that are essentially the end products of a system of domestic power relationships.

Marxists and radicals have always shown the keenest awareness of this domestic background of foreign policy. Indeed, the very idea is inherent in the traditional marxist theory of class, which takes for granted that the purposes and actions of the state abroad will reflect directly the system of power relationships at home. The only difference is that in the marxist scheme of things the power system is monopolized by a monolithic capitalist class, with the result that foreign policy equates the conception of overall national interest with the particular interest of the bourgeoisie. That, of course, is what leads marxists and radicals to concentrate on Waltz's second image of international relations: the defect derives directly from the internal organization of the state, which exists solely to guarantee a given set of property relations.

The weaknesses of the traditional marxist theory of class have been frequently noted. It is enough here simply to repeat that, in advanced capitalist countries at least, political rule in practice has been a good deal more pluralistic than the theory would have us believe. Governmental processes have operated to reconcile the conflicting interests of all groups with bargaining power within the system. Consequently, state action abroad usually turns out to be less monolithic than marxists and radicals generally allege. Often, in fact, it seems to be random, haphazard, or even irrational. Foreign policy will frequently take the form of an uneasy compromise as a result of deadlocked judgments. Sometimes a nation will adopt no foreign policy at all, but will instead, owing to indecision or unwillingness or inability to act, simply drift with the force of events.

The second reason why translation of the basic security objective into an operational strategy is not easy is that the concept of national security is not a precise or well defined guide for action. In fact, it is highly ambiguous. The presence or absence of external threats to a state's independence and territory can never be measured objectively. This must always remain a matter of subjective evaluation and speculation. National security is measured by the absence of *fear* of external threats, and fear is an obviously idiosyncratic element in international affairs. For reasons only partly explained by special interest, groups within nations and even nations themselves differ widely in their reaction to the same external situation. It is not surprising, therefore, that they differ as well in their choice of preferred foreign-policy strategy.

Furthermore, the concept of national security is usually interpreted to imply not only protection of national independence and territorial integrity, but also preservation of minimum national "core values." Tucker distinguishes between physical security per se, and security "in the greater than physical sense."[15] For the nation as for the individual, mere physical survival is not normally valued highly unless accompanied by cultural survival as well. Nations have been known to risk biological extinction through war rather than risk cultural extinction in peace. Even short of war, they tend to design and implement their foreign policies to protect not only their sovereignty and borders, but also a certain range of previously acquired values, such as rank, prestige, material possessions, and special privileges. The difficulty for foreign policy is that such values—security "in the greater than physical sense"—are by definition subjective. Not only are nations and groups within nations likely to differ in their estimation of the range of values considered "basic"; that range is apt to prove elastic over time even for any single nation or group.

Finally there is the problem of what constitutes the "nation" that this concept of security is all about. Being a sociocultural and perceptual phenomenon, the nation is neither clearly definable nor necessarily stable in terms of either space or time. Nations are not always coterminous with the geographic boundaries of states (despite the convenience of the expression nation-state). Accordingly, there is a legitimate ambiguity regarding just what it is that foreign policy is meant to preserve: Whose territorial integrity? Whose political independence? This ambiguity only serves to heighten the general uncertainty prevailing in the system as a whole. National survival, to repeat, cannot ever be taken for granted.

The role of power. Despite all these difficulties, the nation must at least *try* to develop an operational strategy of foreign policy. It must attempt to define, for the purpose of guiding its own actions, a set of proximate foreign-policy goals and objectives. To see how this is done, it will be useful to draw an analogy between the behavior of states in the international arena and that of competing firms in an oligopolistic market. Both situations are particularly apt examples of a nonzero-sum game in operation.

Like the community of nations, the oligopolistic market is characterized by interdependence and uncertainty. The competitors are sufficiently few for the behavior of any one to have an appreciable effect on at least some of its rivals; in turn, the actions and reactions of its rivals cannot be predicted with any degree of certainty. The result is an interdependence of decisionmaking which compels each firm to be noticeably preoccupied with problems of strategy and gamesmanship. The oligopolist's principal worry is to survive in the competitive struggle of the marketplace. He or she must scrutinize every move for its effects on the long-term market position of the firm, its implications concerning the firm's future freedom of action, and the probable countermoves of all rivals. Rarely is any move undertaken that is likely to threaten the existence of the enterprise.

For the individual oligopolist, a position of monopoly would obviously be preferable to the uncertainty and risk of his or her current status. But the goal of total market domination is not operative in the competitive strategies of many firms, for even apart from the constraint of antitrust legislation, each oligopolist knows that rivals, singly or collectively, are also strongly armed with the weapons of competition—price reductions, aggressive advertising, product improvement, and so on. Oligopolistic corporations do occasionally attempt to improve their position or dominate a large part of the market by means of such predatory policies as price-cutting, monopolizing raw materials or distributive outlets, or tying arrangements. However, most oligopolists prefer to rely on less aggressive strategies that are correspondingly less likely to provoke challenge and retaliation. Some of the larger firms seem content to settle for a position of previously acquired preeminence, perhaps considerably short of total dominance, but acknowledged by at least a part of the market as one of price leadership. Their strategy is to maintain their position, not augment it. Smaller enterprises find security in associating themselves publicly with the acknowledged price leader and conforming readily to the latter's observed market behavior. Others, both large and small, enter tacitly or explicitly into collusive arrangements for setting prices and dividing markets; their strategy is to ensure individual survival through mutual compromise and accommodation. Another group adopts a policy of maximum independence, eschewing any consultation or prior agreements with groups of rivals in the process of deciding on their output and prices; their strategy is to ensure survival through neutrality.

There are many variations on these few themes, but the point is that they represent the basic poles of conduct in an oligopolistic market. They also represent the basic strategies of conduct in the game of international relations: predation, preservation of existing hegemonies, association with a great power, compromise agreements and alliances, and neutrality. What determines the choice of basic strategy? Clearly, a multitude of variables is operative. In an oligopolistic market, the ideological inclinations and moral convictions of the corporate management are not unimportant, nor are expectations concerning psychological and commercial developments elsewhere in the market. But undoubtedly most important is the relative bargaining strength that the firm can exercise within the system as a whole—in other words, the general market power it can bring to bear to achieve its ends.

The main problem is for the individual firm to choose a set of proximate goals consistent with the resources at its disposal (its market power). A small firm with little public enthusiasm for its product, no monopoly of any raw material or distributive outlets, and no special access to financial backing, is hardly in a position to elect a policy of immediate market domination. Such behavior, however psychologically gratifying, would not be rational. Much more rational would be a policy of slow accumulation of market power through price "followership," or perhaps tacit collusion. Conversely, a large firm in a dominant market position cannot adopt a policy of maximum independence since its actions have such an immediate effect upon, and hence are so closely watched by, all of its rivals. For such a firm, predation or accepting the role of price leader would be more rational choices.

Firms in the marketplace tend to be much more rational in their behavior than states in the international arena. I have already emphasized that foreign policy, being largely the product of an internal political process, often seems anything but rational. All kinds of variables enter into its determination. Nevertheless, as trustee of the interests of the national community, the government must steer the state away from destruction; national survival is its first responsibility. Therefore, even though there is a wide latitude for irrational elements in foreign policy, that latitude is not without limits. Small, poor states cannot rationally aspire to dominate the world; large, rich states cannot effectively isolate themselves. The proximate goals of foreign policy must fit the resources available, however tenuously. Ultimately, national power sets the limits to the state's choice of a strategy of foreign policy, just as market power sets the limits to the oligopolist's choice of a strategy of competition.

The key word is choice. In a situation of competition, interdependence, and uncertainty, the survival of any one unit is a function of the range of alternative strategies available to it. The oligopolistic firm with only one strategic option leads a precarious existence: if that strategy fails to result in profit, the firm will disappear. Likewise, the state with only one strategic option can never feel truly secure: if that strategy fails, the state will disappear, be absorbed by others, or, more likely, be compelled to abandon certain of its national core values. For both the firm and the state, the rational solution is to broaden its range of options—*to maximize its power position*, since power sets the limits to the choice of strategy:

> [S]o long as the notion of self-help persists, the aim of maintaining the power position of the nation is paramount to all other considerations.[16]

This does not mean that more power must be accumulated than is available to any of one's rivals, or that this power must be used coercively. It only implies that power must be accumulated

ver others increased, only insofar as national resources permit.
Foremost among these is the military establishment—the
organizational and physical entity that wages war. However,
national power is more than just "forces in being"; it is a function of all the nation's other resources as well—its industries,
population, geographic location and terrain, natural resources,
scientific, managerial, and diplomatic skills, and so on. In
addition, it is a function of the resources available to the
nation's principal rivals, for power is potent only insofar as it
balances or outweighs power elsewhere. What truly matters is
not so much influence in absolute terms as influence in relation
to that of others. In a nonzero-sum game, strategy depends on
the player's *relative* bargaining strength.

In short, resources available or potential determine the *cost*
of alternative foreign policies. Imperialism may be a rational
strategy for behavior, but only as far as costs permit. As Robert
Tucker writes in his important recent book, *The Radical Left and
American Foreign Policy* (1971), "it is apparent that the costs of
imperialism to the collective must be taken into consideration."[18]   That explains why it is misleading to speak simply
of the temptations to domination. It is necessary to distinguish
between opportunity and necessity. Tempting though it may be
to take advantage of disparity of power, nations will not
actually yield to the temptation unless the benefits (however
perceived) exceed the costs (however perceived). International
inequality may be a fact of life, but it will not be actively
affirmed unless, in some meaningful sense, it pays.

For example, I emphasized above that the definition of what
constitutes a nation's "core values," being subjective, is often apt
to prove elastic over time, particularly if the nation's available resource base is growing at all rapidly. Again quoting
Tucker, "the interests of states expand roughly with their
power."[19]   It is a familiar phenomenon that military bases,
security zones, foreign investments, commercial concessions, and
so on, which may be sought and acquired by a state to protect
basic national values, themselves become new national values
requiring protection. The process works very much like the
imperialism of the "turbulent frontier" of the late nineteenth
century.[20]   The dynamic of expansion acquires its own internal
source of generation. Pushed to its logical conclusion, such an
expansion of the range of national interests to include more and

to the extent possible in order to maximize the rang
able strategies. In a nonzero-sum game, the crucial im
always to make the most of one's relative bargainin;
This is the conduct we observe of firms in a oligopolis
To the extent that governmental processes are rational,
the conduct we observe of states in the international a;

Dominance and dependence. We are nearing the e
argument. It remains only to ask what constitute;
power, and what determines the extent to which
accumulated.

Essentially, power represents the ability to control ;
influence the behavior of other nations. Such an ability
actually be exercised; it need only be acknowledged
rivals to be effective. The ability derives from
dependence which is inherent in the international sta
Interdependence is often asymmetrical, thus aut;
implying a measure of influence for those who are the
participants. Albert Hirschman has spoken of the
interrupt relations of a specifically commercial or
nature;[17] we may in fact speak of any type of
between nations. *Ceteris paribus*, the greater a state's
threaten stoppage of relations which are considered
importance by others, the stronger will be its power ;
the international arena. Conversely, the more exposed
to interruption of relations which it regards as ess;
more dependent it is on others—the weaker will be
position in the international arena.

It follows that if a state is to enhance its national s
must, to the extent possible, try to use its foreign
reduce its dependence on others. At the same time, in
counterbalance forms of dependence that cannot be a;
must try to enhance its *net* power position by *increasin;*
influence on others—that is to say, its *dominance* o;
This means that *imperialistic behavior is a perfectly*
strategy of foreign policy. It is a wholly legitimate an
response to the uncertainty surrounding the surviva
nation.

But, of course, there is a limit to the extent to whic
can behave in this way. This is determined by the ent
of resources available or potential, particularly those
that have been or could be placed at the disposal of th;
foreign policymakers. Dependence can be reduced, and d

more marginal values would not stop short of the goal of total world domination. Yet in practice, at any single moment in history, world domination has rarely figured in the operational foreign policy strategies of nations. The reason is, simply, that the cost was far too high.

When the cost is not too high (in relation to benefits), superiority over dependent nations will be actively affirmed. Then it is perfectly logical to behave in an imperialistic fashion—to subordinate, influence, and control others. Tucker said that "dominion is its own reward."[21] We now see that this means that dominion is prized because it maximizes the collectivity's range of choice in the international arena. It makes both territorial integrity and political independence more secure in an insecure and uncertain world. Above all, it enables a country to preserve the entire range of values that it has come to consider basic. As Tucker also remarks, one of the main reasons for imperialism:

> must be sought in the variety of motives that have always led preponderant powers to identify their preponderance with their security and, above all, perhaps, in the fear arising simply from the loss of preponderance itself. The belief that the loss of preponderance must result in a threat to the well-being of the collective, and this irrespective of the material benefits preponderance confers, is so constant a characteristic of imperial states that it may almost be considered to form part of their natural history.[22]

The taproot of imperialism. Tucker is perhaps putting it a bit strongly when he speaks in terms of "natural history." This smacks of the determinism of marxism and its "iron laws." But there can be no doubt that this and his other remarks point in the right direction. Though he too tends to rely more than he should on the hasty generalization and the pithy aphorism, Tucker makes an important contribution to our understanding of the imperialism phenomenon. He identifies many of the elements of the problem, and goes far enough to suggest a final answer to the question of what lies behind the nation's will to power. That answer, he says, must be found in the "dynamics of state competition," "the compulsions of the international system":[23]

> It is not only the division of humanity into the rich and
> the poor that gives rise to the various forms of unequal
> relationships the radical equates with imperialism. It is
> also the division of humanity into discrete collectives.[24]

In short, the answer must be found in the character of the
international political system. Other writers, following their
own lines of argument, have arrived at precisely the same
conclusion. British economist Lionel Robbins (now Lord Robbins),
for instance, said very much the same thing:

> There are inherent in the fundamental principles of
> national collectivism certain basic assumptions which
> make conflict with other national units almost inevitable. .
> . . The ultimate condition giving rise to those clashes of
> national economic interest which lead to international war
> is the existence of independent national sovereignties. Not
> capitalism, but the anarchic political organization of the
> world is the root disease of our civilization. . . .[T]he
> existence of independent sovereign states ought to be
> justly regarded as the fundamental cause of conflict.[25]

Similarly, in a 1944 essay American economist Jacob Viner
wrote that "war is a natural product of the organization of
peoples into regionally segregated political groups."[26]
Historian E. M. Winslow, using almost identical phraseology,
also argued that "imperialism is a political phenomenon":

> [T]he organization of peoples into regionally segregated
> political groups is the most potent cause of modern war.[27]

Here is the real taproot of imperialism—*the anarchic organization of the international system of states*. Nations yield to
the temptations to domination because they are driven to
maximize their individual power position. They are driven to
maximize their individual power position because they are
overwhelmingly preoccupied with the problem of national
security. And they are overwhelmingly preoccupied with the
problem of national security because the system is formally in a
condition of anarchy. *The logic of dominion derives directly
from the existence of competing national sovereignties.* Imperialism derives directly from this crucial defect in the
external organization of states.

Some Possible Objections

This completes the main body of my argument. I have now constructed a single analytical framework within which it is possible to account for all of the various forms of imperialism. The remainder of this essay will be devoted to an examination of some possible objections to the theme I have developed.

Too narrow. One possible objection might be that the theme depends too much on a single explanatory variable. Most social theories that attempt to reduce reality to a single causative factor can be seriously faulted on grounds of excessive consistency and limited applicability. Some readers might argue that the same seems true of the political interpretation of imperialism. The explanation seems *too narrow*.

However, this would not be a valid objection. Although the explanation depends ultimately on a single causative factor, this does not mean that the theme thereby does serious violence to the complexity of reality. While I have argued that the key to understanding the behavior of nations is their preoccupation with national security, I have also argued that what actually guides the actions of governments is their operational strategy of foreign policy—and this comprises a whole set of proximate goals and objectives. Therefore, imperialism can arise for any number of practical reasons, not just for a single one (such as, for instance, material need). At a more immediate level, the explanation depends on a multiplicity of operationally causative factors. In this sense, the political interpretation is not at all limited in analytical applicability. It is sufficiently comprehensive to encompass virtually all possible subtypes or special cases. Viner put the point best (read *imperialism* for *war*):

> In my view, therefore, war is essentially a political phenomenon, a way of dealing with disputes between groups. Every kind of human interest which looks to the state for its satisfaction and which involves real or supposed conflict with the interests of other peoples or states is thus a possible source of contribution to war. Every kind of interest which can conceivably be served by successful war will be in the minds of statesmen or will be brought to their attention. Given the existence of nation-states, the factors which can contribute to war can be as varied as the activities, the hopes and fears, the passions and generosities and jealousies, of mankind, in so far as

they are susceptible of being shared by groups and of being given mass expression.[28]

Too broad. This suggests an alternative objection. Perhaps, rather than being too narrow, the explanation is really *too broad*. This objection, converse to the first, is frequently stressed by marxist and radical writers. By allowing for such a multiplicity of causative factors, they say, the political theme gets so lost in ambiguity and vague generalities that it is devoid of any genuine analytical value. As one young radical argues: "By associating imperialism with a phenomenon that has characterized international political relations since the beginning of time, this conception is so broad as to deprive the term 'imperialism' of any specific meaning."[29]   Or as the Marxist Harry Magdoff puts it: "This interpretation, correct or incorrect, is at so high a level of abstraction that it contributes nothing to an understanding of historical differences in types and purposes of aggression and expansion. It is entirely irrelevant. . . ."[30]

The best answer to this objection has been suggested by Tucker:

> That a general interpretation of expansion may contribute little to an understanding of historical differences in types of expansion is no doubt true. It does not follow, however, that general explanations are therefore irrelevant. All that follows is that specific cases cannot be understood in their specificity merely by applying to them otherwise valid general explanations.[31]

In other words, a general theme does not relieve the analyst of the responsibility for identifying the specific causes of particular historical variations. But it does give him a common thread with which to sew them all together in the "seamless web of history." The proper test of a social theory is not whether it is at a higher or lower level of abstraction, but whether the theory offers a useful insight into a variety of historical experiences. The political interpretation of imperialism does just that. The economic interpretation favored by marxists and radicals, on the other hand, fails to pass the test.

Too shallow: 1. A third possible objection might fault the political interpretation for being not too narrow or too broad, but *too shallow*. Marxists and radicals frequently stress this objection. The problem is not in attributing imperialism to the anarchy of the international state system, but in not going deeper, to ask what lies behind the anarchic organization of relations. As one young marxist writes, "it is necessary to ask more fundamental question—about why nations struggle for power or come into conflict with one another, why they seek to increase their rank in the international system."[32]

There may be some validity to this objection, but *not* for the reasons that marxists and radicals typically suggest. What these writers see lurking behind the anarchy of international relations is, of course, the omnipresent hand of business. Nations come into conflict, and seek to increase their rank in the system, because of the selfish desires of private enterprise. To quote the same marxist: "The struggle for power is now seen for what it is—the ideological mask of monopoly capital."[33] These writers are suggesting, in effect, a return to Waltz's second image of international relations: the objection merely paraphrases the traditional marxist theory of class. However, by now the flaws of this discredited theory of politics should be more than clear. In fact, the approach makes the error of inverting ends and means. Governments do not play "the good old game of power politics" for the sake of corporate interests. Most available evidence indicates that the situation is, rather, the reverse—corporations being influenced to play the international power game, whenever possible, in ways that will serve government interests. If governments come into conflict over economic issues, it is because they are concerned about the security of the nation, not because they are trying to protect the security of corporate profits.

The question of the connection between economics and politics in the behavior of nations is an old one in the study of international relations. It would be rash to try to provide a definitive answer here. For the purpose of this essay, it is enough to emphasize two particular points. First, there can be no doubt of the *importance* of strictly economic factors to any conception of what constitutes national security. Security depends on power, and power depends on resources. Consequently, it is only natural that nations would define their minimum core values to include at least some values that are obviously economic in nature, such as investments, commercial and financial concessions, and so on. To this extent, there is little point in distinguishing at all between economics and politics in a discussion of international relations, since both are essential elements in the perpetual struggle for survival.

However, this does not mean that economic factors are therefore the ultimate *driving force* in the struggle for survival. This is the second point to be emphasized. To assume that economics is the end rather than the means of international politics, it is necessary to make one of two key assumptions. One must assume either that governments exist exclusively to serve the interests of the bourgeoisie, a view which is now discredited, or that national security is sought for no other reason than to enhance the nation's income and material possessions, a view which is equally indefensible. Greed is hardly the sole motivation of state action in the international arena. Nations, and the people in them, appreciate many objects of value for their own sake, apart from their transferability into current consumption or future wealth. These include international rank and prestige, and even the nation's domestic culture and religion, its "way of life" and language. (Consider, for instance, France's determined efforts to promote use of the French language in international organizations and around the globe.) They even include the exercise of power itself. All go into the conception of what constitutes national security.

This suggests why marxists and radicals are so misleading when they try to explain, for example, U.S. policy in Vietnam in the 1960s. Some writers have tried to find a specific economic motivation for our prolonged military involvement (so reminiscent of the bloody "sporting wars" of Bismarck's day). However, even many marxists and radicals concede that such "scandal" or "devil" theories are hardly persuasive. For marxists like Harry Magdoff or Arthur MacEwan, the real explanation was much more subtle, having to do with concern over the system as a whole, rather than with a particular set of interests. As MacEwan put it:

> In terms of particular interests, there is simply not much at stake for U.S. business in Vietnam.
>
> However, in terms of the general interest of maintaining South Vietnam as part of the international capitalist system, there is very much at stake. . . . *What is at stake in Vietnam is not just a geographic area but a set of rules, a system.*[34]

I could not agree more with MacEwan's concluding sentiment.

What was at stake in Vietnam *was* a set of rules, a system in which the United States enjoyed an exceptional position of preponderance. But does this mean that the capitalist system was the ultimate driving force of policy, as MacEwan and others like him consequently argued? Not at all; with that sentiment I could not be more in disagreement. It means that the system was viewed as the necessary means to achieve other ends—specifically, to protect the whole range of national values that America, in its preponderance of power, had come to consider "basic." Defeat for our clients in Vietnam, it was somehow decided, would threaten our national security "in the greater than physical sense." As Tucker summarized:

> The threat held out by Vietnam was real. It was not America's physical security that was threatened, but the security of an economic and social system dependent upon the fruits conferred by America's hegemonial position. A world in which others controlled the course of their own development, and America's hegemonial position was broken, would be a world in which the American system itself would be seriously endangered. To prevent this prospect from materializing, to reveal to others what they can expect if they seek to control the course of their own development, the United States intervened in Vietnam.[35]

Too shallow: II. This brings us to a fourth possible objection to the political interpretation of imperialism, which can perhaps be best phrased in the form of a question: Would a socialist (or communist) America have done the same thing? Marxists and radicals argue that it would not have. More generally, they argue that no socialist state would have done the same thing. Imperialistic behavior would be impossible, *by definition*, in a world of socialist states. The argument is implicit in the modern economic theory of imperialism. As one young radical has written: "Imperialism is capitalism which has burst the boundaries of the nation-state. . . . [The] two phenomena are inseparable: there can be no end to imperialism without an end to capitalism and to capitalist relations of production."[36]

In effect, this line of argument simply repeats the third objection above, that the political interpretation is *too shallow*. The question still involves what lies behind the anarchy of the international state system, with the answer still framed in terms of Waltz's second image of relations. The only difference is that in this instance the logic is reversed. Instead of insisting on the reasons why survival of capitalism must necessarily mean perpetuation of imperialism, the converse is implied—that the demise of capitalism must mean the end of imperialism. Socialism would correct the basic defects in the internal organization of states. Accordingly, in a socialist world there could be no serious problems of war or international conflict. No state would have reason to fear for its territorial integrity or political independence. No nation's security, physical or otherwise, would be threatened by any of its neighbors.

The fallacy of this sort of logic should be clear. As Waltz puts it: "To say that capitalist states cause war may, in some sense, be true; but the causal analysis cannot simply be reversed, as it is in the assertion that socialist states mean peace."[37]   It is necessary to supply some sort of proof, at the level either of logic or of empirical observation. Unfortunately, marxists and radicals can do neither.

At the level of empirical observation, it is difficult to prove that socialist states mean peace, especially since the record shows very much the opposite. The Soviet Union in particular has obviously been guilty of imperialistic and warlike behavior—not only in relation to its sphere of influence in eastern Europe through the years since World War II, but especially, in more recent years, in relation to its Chinese neighbor in the Far East. Marxists and radicals retort that this demonstrates nothing. If the record shows "social imperialism," it is for one of two reasons—either because no socialist state in a predominantly capitalist world is free to realize its true nature, or because the "social imperialists" are no longer truly socialist. Magdoff has written that in his opinion the imperialism of the Soviet Union is simply a symptom of the degree to which the Russians have departed from socialism and adopted some form of sociocapitalism.[38]   For Magdoff, as for most marxists and radicals, it is impossible to conceive of imperialism persisting in a world of *genuine* socialism.

This suggests that the proof must be sought at the level of logic. However, here, too, marxists and radicals have a difficult time. If conflict and war are to be ended, it must be because there is some automatic harmony, some automatic adjustment of interests. Where would this come from in a world of *genuine* socialism? The usual answer is from the change in the attitudes of men and institutions. With all states becoming socialist, the elements of competition in the system would be eliminated. Cooperation, harmony, and mutual collaboration would become the hallmark of international relations. The minimum interest of each state in its own self-preservation would become the maximum interest of them all. The strategical game, in a sense, would be finished forever.

Merely to state the answer is to make obvious the utopian quality of the marxist and radical argument. It assumes a possibility of the existential perfection of all players in the game that goes far beyond anything the evidence of history would lead us to believe is feasible. In effect, it simply assumes the past to be irrelevant in projecting into the future: men and institutions are viewed as they might become, rather than as they have been. Ultimately, as Tucker notes, it "rests on the assertion—a tautology—that if men are transformed they will then behave differently."[39]

But would socialist states behave all that differently? Such a leap of faith is courageous, even touching, but it is hardly a persuasive tool of intellectual debate. In fact, a strong case in logic can be made that socialist states would not behave differently, indeed, they might behave in even a worse fashion. Once sovereign states become socialist and take over the means of production within their borders, all distinctions between territorial jurisdiction and property ownership disappear. As a result, the inherent inequality of nations becomes a permanent source of potential disharmony in the system. A political element is injected into all important forms of international economic relations. Any dispute over commercial or financial interests automatically implies a measure of friction between states; if disputes are serious enough, they might even achieve the status of *casus belli*. Within a single nation, economic conflicts are ultimately resolvable through the fiscal mechanisms of the state or through legislative or judicial processes. Between nations, however, these same conflicts are ultimately resolvable (in the absence of world government) only through force or the threat of force.

The situation just described bears a striking resemblance to classic laissez-faire capitalism as outlined in traditional marxist analysis. Like a nation organized along capitalist lines, a world system of socialist states would consist of a number of "sovereign" property owners, all formally "equal" partners in a network of "free" exchange relationships. According to marxist analysis, at the national level these conditions necessarily lead to dominance for capitalists (who own the means of production), dependence for workers (who have correspondingly less control over resources other than their own labor power), and exploitation of the latter by the former. By analogy, it may be argued that the same outcome would obtain at the international level— dominance for large, rich countries, dependence for small, poor ones, and exploitation of the latter by the former. Of course, it is possible that cooperation among socialist states would act to moderate and limit the antagonisms generated by international differences of wealth and development; socialism is intended to be a humane system, after all. But it is improbable that mutual collaboration would succeed in eliminating tensions entirely. As one scholar has pointed out:

> [T]he "fraternal assistance" and "mutual aid" allegedly informing the relations among Socialist states do not essentially change the character of these relations, but leave them, in marxian terms, fairly and squarely at the level of typical capitalist relations. . . . The point is that nations *cannot help but be* self-regarding, as long as their position is that of owners of property in a wider community characterized by economic interdependence.[40]

Too shallow: III. This leads us to a fifth, and final, possible objection, which can also be phrased in the form of a question: *Why is it* that nations cannot help but be self-regarding.? Why must the world community be divided into distinct, and potentially antagonistic, national units? In effect, this objection also faults the political interpretation of imperialism for being *too shallow.* The existence of separate national collectivities is simply assumed. The deeper question is: Why do these horizontal distinctions persist?

Marxists and radicals are unable to give a truly satisfactory answer to this question, since the focus of their analysis is generally directed toward a different kind of distinction—not the horizontal division of mankind into nations, but vertical division into classes. Here, they insist, is the true source of conflict. If horizontal group diversity tends to persist, it is only because of the antagonisms generated by the warfare between classes, between capitalists and workers; the idea is inherent in the marxist class theory of politics. Conversely, if class warfare is ended by the coming of socialism, all conflicts and tensions will be eliminated in the international arena as well. As Marx himself put the point: "Is the whole inner organization of nations, are all their international relations anything else than the expression of a particular division of labor? And must not these change when the division of labor changes?"[41]   In other words, nations are self-regarding only because they are capitalist. Will they not stop being self-regarding as soon as they stop being capitalist?

Once again, merely to state the argument is to make obvious its utopian quality. All the evidence of history argues to the contrary. Horizontal distinctions in human society have prevailed since long before capitalism came into existence, in fact since the birth of time; they have persisted long after capitalism has been overthrown. As even Soviet spokesmen now willingly admit, national differences seem every bit as enduring in this world as class distinctions, if not more so. Certainly the experience of communism in more than a dozen nations since World War II has demonstrated that the centrifugal pull of national identity is at least as strong as the centripetal attraction of socialist fraternity. The leap of faith implied in the marxist and radical analysis is simply not justified by the facts.

What accounts for the persistence of national differences in this world? Unfortunately, *no* satisfactory answer is possible here. To account fully for the phenomenon would require at least another entire volume, drawing at a minimum on the combined insights of sociology, anthropology, and psychology. All that is possible here is to note that for whatever reasons one might conceivably imagine, men have always preferred to group themselves into distinct national units, and seem content to continue doing so. Separate nations are *a given fact*, and what characterizes them is a feeling of homogeneity. This means not only that the members of a nation feel a sense of belonging to one another; more significantly, they feel little or no sense of obligation to others. Accordingly, as members of national collectivities, men find it most convenient to reconcile their own internal conflicts and tensions, whenever possible, mainly at the expense of outsiders. This is the meaning of "self-regarding." Foreigners don't vote, but nationals do. Even the most genuine socialist nation, maintaining the highest standards of justice and equity at home, is apt to act with less justice and equity in most of its relations abroad. The best definition of a nation I have ever seen is: "A people with a common confusion as to their origins and common antipathy to their neighbors."[42]

This implies that there is some validity to the objection that the political interpretation of imperialism is too shallow. In this sense, it *is* too shallow. By concentrating on Waltz's third image of international relations, it takes the persistence of self-regarding nations for granted, and therefore takes the nature and behavior of man for granted. But what is suggested now is that it is precisely with the nature and behavior of man that we ought to be most concerned—in other words, Waltz's first image. In the end, it is a question of the defects in ourselves, not in our national or international systems—our selfishness, our aggressiveness, our prejudices. We cannot relieve ourselves of the blame merely by blaming "society." Real solutions are never as simple as that.

> The fault, dear Brutus, is not in our stars,
> But in ourselves . . .

Shakespeare

Notes

1. John A. Hobson, *Imperialism: A Study* (Ann Arbor, Michigan: University of Michigan Press, 1965), p. 81. This classic work was first published in England in 1902.

2. Richard J. Hammond, "Economic Imperialism: Sidelights on a Stereotype," *Journal of Economic History* 21, no. 4 (December 1951): 596.

3. W. H. B. Court, *Scarcity and Choice in History* (London: Edward Arnold, 1970), p. 193.

4. Hans J. Morgenthau, *Politics Among Nations*, 3rd ed. (New York: Alfred A. Knopf, 1960), p. 51.

5. Raymond Aron, "The Leninist Myth of Imperialism," *Partisan Review* 18, no. 6 (November-December 1951): 648.

6. Court, *Scarcity and Choice*, p. 194.

7. David S. Landes, "The Nature of Economic Imperialism," *Journal of Economic History* 21, no. 4 (December 1961): 510.

8. Robert W. Tucker, *The Radical Left and American Foreign*

Policy (Baltimore: Johns Hopkins Press, 1971), p. 151. To be fair to Tucker, he does go further than authors such as those previously cited, to ask what lies behind the logic of dominion. In fact, in many repects his analysis of the imperialism phenomenon anticipates the substance of my own argument.

9. Landes, "Nature of Economic Imperialism," p. 510.

10. Kenneth N. Waltz, *Man, the State and War* (New York: Columbia University Press, 1959).

11. Ibid., p. 125.

12. A considerable part of the subsequent argument is adapted from an earlier essay of mine in my book, *American Foreign Economic Policy: Essays and Comments* (New York: Harper & Row, 1968), pt. 1.

13. Waltz, *Man, the State and War*, p. 209.

14. Nicholas Spykman, *America's Strategy in World Politics* (New York: Harcourt, Brace & Jovanovich, 1942), p. 17.

15. Tucker, *The Radical Left*, pp. 62-63.

16. Frederick S. Dunn, *Peaceful Change* (New York: Council on Foreign Relations, 1937), p. 13.

17. Albert O. Hirschman, *National Power and the Structure of Foreign Trade* (Berkeley: University of California Press, 1945).

18. Tucker, *The Radical Left*, p. 114.

19. Ibid., p. 73.

20. See John S. Galbraith, "The 'Turbulent Frontier' as a Factor in British Expansion," *Comparative Studies in Society and History* 2, no. 2 (January 1960): 150-168.

21. Ibid., p. 151.

22. Ibid., p. 69.

23. Ibid., pp. 11, 38.

24. Ibid., p. 143.

25. Lionel Robbins, *The Economic Causes of War* (London: Jonathan Cape, 1939), pp. 95, 99, 104.

26. Jacob Viner, "Peace as an Economic Problem," in Viner *International Economics* (New York: The Free Press, 1951), chap. 16, p. 247.

27. E. M. Winslow, *The Pattern of Imperialism* (New York: Columbia University Press, 1948), p. 237.

28. Viner, "Peace as an Economic Problem," p. 248.

29. Susanne Bodenheimer, "Dependency and Imperialism: The Roots of Latin American Underdevelopment," in K. T. Fann and Donald C. Hodges, eds., *Readings in U.S. Imperialism* (Boston: Porter Sargent, 1971), p. 171.

30. Harry Magdoff, *The Age of Imperialism* (New York: Monthly Review Press, 1969), p. 13.

31. Tucker, *The Radical Left*, p. 78.

32. Robin Jenkins, *Exploitation: The World Power Structure and the Inequality of Nations* (London: MacGibbon and Kee, 1970), p. 166.

33. Ibid., p. 167.

34. Arthur MacEwan, "Capitalist Expansion, Ideology and Intervention," *Upstart*, no. 2 (May 1971): 36. Emphasis in the original.

35. Tucker, *The Radical Left*, p. 52.

36. David Horowitz, *Empire and Revolution: A Radical Interpretation of Contemporary History* (New York: Random House, 1969), p. 38.

37. Waltz, *Man, the State and War*, p. 157.

38. Private correspondence to the author, January 30, 1971.

39. Tucker, *The Radical Left*, p. 145.

40. R. N. Berki, "On Marxian Thought and the Problem of International Relations," *World Politics* 24, no. 1 (October 1971): 103. Emphasis in the original.

41. As quoted in ibid., p. 82.

42. Herman Harmelink III, in a letter to *The New York Times*, January 12, 1972, p. 38.

About the Book and Author

International political economy is the increasingly important research agenda that emphasizes both the interdependence of politics and economics and the interdependence of national economies. It insists that politics be informed by economics (and vice versa) and that local issues be understood in their global contexts.

For more than a quarter of a century, Benjamin J. Cohen has been one of the few economists to venture systematically into this emerging field, an area traditionally dominated by political scientists. *Crossing Frontiers*—the title refers to both national and disciplinary boundaries—brings together for the first time a dozen of his best and most enduring essays.

Eight of these essays address issues in the formation and implementation of foreign economic policy by individual governments, and four others focus on the organization and management of economic relations between sovereign nation-states. Throughout, Cohen exhibits an adventurous pragmatism, a preference for practical applications over abstract theory, and a willingness to face the complexity of the real world rather than adopt simplifying assumptions.

All scholars and students of international political economy will profit from this collection of papers from one of the pioneers of their field.

Benjamin J. Cohen is professor of economics at the Fletcher School of Law and Diplomacy, Tufts University.

Index